To: Phyllis

God's peace + joy
be with you always.

Yours in Christ

Renee Splichal Larson

A Witness

Third Sunday in Lent: March 24, 2019

Worship at 8:30am & 10:15am | sanctuary

Guest Preacher – Rev. Renee Splichal Larson

12:15pm – Light lunch | ULC lounge

1pm - Book Talk by author, Pastor Renee Splichal Larson
ULC fellowship hall

We are excited to welcome Pastor Renee Splichal Larson to United this **Sunday, March 24th**. Pastor Renee is the author of the book *A Witness: The Haiti Earthquake, A Song, Death and Resurrection*. Renee will be leading a Book Talk and you are invited to attend this special event!

About the book: The 2010 earthquake in Haiti buried Renee Splichal Larson in concrete rubble, killing her husband and leaving her a widow at age 27. Surviving only to be overwhelmed by loss and trauma, she wondered if life was still possible for her. Even as she trained to become a pastor, her faith in a loving God was shaken and battered by the earthquake that devastated Port-au-Prince and took the lives of many thousands.

This Renee's moving story of love, grief, survival, and new life. It is an account of the lives of three young people, their experience of the challenges, beauty, and hospitality of Haiti, and the tumult that overthrew all they held dear. After years of struggle and healing, aided by remarkable signs of the love and presence of God, Renee offers us an intimate look at her young romance, her experience of the earthquake, and the journey that followed. Most of all, she proclaims her hard-won witness: that in Christ, love and life conquer death.

Pastor Renee Splichal Larson has been serving as pastor of Heart River Lutheran Church in Mandan, ND, since September 2010. She is married to Pastor Jonathan Splichal Larson who serves as the senior pastor of Faith Lutheran Church in Bismarck, ND. They have two sons, Gabriel and Elias.

Non-Profit Organization
U.S. POSTAGE
PAID
Grand Forks, ND
Permit No. 163

PHYLLIS TRELFA
407 CRESTWOOD CT SE
EAST GRAND FORKS 56721

Book Talk with author, pastor Renee Splichal Larson - This Sunday, March 24, 2019 at 1pm.

A Witness

The Haiti Earthquake, a Song,
Death, and Resurrection

Renee Splichal Larson

EDITED BY
Jennifer Agee

FOREWORD BY
Norma Cook Everist

RESOURCE *Publications* · Eugene, Oregon

A WITNESS
The Haiti Earthquake, a Song, Death, and Resurrection

Resource Publications
An Imprint of Wipf and Stock Publishers
199 W. 8th Ave., Suite 3
Eugene, OR 97401

www.wipfandstock.com

PAPERBACK ISBN: 978-1-4982-2606-6
HARDCOVER ISBN: 978-1-4982-2608-0

Manufactured in the U.S.A.

For Ben, and all those who died in the Haiti earthquake;
for Jon, and all those who are still surviving January 12, 2010

Suddenly there was a great earthquake..."I know that you are looking for Jesus who was crucified . . . He has been raised from the dead."

—MATTHEW 28:1–10

Contents

Foreword

THIS BOOK COULD HAVE been titled so many different ways: *A Love Story*; *Tragedy in Haiti*; *Loss and Grief*. But I think *A Witness* is just right. Renee Splichal Larson is a participant witness. She saw and experienced what we, the readers, did not, and yet we connect with her witness.

A Witness is a very personal and also a very global book. In telling her painful yet hopeful story, Renee invites us to enter, from wherever we are; to see, to feel, to question, and to understand more deeply the power, grace, and love of God. There are many entry points for us readers, whatever our age, station in life, or place in the world. We read alone, and possibly feel as alone as she does at times. And yet we read together, because this is a communal story. It is about accompaniment and relationship, about Ben, Renee, and Jon, who went to Haiti to be with the people of Haiti and who became part of the shaking of the earth with them.

This book is about a few minutes in history and about the years that surround them. It is not a short book, but you won't want to put it down. So, too, our lives. We live in the moment and yet sometimes, suddenly, swiftly, some event changes everything. How do we respond? In that moment? In the months and years to come? Because Renee cares enough to share her story, including the difficult details, she ministers to us readers who know love and loss. The book is intimate, deep, and profound, but not heavy; there is even some humor. We laugh as well as cry. We see people who go to amazing lengths to care for each other. Care across boundaries: accompaniment!

As the book begins, we meet these three young people and enjoy setting out on life's journey with each of them. Ben and Jon are cousins who are closer than brothers. We hear Renee's own story about her early years. I have witnessed in Renee an incredible woman. You will discover this, too, as you come to know her and see how she views life and the people whom she comes to cherish. We see Christ in people, because Renee is a witness to Christ in their lives and to Christ at work in the midst of tragedy, care, connection, and the renewal of resurrection.

The story's focus is on one very gifted young man who died too soon. But the story is also about two people, and three, and about the families of Renee, Ben, and Jon. This is a book about family. Yet we also meet strangers, and we learn from them, and learn what it means to be served by them as much as serving among them. We see, really see, the people of Haiti: Belinda, Livenson, Naomi, Louis, Mytch, and more. Soon we are a witness to hundreds and yes, thousands. This story is about the global church, not just as an idea, but the reality. It is about faith and what it means to be church together in life and death, and in new life.

This book is also a call to accompaniment and to advocacy: to be in relationship with people and to really learn to know one another. We learn about Haiti, its history, and the misrepresentations *of* and misunderstandings *about* this beautiful country. Renee the writer is Renee the teacher, introducing us to the Haitian people, who have suffered so much and continue to care for the outsider. We hear their faith and song in the midst of despair. We see their resilience, but dare not romanticize the complex issues. In our own ignorance and arrogance, we who live in affluent countries benefit from countries that remain poor and dependent. These are the causes and ramifications of poverty. The call of *A Witness* is a call to community and justice.

Poetry from fellow witnesses (friends and classmates) comforts us as well as the author as we walk and weep with each step from earthquake to resting place. This is a book for all who have suffered trauma, sudden tragedy, or the sadness of long suffering. You are invited to bring your own experiences and witness to these pages, because this is not just one woman's personal narrative made public, but a much broader work that includes us all as we share the long journey of love, grief, and healing.

Renee is a theologian—of the best sort—who lives life fully, and is forever asking questions. (So the title could also have been *A Theology*.) Her reflections are existential and challenging, and she invites her readers to reflect theologically with her. She does not simply summarize, "I had a faith struggle," or "I wrestled with God," nor glibly accept, "All things work out for good in the end." Renee knows that death is real. She also knows that the resurrection of Jesus Christ is true, and that new life in Christ is real. But this new life comes only after lamentation and loneliness and deep grief.

Together with Renee, we become witnesses to the importance of pastoral care and of a worshipping and caring community. Among the questions are dreams and visions and vision . . . and friends. Friends carry a body out of Haiti, and all are carried by the body of Christ. This is a theology of grace, of the cross and resurrection, of Christ with people in their dying as much as with the living. This power of God, God's own commitment to us, empowers us for commitments to all of God's global family. Love given opens us to love shared—beyond imagining.

And so there are more ministry opportunities for this now-ordained pastor and for us all. Renee goes where God leads, including to the people of Heart River. I have been so privileged to walk with Renee as she drew on God's strength for the emotional and physical courage to relive this story, to walk again through those days, and to write this book. I believe this work is and will be a blessing to all who read it, to all for whom she is a witness to Christ and to his cross and resurrection.

—Rev. Norma Cook Everist,

Professor, Wartburg Theological Seminary

Introduction

I AM A WITNESS. I am just one among millions of witnesses of the Haiti earthquake of January 12, 2010. Hundreds of thousands of people became martyrs that day. I lived, and I am called to share my story.

The Greek word *martyr* is often translated as "witness." A witness tells others about something they have seen or heard or experienced. What if the women never shared what they saw (or did not see!) when they went to the tomb in the early morning dawn on the third day? Without the first witnesses to the resurrection of Christ, there would be no gospel, no knowledge of victory over death. There would be no Christianity. The women were not responsible for explaining what they saw and experienced. They were simply called to tell their story—that they had seen the empty tomb and the risen Lord—and let the Spirit of God do the rest.

I tried to write this story many times in the first few years following the earthquake, but I was not ready. The trauma and grief were too overwhelming. I am ready now.

A dear friend of mine, who happens to be Haitian, once told me: "I don't think the earthquake will be erased from anybody's mind. This is something that will stay with people forever, from generation to generation. I don't think our lives will ever be the same."

My life was one of the millions that were changed forever because of the Haiti earthquake. In January 2010, I was twenty-seven years old and had just celebrated my second wedding anniversary with my husband, Ben. We planned to graduate from seminary later that spring with our four-year master of divinity degrees. We were preparing to become pastors in the Evangelical Lutheran Church in America (ELCA), along with Ben's cousin, Jon, who accompanied us to Haiti that January.

The three of us were sitting together at a table at 4:53 p.m. on Tuesday, January 12, at the St. Joseph's Home for Boys in Pétionville, when the earth began to shake. Less than a minute later, I saw Ben for the last time and Jon and I were trapped under concrete rubble. Before Ben breathed his last, I heard him singing about the Lamb of God who bears the sin of all the world away.

It is true that "too many people die with their music still in them."[1] Many beautiful, gifted, faithful people died in the Haiti earthquake, and Ben was one of them. Those of us who lived strived to make sense of all we had seen and survived, and ultimately, to continue living in an unpredictable world created and loved by God. Yes, this is a story about three people—Ben, Jon, and me—but more important, it is a story about death and resurrection, the suffering and faith of the Haitian people, despair and healing, and the power and grace of God. This is a story about survival; it is a witness to a song, and a confession of the profound mystery that in Christ, new life comes forth from death and despair.

Ben's sister Katie told me while I was writing this book: "I feel like this is my story, too." This story belongs to anyone who has loved and lost, anyone who has cared about the event and aftermath of the Haiti earthquake, and anyone who is struggling to keep faith in a loving God in an unfair world. I have intimately learned that the new life God promises and gives in and through suffering and loss does not mean better life or back-to-normal life. New life is *new,* but it is life.

For a while it seemed that the earthquake and Ben's death would define me, as well as Jon. For a long time I felt as if people who did not know me before the earthquake just saw me as Ben's widow, or as the one who survived. And Jon was the family member who came home, not Ben. It took Jon and me a while to claim who we had been and who we were becoming after the earthquake. But I had my call from God to ordained ministry before I met Ben; I started seminary on my own. Yes, the earthquake and Ben's death are highly significant for Jon and me, but they do not direct our lives or define us. Our family and close friends have helped us remember who we are as beloved children of God and that we have our own worth in this world.

For Ben, "new life" means something I can only hope for and have faith in. I have every confidence that Ben is with Christ and is alive and well. I wish everyone could know Ben today. A mutual friend wrote this poem about his personality:

---

1. Quote commonly attributed to Oliver Wendell Holmes.

contagious joy
Corrine Denis

I caught your joy
like a head cold
contagious joy
endearing spontaneity
joy skipping out of control
over the river of life
jumping, springing, shooting up
from the font
water dancing
spilling and splashing
all.
you doused us with your joy
justice joy
and I still have water
laughing in my ears.

I have story after story of Ben and our life together, but it is impossible to capture him in language or describe our deep love. Ben always said, "I have never kept a diary, so if you want to know me, listen to my music." Ben was a gifted singer and composer; he wrote more than 130 original compositions, including a couple of liturgies. In his song "Grace and Peace," he sings about the love of God:

> And when I go out, I'll go out in your love
> And if I fall it will not be in vain
> I know how I feel; Your love is so real
> And I know that I am loved by you.

I do not believe that Ben, and the estimated 158,000[2] other beloved people of Haiti, died in vain in the earthquake. For me, one way to ensure that is through my witness: writing our story. Even more important is to live and continue to serve God and the people of this world.

The truth is, God is the one who inspires and empowers us survivors, but God does so through the ordinary and extraordinary lives of everyday people. Yes, Ben sang as he died, but it is not just his song that inspires us. It was who he was, how he treated people, his contagious joy, and how he lived his life as an expression of God's grace and love in the world. All of us in God's good creation are capable of this, too, through the power of the Spirit.

---

2. This number has been debated; see chapter 21 for more information.

What you will read in the following pages is not a theological dissertation, but a witness. As with every story, there is always more to tell, but what follows is an honest account of the events leading up to the earthquake, the earthquake itself, and the journey that followed. It is frightening to be so vulnerable, to invite so many others to read my most intimate thoughts and know my despair, but it has given me hope to know that perhaps my story will be an encouragement or a source of hope for others, particularly in times of grief.

The story of Ben's life and his dying witness is certainly worth recording so that others can read it and rest in the love of the Lamb of God, but I also find it to be my responsibility and in my power to write about the incredible hospitality, courage, and faith of the Haitian people. I by no means speak for them, and what I share in this book is not universal, nor is it a comprehensive picture of the complex realities of Haiti. Instead, it reflects my limited experience of traveling to Haiti a few times and my ongoing relationships with the people I love there. We were there in the heart of the chaos that deeply changed Port-au-Prince, its surrounding area, and its people. The earthquake has forever bound Ben, Jon, me, and our families to Haiti.

If I had known what would befall us on January 12, 2010, I would not have believed that I could survive such trauma and loss. We never know what we are capable of enduring and surviving until the cross is on our shoulders. I have learned that I have an inner strength that can come only from the Spirit of God, and faith that not even an earthquake can shatter. I have also learned that grief is a lifelong companion that ebbs and flows. Above all, I have come to more fully understand the truth of the gospel: that in Christ, life and love conquer death.

PART I

Context and People

Ben's Church
Corrine Denis

there was always room
at the table.
class notes, music sheets, and half-opened mail,
your arm ushered away with one gracious swoop
creating space
at the table.
finest china for ordinary friends
candles even
feeling like we mattered
giving us each a distinguished place
at the table.

You said you wanted those who
never felt like anyone
to feel like they mattered to Jesus;
you said, "That's what I want my church to be."

dear one, you lived your church
you carried your church with you
in a song
at the table
the table you and Renee grew
joyfully placing leaf and leaf and leaf
a love feast spread for all
edamame, new bread, dumplings, real butter, five-dollar organic vanilla yogurt,
and coffee so strong you could chew it.

1

The Journey to Seminary

I FIRST CAUGHT THE contagious joy of Benjamin Judd Ulring Larson in July 2006 during an intensive summer Greek class at Wartburg Theological Seminary in Dubuque, Iowa. We were both newly enrolled in the master of divinity degree program, preparing to become pastors in the Evangelical Lutheran Church in America (ELCA). During one of the first few weeks, I stole a glance in Ben's direction during daily chapel. He was staring at me. Our eyes met and I looked down quickly, embarrassed. I felt as if I had been transported back to junior high, complete with racing heart and sweaty palms. I raised my eyes again. He smiled at me.

Soon we were dating. After about a month, Ben took me aside. This was something serious. Taking a deep breath, he sheepishly confessed: "When we first started dating, I really struggled with the fact that you are not Scandinavian."

What! I thought. *Is he serious?* Never in a million years did I see that one coming. Not that I knew Ben well yet, but he was the last person I would have thought could be so picky. How could Ben seriously struggle with the fact that I was not Scandinavian? I didn't care at all that he was Norwegian. I hardly knew what to say, since it was something I had absolutely no control over and could not change, so I simply said, "What?"

"Well," he gulped and tried to explain, "my Norwegian heritage is very important to me and it really bothered me at first that you were not Scandinavian at all, but rather German and Bohemian. But! I want you to know that I am totally over it now and I love who you are in all of your wild Bohemian-ness."

I was still trying to take it in. I could tell that it really did bother him at first, and yet at the same time his mind had changed. It seemed that he now fully rejoiced in my heritage and that we had somehow crossed a threshold in our relationship that I had not known was there. Now he was relieved and smiling so lovingly at me, ready to step more fully into a relationship with this structured, rule-following, yet slightly wild, long-dangly-earrings-wearing woman.

I grew up dancing the polka, waltz, schottische, and butterfly, and I certainly knew about and had eaten lefse. I even had a Norwegian step-grandmother. Sure, when I asked for half a cup of coffee, I wanted half a cup of coffee, and when Ben asked for half a cup of coffee, he actually wanted a full cup. But how different could we really be? In a very German, direct way I said to the cute, bearded Norwegian in front of me, "Oh, get over yourself!" Thus ended our first confession and absolution.

I grew up in Garrison, a town of 1,350 people in west central North Dakota. My last name, Splichal, means "splashes" in Czech, which my family has lived into well, practicing our "splashing" through boating, fishing, tubing, kneeboarding, and swimming on Lake Sakakawea. I practically grew up on that lake and loved every minute of it, completely oblivious to the devastation it caused to the native tribes and my maternal great-grandparent farmers when the Missouri River was dammed for recreational purposes, creating one of the largest man-made lakes in the world.

Garrison claims to be the "Walleye Capital of the World" and the "Christmas Capital of North Dakota." The main street of Garrison turns into an old English market between Thanksgiving and Christmas, bearing signs that read, "Ye Olde Malt Shop" and "Ye Olde Barber Shop." Men wearing top hats and women in big dresses are on the sidewalks ready to sell anyone a turkey leg, knoephla soup, fleischkuechle, pickled fish, lefse, or cheesecake on a stick. If you happened to purchase a sausage on a stick, you would be buying it from my dad, decked out in a top hat and supporting Garrison High School's Future Business Leaders of America chapter. In my high school years, you'd find me right next to him, shivering in the cold—sometimes twenty degrees below zero (Fahrenheit).

I'm not kidding about that temperature, although it's not always so extreme during what seems to be six months of winter. Even now with North Dakota's influx in population because of the booming oil industry, not many people stay permanently. I resonate well with Kathleen Norris's book, *Dakota: A Spiritual Geography*. She is very honest and accurate when she writes: "The Plains are not forgiving. Anything that is shallow—the easy optimism of a homesteader; the false hope that denies geography, climate, history; the tree whose roots don't reach ground water—will dry up and blow away."[1]

Growing up in North Dakota has undoubtedly shaped me in more ways than I probably know myself. I once heard someone say, "The women

---

1. Norris, *Dakota*, 38.

in North Dakota stand up in the wind and don't blow over." I like to think growing up in North Dakota gave me strength and perseverance, especially during those occasional blizzards in May, when all everyone longs for is spring green and the warmth of the sun.

Family and Faith

I am the oldest of three siblings and considered it my responsibility to care for my younger brother, Eric, and younger sister, Jessie. They may have viewed my interference as bossy and worried. Despite my hovering, they managed to grow up and turn out perfectly normal, making all kinds of good, independent life choices.[2]

I was raised by incredible parents, Dan and Joleen. They both grew up in Garrison as well; my dad's parents lived one block away, and my mom's folks lived five blocks away. This meant many days with grandpas and grandmas when both my parents worked to provide for us. I have countless memories of polka and waltzing on the patio as my paternal grandfather played a beautiful mother-of-pearl full accordion by ear, and summer days on the farm with my maternal grandparents picking chokecherries, tearing around on the four-wheeler, and helping in the garden and in the field.

My dad's family (the Bohemian ones) were Roman Catholic, and my grandfather was a jeweler in town after serving in World War II in the Philippines. My mom's family (the Germans from Russia) was Lutheran and farmed some land seventeen miles west of Garrison. Had my dad been more active in his Catholic faith, I would have been raised Catholic. As things were, however, I was baptized into the Body of Christ at St. Paul Lutheran Church, August 10, 1982.

My parents, especially my mother, were faithful in their baptismal promises to me and my brother and sister. She woke us three kids up every Sunday, endured our picking on each other all through worship, and had us attend Sunday school, confirmation, and sing in the Sunshine Choir, all so that we would grow to love and trust God. I participated in youth events, went to Camp of the Cross just outside of Garrison every summer, attended two national youth gatherings, and played organ and piano for worship starting in middle school.

I never had a "conversion" experience other than my baptism when I was one month old. My faith life was quite ordinary. I participated every

---

2. Eric married his high school sweetheart, Janessa Giffey, and now works for Microsoft in Fargo, North Dakota. Jessie married Nate Watson and is a nurse at Sanford in Bismarck, North Dakota.

Lord's Day in the liturgy from the *Lutheran Book of Worship*, settings one and two. I had the liturgy memorized as far back as I can remember because it was simply ingrained in me since infancy. I remember I would always check the hymn board first thing when I sat down in the pew and look up all the hymns to see which ones they were. Under my breath I would rejoice, "Yes!" when I saw "Beautiful Savior," "Come, Let Us Eat," and others I loved.

Later in life fellow brothers and sisters in Christ would ask me: "What day were you saved?" and "Have you accepted Jesus as your Lord and Savior into your heart?" These seemed like strange questions to me as a follower of Christ raised in the Lutheran tradition, because I have always understood myself to be a recipient of God's grace and saved already through the death and resurrection of Jesus. Every day God was saving me and renewing me. As far as accepting Jesus as my Lord and Savior, I had the affirmation I needed in my baptism that I was his and he was mine. Growing up in the Lutheran church gave me a solid foundation of everyday, sustaining, even "boring" faith that nevertheless provided joy, excitement, and hope. This faith carried me in my early life as I witnessed the death of many of my loved ones.

Those Claimed by Cancer

On May 28, 1990, my maternal, non-smoking grandmother died of lung cancer at the age of fifty-six. I was seven years old and still remember the moment my parents sat my brother, sister, and me on their laps and told us Grandma Adeline had died.

Every night in bed, I thought of her and wondered if she knew how sad I was that I could no longer see her. I used to lie in the grass of my front yard gazing up at the moon and stars, imagining her looking down at me. I would speak out loud to her and to God. I asked God what life and death meant, whether or not I would see my grandmother again, whether or not the ache in my chest would ever go away, and why it was that my beloved grandmother had suffered and died the way she did. As far as I can remember, I never received a clear answer to any of these questions.

In the spring of 1999, my paternal grandfather died after spending seven years in a nursing home, suffering from Alzheimer's and accompanied horrid illnesses. He did not always recognize me, and he no longer played the accordion. I watched my father and grandmother make painful decision after painful decision about a person who hardly knew them any longer. It was actually a sorrowful relief when my grandfather, a shadow of the person I knew and loved, breathed his last.

In his mid-thirties, my dad's oldest brother, Dave, was diagnosed with melanoma. I remember when my father and I cried together in our breakfast nook at 1:30 a.m., knowing that Dave's suffering was beyond our comprehension and there was nothing we could do. He died in the spring of 2000, two days before my high school graduation, at the age of forty-six.

In the fall of 2001, my paternal grandmother died. Lung cancer ravaged her body as well. I watched her struggle for breath and moan with pain. How I hated cancer! A few nights before she died, she told my parents that Dave had visited her. They reminded her that Dave had died, but the next day and the next she told them that Dave visited her each night. When she died she sat straight up in her bed, arms outstretched to the sky, and released her life breath.

Cancer was not finished with our family. My dad's bachelor younger brother, Tim, had lived with my grandmother, but got married two years after her death. On July 11, 2004, Tim died of liver and pancreatic cancer at the age of forty-two, after being married for less than a year. The day before my Uncle Tim died—my birthday—I spoke to him on the phone. I said, "Give Jesus a hug for me." I suppose it helped me to rest in the hope that Tim would be able to embrace Christ and lay his head on His shoulder soon after we hung up.

Leaving Home

After I graduated from high school, Concordia College in Moorhead, Minnesota, beckoned me out of Garrison. I was excited, although I cried a little when my parents left after lofting my bed in my little dorm room and buying me my first Concordia sweatshirt.

In college, the possibilities in life seemed endless. I loved the liberal arts education that allowed me to explore a vast range of subjects and be challenged to think critically, yet also exercise my body and spirit through other groups and activities. I became involved in campus ministry, intramural sports, music groups, work study, and track and field. As a heptathlete and pole vaulter, I sometimes spent more time on the track than I spent sleeping. I earned a teaching license for the state of Minnesota with my physical education major and rounded out my degree with a minor in religion.

While in college I worked as a youth director for 120 middle-school youth at Trinity Lutheran Church in Moorhead. There is nothing like taking ninety-five pre-teens out ice blocking (that is, "sledding" using a block of ice rather than a sled) or on hayrides and bonfire trips. Every summer I worked as a counselor at Bible camps. I loved those summers with children and other young adults, sharing the gospel as I understood it, and being in God's good creation. For the first time, I began to seriously consider a career in pastoral ministry.

In the spring semester of my senior year of college, I had a minor crisis. What on earth was I going to do after graduation? Even though I had a degree in education and a teaching license in hand, I wasn't ready to apply for first-year teaching positions. I had spent so much time focusing on myself in college that I now felt ready to volunteer for others and explore new places and opportunities. So I did the most practical thing any college graduate could do: I decided to volunteer full-time and defer my student loans. After months of prayer and searching, I signed up with the ELCA volunteer organization Urban Servant Corps and made plans to move to inner-city Denver, Colorado.

I'll never forget saying goodbye to my parents. My dad mourned, "Why are you moving so far away?" I told him, "This is what I need to do," but in reality I was thinking, *What in the world* am *I doing?* I got in the car and cried through the whole state of North Dakota. I remember hitting the steering wheel and yelling at God, shouting things like, "This better be right!" and "I'm trusting you!"

Denver

Soon I arrived at my new home in Denver and met the nine roommates I would be living with in intentional community for the next year. We lived on Ogden Street, less than two blocks north of Colfax Avenue, the longest street in the U.S. It stretches a marathon length of twenty-six miles, and it's said that *Playboy* magazine once described it as "the longest, wickedest street in America."

It was certainly a different world. I felt powerless to do anything about the drug use I saw every day and its effects on people, the rampant home-lessness, the mental suffering of war veterans I talked to in our alleyway, and the neighborhoods in which gunshots and gang activity were commonplace. Even in winter, people lined the sidewalks in front of the Denver Rescue Mission, sleeping under tarps. In Denver I learned about complex situations, chronic homelessness, and the effects of poverty on human beings.

I wrestled with how to respond when someone on the street asked me for money, which happened often. One afternoon I pulled into the parking lot of the building where I volunteered and a man in his forties approached me. He said, "Excuse me, my father over there is sick and we need money to take the bus. As you can see, I'm not well myself, having just been in the hospital." He showed me his arms, which revealed, not a recent trip to the hospital, but rather years and years of drug use. His clothes were worn, but I mostly remember his eyes: ashamed, tired, and deep with heartache, yet hopeful for a green piece of paper I might give to him. I listened to his story and told him I had no money on me, but would go inside to look for some and come back.

Once I was inside, I had the usual battle with myself. If I gave the man money, it would more than likely go toward drugs. Yet I also felt compelled to simply give, not knowing how God might work. I asked my coworker if I could borrow a dollar. Then I went to my desk and got two bagels I had wrapped that morning and went back outside.

I could tell the man was surprised to see me again. He came running back across the street. I said, "I only have a dollar to give you, but I also have these two bagels for you and your father." He stared for a while at the items and then said, "You know . . . my life is so messed up. I haven't been into good things. I'm not a good person. I just need . . ." He seemed to be searching for what he believed he needed. Tears started in his eyes. Then he asked me, "Could you just pray for me sometime, just remember me in your prayers?"

Then, as if I was not in control of my own words, I said, "Well, how about right now?" He hesitated a bit but agreed, so I took his hands in mine and I prayed. I don't remember what I said, but even before I was finished with the prayer, the man started to back away, tears streaming down his face, saying, "Thank you, thank you." I never saw him again.

I learned a lot from my nine roommates, all of whom were volunteering at various nonprofit agencies in the city. Because we lived in "intentional" community, we spent one night a week processing and talking about our experiences, sharing our stories, and ironing out our issues with one another. We were all very different people and were volunteering in stressful situations—we all worked with the homeless population, people struggling with mental illness and narcotics, abused women and children, and people fresh out of prison. Yet, I came to love my roommates deeply, and some of my best friends are those I met in Urban Servant Corps.

I worked at a nonprofit called Girls Inc., whose mission was "to inspire all girls to be strong, smart, and bold." I learned so much from those young girls, who ranged from ages six to eleven. They taught me about life, particularly life that is hard. I saw fear and disappointment on their faces when their dads showed up drunk to pick them up from the afterschool program. Girls worried about an eleven-year-old friend who had been cutting herself. I learned that pregnancy and dropping out of high school could be an expectation of life at the age of sixteen. That graduation from high school, let alone college, was fought for and hard-earned against great odds for some of those gifted, beautiful girls.

When a seven-year-old girl with a colorful vocabulary told me, "I live in the 'projects' with my grandma," I could only wonder about her chances of avoiding alcohol or drugs in the years to come, of avoiding sexual assault or unplanned pregnancy, or even of having enough food. And yet, all of us who worked at Girls Inc. said to her each day through our relationships, classes, and our words: "You are strong, smart, and bold!" We did our best to build the girls up and affirm who they were and were going to be.

As much as these girls taught me about the hardships of life, they also taught me about innocent joy and about the laughter and play that are possible in the midst of homelessness, of being bullied, and of being exposed to drugs more readily than a glass of milk. They were kids. They defied amazing odds and brought smiles, play, creativity, and beauty to every day.

To the Border . . . and to Seminary?

As much as I loved teaching in the after-school program and living with my nine roommates in the Ogden house, I soon discovered that I was being pulled in another direction. At my midyear check-in with the director of Urban Servant Corps, Pastor Barb, she looked me straight in the eye and asked, "What do you want to do with your life, Renee?"

This after patiently listening to me discuss all of my many options after completing my volunteer year, including moving to Central America to improve my Spanish or applying for the ELCA Young Adults in Global Mission program. I shook my head and said, "I don't know."

Pastor Barb had a surprise in store. She said: "We're going to help send you to tour Luther and Wartburg Seminaries. You need to explore a life in public ministry, Renee, and visiting seminary will help you do this."

I had never seriously considered seminary, and certainly not ordination. Four more years of school didn't sound so great, and I wasn't sure I wanted the responsibilities that come with being a pastor. Despite my doubts and reservations, though, I accepted Pastor Barb's offer and purchased a plane ticket.

I have had very few moments of total clarity in my life, but as soon as I stepped onto the campuses of Luther and Wartburg, I knew seminary was where I was being called. Standing in front of the entrance to the chapel and refectory at Wartburg, I read Jesus' words embossed on the great copper-plated double doors: "As you did it to one of the least of my own so you did it to me." Below these words, acts of ministry were illustrated on the doors:

feeding and clothing people, visiting the sick and those in prison, offering hospitality to a weary traveler. These were the kinds of things I wanted my life to be about. I felt the desire to shepherd others to do the same pulse through me as I stared at the copper doors of discipleship.

I immediately contacted the Western North Dakota Synod to start the ordination candidacy process and started filling out seminary applications. But in my prayer life and Scripture reading that spring, I came across Luke 12:48, which reads: "From everyone to whom much has been given, much will be required; and from the one to whom much has been entrusted, even more will be demanded."

Reality check! These words nearly prevented me from entering seminary. Did I really want to hold the office of pastor, to be entrusted with proclaiming the Word of God and administering the sacraments, and to bear the responsibility of caring for the people I would shepherd? I decided I did not—at least, not yet. I deferred my seminary application and looked for something else to do while I spent more time in prayer and discernment.

In August 2005, I moved even further south—this time to the Land of Enchantment, beautiful New Mexico. I liked volunteering and living in community so much that I joined Urban Servant Corps' sister program, called Border Servant Corps, and moved into their Las Cruces house to join three roommates.

I accepted a position at Mesilla Valley Habitat for Humanity as the assistant to the director—a catch-all role that included a myriad of odd jobs. Instead of working with six- to eleven-year-old girls, I now worked with a bunch of retired men.

I also worked closely with a group of courageous Latina women. Some of them had bravely left abusive husbands—children in their arms, barely able to speak English—and headed into an unknown world without a place to call home. These women taught me the definition of perseverance.

Before my year was up we handed the keys of brand-new homes to four single mothers and a married couple with children. Two of the women took me to dinner at the Golden Corral as a thank-you. We spoke of dreams for their new homes and their children in their broken English and my broken Spanish. When it came time to pay for our meal, one of the women took out a crisp fifty-dollar bill. The pride on their faces in taking me out to dinner was so humbling and will forever remain stamped in my memory.

I also participated in a border women's group of nuns who had dedicated their lives to the people and politics of the boundary that separated so many and could mean life or death. Thanks to these sisters, I had a number of opportunities to go into Juarez, Mexico, where I witnessed a more extreme form of poverty and met and heard the stories of people who lived south of the forbidden border, including the story of one couple who traveled on foot from Guatemala fleeing gang violence. The woman was eight months pregnant.

The border and immigration issues were incredibly complicated and there were no easy answers, but I met Jesus in the stranger, exhausted and worn out from a long and desperate journey.

I worshipped once along "la frontera," the border. People from Juarez stood on one side of a tall fence topped with barbwire as the faith community I was with stood on the other side. Children wrapped their tiny fingers around the chain links, looked up at me, and smiled. We sang hymns and prayed for one another as brothers and sisters in Christ.

My internal call to public ministry was gaining strength. As I observed and participated with the nuns, visited people living in Juarez and on the border, and joined the faith community of Peace Lutheran Church in Las Cruces, I began to feel that I might be ready to be entrusted with pastoral ministry and to work on giving up my own life for the sake of something greater. I wanted to serve the kingdom of God on earth as found in the poor, the stranger, and the people of God who comprise the church.

I will never forget the joy and peace I felt when I woke up one Sunday morning in May 2006 overwhelmed with a feeling of clarity. I must and would attend Wartburg Theological Seminary in Dubuque, Iowa, and become a pastor.

I had been agonizing, discerning, and praying for so long about whether to attend seminary (and which one) that when the peace of the Spirit of God finally descended upon me, I just relaxed into it and let it encompass me. It seemed that one of my greatest adventures was still ahead.

At the end of July I shoved everything I owned into my car, said goodbye to my three roommates (who had become like sisters to me), and took off on my solo, three-day trek to the land of corn.

2

Falling in Love

I WAS DRAWN TO Wartburg Theological Seminary because of its emphasis on communal life centered around worship and the Word. I was confident that Wartburg's formation and education would make me a sound theologian and the best pastor I could be. I didn't know it was also where I would meet my husband.

There is nothing like a summer Greek romance! Studying ancient participles begs for something more exciting in one's life. The guy with green eyes and the multi-colored beard merited my particular attention.

One weekend I went camping with a number of my seminary classmates, including Ben. We played a game around the campfire called "Two Truths and a Lie." The object was to guess each person's lie out of three things they said about themselves. It was Ben's turn. "I can pull lint out of my belly button at any given moment of every day. I have gone scuba diving. I have dated twenty-two women and have been dumped eighteen times."

Oh my goodness, I thought. *If the last one is true, I am* not *going to date this guy.*

"I haven't gone scuba diving!" he boasted. My mouth dropped open, and I hoped no one could see it in the campfire light. *Why on earth has he been dumped so many times? I can deal with the lint, but that's it . . . no dating this guy.*

We started dating a week later.

I knew Ben was a songwriter and a gifted musician, but I did not realize at first how many songs he had written, the depth that he poured into his music, and how it reflected his profound faith and love for God. I knew Ben's silly songs, like the one titled "Cheese Curds." I also knew he had a reputation at Luther College for serenading girls he hoped to date. This seemed pretty romantic, but I was still determined not to fall for Ben and be number twenty-three. His heart had already been broken so many times. Why?

It took me a couple of weeks to convince Ben to give me a CD of music he had written and recorded. I listened:

Your eyes are the most beautiful I've ever seen
Glistening blue[1] I've seen them in my dreams
I look at them, I see peace
I look at them, I see love
Ohhhhhh . . . why does my heart beat this way?
Ohhhhhh . . . why does my heart beat this way?
Your eyes, your smile, your touch

Ben's voice, life, passion, and faith poured into my ears, and my heart opened wide to this extraordinary person. I bathed in the lyrics and music. I thought, *This guy just loves! Loves God, and loves people.* I recognized the self-confidence that drove him to take risks and be vulnerable enough to ask a woman he hardly knew on a date. I also thanked the heavenly stars that those other eighteen women didn't date him long enough to appreciate the way his heart beat.

When I listened to Ben's music I saw into the window that was his soul and his being. I wanted to be a part of his life and know deeply the person who could create such beauty and melody. My whole life changed the night I listened to thirteen of Ben's songs. From that moment on I loved Ben: his silliness, his compassion, his faith . . . everything.

As for Ben, apparently his life had changed that night we went camping. It was all because of a dog.

After our campfire games, some of us decided to sleep out under the stars. A few hours later, we were awakened by a low, threatening growl. I opened my eyes and saw a Rottweiler, teeth bared, just a few feet from our heads. We laid there stiff for what seemed like hours as it snarled and barked at us. I looked in vain for a stick or anything we could use to defend ourselves. Finally I got fed up. I whispered to the others, and on my count, we all sprang up and darted into the tents with the dog on our heels.

The next morning I told the dog's owner what had happened. "Sorry about that," he said. He turned to the dog and yelled, "Rubber Nuts, you damn dog!"

It was the night I took on Rubber Nuts the Rottweiler that won me the heart of Ben Larson. Looking back on it later, he told me, "My family is full of strong women, and I loved seeing that fearlessness in you."

---

1. After we had been dating for a while, Ben changed the lyric of "blue" to "dark" since my eyes are brown and re-recorded "Eyes, Smile, Touch." When on a mission trip to help rebuild New Orleans, and after playing one of his songs at night, one of Ben's youth group asked him if he wrote the song for me. Ben said, "Not originally, but now all my songs are for Renee."

Ben's Family, Music, and Faith

I didn't know it, but our relationship was forbidden. Ben's mother, April, had given him three very strict rules before entering seminary, including: "Absolutely, under no circumstances, fall in love with another seminarian."

April Larson was a bishop—the first Lutheran woman bishop in the western hemisphere, to be precise. (Ben loved to refer to himself as a "son of a bish.") She knew how difficult it was for clergy couples to get placement within a synod. She would say, "There is always one of the couple who is unhappy with their call." Her pastor husband, Judd, would grin and respond: "I'm happy."

I think "No seminarians" was the only parental rule Ben ever broke. He respected his parents more than any other people on earth. Because they were both pastors, he had all the pressures of a "pastor's kid" growing up, and then some. He once told me, "I could have disobeyed my parents and done all kinds of things that would have disappointed them, but I could easily see that the people they were on Sunday morning were the same people they were at home. There was no hypocrisy in them whatsoever, and I never doubted my parents' call to ministry." Ben fully embraced the identity of a pastor's kid. He understood the life of ministry from a young age.

Ben was born to Judd and April Larson on February 27, 1984. His twin sisters, Katie and Amy, were already five when he was born, and were like another set of mothers to him. I once asked Ben if he ever fought with his sisters growing up. He thought about this for much longer than I would have to think about such a question and finally said, "We had an argument once in the car about whether Monticello is pronounced 'Monti-sell-o' or 'Monti-chell-o.'"

One of the first things Ben shared with me about his sisters was that they were already reading medical journals at the age of five—only a slight exaggeration. They were doctors from the start.[2] Amy and Katie nurtured Ben and he entertained them. He rarely had to help with the dishes, because they all agreed that if Amy and Katie would do them, Ben would entertain them with stories, jokes, and plays. Everyone was happy with this arrangement.

Even though Ben was on track to be a pastor, it was not what he had in mind for himself. Ben loved music from the beginning. When April was seven months pregnant with Ben, she conducted a performance of "Hodie Natus Est" by Heinrich Schütz for Advent. When Ben was old enough to

---

2. Katie is now a pediatric endocrinologist at University of Iowa Children's Hospital and married Seth Ode. Amy is a pediatric geneticist at University of Minnesota Masonic Children's Hospital and married Peter Calhoun.

walk, April was astonished to realize he was moving around the house humming the melody of "Hodie Natus Est." There was nowhere he could have heard that music except in the womb.

Ben was an infant when he attended his first Women of the ELCA Triennial Gathering with his mother, and was present at the age of five at the very first ELCA Global Mission event in 1989, where April helped lead music. Being part of the larger church was simply a way of life for Ben, and he quickly followed in his mother's footsteps and began to help lead music at Global Mission events in his high school years in the late 1990s.

Ben sang in choirs while growing up and was active in his La Crosse Central High School's show choir. He also sang in a barbershop-style quartet in high school that won awards. His dream was to sing in the celebrated Nordic Choir at Luther College in Decorah, Iowa.

Ben was introduced to songs of faith from around the world at an early age. Because his parents were pastors (and his mom a bishop), church leaders from different countries were frequent guests in their home. At night they would tell stories and sing songs from their faith communities. Ben gravitated toward African songs with their strong drum rhythms and four-part harmonies. He also loved to dance and move to the Latin beats of South America, or close his eyes to enjoy the Celtic whistle.

One of Ben's most transformative moments came was when he was fifteen. It was Easter Sunday, and Ben had traveled to Ethiopia with his father and others from the La Crosse Area Synod. They were there to form relationships with the people of the Ethiopian Evangelical Church Mekane Yesus (Place of Jesus), their companion church.

On Easter morning, Ben and his dad were staying in a guesthouse in a local village. Around 3 a.m. they awoke to the faint sound of singing. They rose from bed and went outside in the darkness, the kind of pitch blackness that comes with no electricity or street lights. They discovered people were gathering, lifting their voices together in song, and following torches that lit their way through the dark streets.

The singing procession flowed through the streets of the village, adding more and more people as they went along, including Ben and his dad. The whole community, thousands and thousands of people of all ages and from all Christian faith traditions, joined the throng as they made their way up the mountain just outside the village. They walked and sang, following the light of the torches. The sun rose as they reached the top of the mountain, and there they worshipped on Easter morning, celebrating the resurrection of Jesus Christ from the dead.

College and Choir

A few years later, Ben entered Luther College, where he hoped to sing in the prestigious Nordic Choir. His freshman year, he placed in the junior Norscmcn Choir. When he tried out again as a sophomore, Westin Nobel, the conductor of the Nordic Choir, gave Ben tenor parts for his audition. Ben made the choir, but what Westin didn't realize was that Ben sang his audition in falsetto. He was actually a bass.

When Westin found out Ben's range, Ben ended up singing all four men's parts in the Nordic Choir over the next three years. He was elected choir president his senior year.

Predictably, Ben had entered Luther College as a music major, but in the middle of his junior year he had a huge turning point when he was driving home to La Crosse. Ben loved driving his red Nissan Maxima with the windows down and music blaring (usually Dave Matthews or U2). After a few miles on the road, he reached for his radio and pushed the "off" button. Suddenly, he did not want to hear music—any music. It was as though his intense study of music in college had dampened its joy for him. Something needed to change. He thought long and hard and realized that what lit a fire in him now were his religion classes.

He told me about that time: "I wanted everyone to know what I was learning. I became so excited about theology and talking about God. I decided to become a religion major at that moment. For the first time I pondered whether or not I might be headed for seminary." Ben took twenty-one credits through summer school and worked furiously to graduate on time after switching majors. When he graduated as a religion major from Luther College in 2006, music became joy, gift, and life for him once again.

Engagement and Life Together

Ben and I became engaged in July 2007 on the banks of the Upper Iowa River in Decorah, Iowa. We were exhausted from the rigors of our first year at Wartburg followed immediately by our required clinical pastoral education (CPE), which meant that we were both full-time hospital and long-term care facility chaplains for the summer. Tired, yes, but we were bound and determined to go canoeing. As we attempted to carry the heavy canoe down the steep, muddy embankment, Ben suddenly put the front end of the boat down on the ground.

"What are you doing?" I asked. "Put the canoe in the water."

He did not say a word, but climbed the muddy hill in his swimming trunks up to where I was. He pulled out a box and opened it and said, "Will you . . ."

A blue sapphire shone up at me. I could not orient my brain to what was going on. I stood there in my bathing suit, slathered in sunscreen. We had never talked about engagement. It must have been a solid minute before I figured out what was happening. "Well, if you ask me . . ."

He took the ring out of the box and shoved it on my finger as he asked, "Will you marry me?"

With the ring already on my finger, I said, "Yes." Suddenly I was slipping down a muddy riverbank with a number of precious jewels on my hand and a new future ahead of me. We pushed the canoe into the water and started paddling. We passed a couple who were outside on their porch and yelled, "We just got engaged!" They cheered.

I said to Ben, "This ring is so beautiful!"

"I thought of you when I bought it," he replied.

"I certainly hope so," I laughed.

"Ah! My dad told me not to say anything stupid," he mourned.[3]

I loved that day. And, Ben being Ben, wanted to be married right away. If he had his way we would have been married within the month. I lobbied for the following summer and we met in the middle with December 29, 2007.

We thought long and hard about what our last name should be. Should we each keep our family names? No, we did not want to have different last names. Should we both be Splichal? Ben was in favor of this, and he had two solid arguments. First, he said Benjamin Splichal is a really cool name, and second, it's sexist that the woman always takes the man's last name.

Should we combine our last names and make a new one? The best we and our friends at seminary could come up with was "Splarchalson," but that sounded more like a fireworks company than a proper last name.

What about just Larson? It's a simple and common name, especially for two people who are becoming pastors; however, there was the whole "sexist" issue, and Ben would have none of it.

In the end we decided we would each keep our own last names and add them together: Renee and Ben Splichal Larson. Our identities were both changing, yet it was important for both of us to keep our family names.

---

3. When Ben's dad, Judd, asked April to marry him, he dug in his pocket and pulled out a ring among a handful of change. He said, "This is what I got for you after a summer of bagging raisins." (He prepared food for canoeing trips out of Wilderness Canoe Base Camp.) "And I even got it on sale so I had enough left over to buy a pizza."

After we decided, Ben said happily, "Renee, I'm practically African—I just keep on adding names. Benjamin Judd Ulring Splichal Larson!"

I loved Ben's humor. Even from a young age he was witty. One day he came home from first grade and said to his parents, "We practiced writing p's today. I just wrote upside down d's and the teacher didn't even know the difference!"

On road trips I would buy a bag of Laffy Taffy candy and read him the jokes. He would guess the answers at least half of the time, and the other half he came up with better answers to the jokes than what was written. For our first Valentine's Day[4] as a married couple, he made up puns and strategically placed them so that I would find them during my morning routine. On the bananas I found the note: "You drive me bananas!" On the oatmeal container: "You make me flip my lid!" On the milk carton: "I dairy you to kiss me!" In the top bowl in our cupboard: "You are soooo luv-a-bowl." And my favorite one was on the coffeepot: "If you were coffee, you wouldn't be low acid because you give me heartburn!" Ben expressed his love for me in many creative ways, yet none were as dear to me as his daily spoken word of, "I love you so much, Renee, my wife."

The most meaningful gift I ever received from Ben besides my wedding ring and his music was a Bible. I used to lug around a heavy HarperCollins Study Bible complete with commentary and Apocrypha. One day soon after we were married, Ben met me right after chapel. He had a big smile on his face as he said, "I got you a gift." He pulled out a more reasonable, smaller, leather-bound Bible. On the inside cover he had written these words:

> For My Love Renee,
>
> So that the word of God might not weigh you down as much as the HarperCollins version.
> May your faith increase with participation in the Word.
>
> Love, Your Husband,
> Ben

Ben's favorite drink in the world was coffee. He often argued that he did not need to drink water in a given day because coffee was mostly water. As Ben's mother, April, once said: "I could live without coffee; I just wouldn't feel like I was alive."

---

4. For our very first Valentine's Day date before we were engaged, we went to a restaurant on the Mississippi River and got into an intense discussion on the relevance and importance of the Ten Commandments. Ben argued that it's all about grace and there shouldn't be such an emphasis on teaching them, whereas I thought there needed to be more of a balance. Our disagreement carried into the next morning after seminary chapel, when we pulled our homiletics professor into our argument to determine who was right. We never got our answer, because he laughed and said, "Did you spend your whole date talking about this? You two . . . you need to figure it out."

Probably one of the reasons Ben loved coffee so much was because he would usually drink it around a table with others in conversation. One of Ben's greatest joys was to be with others, especially when it involved coffee, a meal, and wine.

Back in college, Ben would receive $100 at the beginning of every month from his parents. This would be all the money he had for four weeks until he got his next $100. The logical thing would be to spend $25 each week and plan well to get himself to the next month, but logic was not high on Ben's priority list. Instead, his priority was: how can I share this money with others, and how can we all enjoy it together? Money was never too important to Ben, and when he did have it he mostly gave it away. When he was little he would receive an allowance every once in a while, and he would take it to his twin sisters and say, "Amy, Katie, can we go to the store so I can buy you something with this money?" They, of course, would point him in the direction of his glass pig and tell him that it was his money and he needed to keep it.

One of the many things I cherished about Ben was the complex nature of his faith in God. When I first met him, it was easy for me to stereotype him as the "guitar worship leader guy" who mostly just loved Jesus because of his general joy for life and love of people. I quickly discovered that real doubt was an intimate piece of Ben's faith life, and tough questions were an important part of his close and beautiful relationship with God.

Ben certainly did not have a blind belief, but rather a profound faith that came out of seeing the painful realities of the world and his own short-comings. Often, during our long car rides to visit family or evenings before bed, we would talk about things like children dying of hunger and how a loving God could allow such travesties. We contemplated the complex issue of free will and how it related to the grace of God. After working through his struggles, Ben came to believe that doubt is not the opposite of faith, but necessary for faith. Ben's sister Katie once said to me: "One reason I think so many people could relate to Ben is that he knew and saw himself as a sinner; yet, he also completely believed in the love of God for him and for all people." I loved this about Ben.[5]

Since I was the oldest of three and Ben was the youngest of three, we differed in a few important ways, especially when it came to money management (see above!) and planning. We were both familiar with the

---

5. He wrote in his song "Pierced Hands": "Oh, I am a sinner Lord, I know I am, I know I am." He also wrote the song "Certainty" for me when I was struggling with my own faith. The song says: "If you are in search of certainty / Then you are on the wrong ship / And if you are in search of control / Then you are sailing in the wrong waters / But in this world not all is uncertain / There's the love of God and my love for you."

Myers-Briggs Type Indicator, a personality inventory tool that was helpful for discovering some of these differences. The Myers-Briggs indicator was created to help people better understand themselves and others, especially others who function differently from themselves in a work environment, a marriage, and so on. We learned that people can fluctuate within their categories (there are four) toward the middle, but no one ever changes dominant characteristics.

Ben's personality type was an ENFP, which basically meant that he was an extrovert who received his energy from being around other people; that he needed plenty of time for play and creativity; that he made decisions with his heart rather than based on logic; and that having a day fully scheduled out would be like a day spent in hell. Ben was a "feeler" through and through (the "F" in ENFP). He also used to brag about being such an off-the-chart "P" ("perception," or being open to many possibilities) that it was "almost a personality disorder."

I, on the other hand, was an ENFJ, with emphasis on the "J" (judgment versus perception). Thus, Ben and I were very compatible in every category except the last one. Unlike Ben, I loved having a plan. I would schedule my day to the minute sometimes and it felt good. I made lists, I crossed things off, and then I made more lists. In contrast, hardly anything depleted Ben's energy more than having a very full day with lots of places to be and things to do within a certain time frame. Making and sticking with a decision was really tough for him because it left no room for creative energy. He felt it was much more interesting to keep options open.

I can roll with the punches and be spontaneous when necessary, but it mostly stresses me out. If I don't know what to plan for in a day, I start to feel my chest tighten and the anxiety monster whispers in my ear, "You could be getting something done!"

When we were in the final week of our seminary internship year in Lincoln, Nebraska, Ben and I were with a small group of people at Our Saviour's Lutheran Church after a Saturday night worship service. Someone suggested that the group should take Ben and me out for dinner to celebrate the conclusion of our internship. People started throwing out suggestions, but no one was making a decision. After about fifteen minutes of, "Where should we eat?" and plan after plan being proposed and discarded, some-one finally decided on the Olive Garden. *Thank goodness!* I thought. *Pasta sounds great. Hmmm . . . I think I'll have their salad and chicken parmesan.* But no sooner did we step out of the church doors than Ben said, "Well, maybe we should go to HuHot."

Not another change of plans! Right there in that church parking lot with about six congregation members within earshot, I blurted out: "Oh, Ben! You and your P-ness!"

Ben put his hand to his open mouth, gasped, and stopped in his tracks. I stood wide-eyed and looked all around to see if any of the people had heard. *Some of them must have heard.* I looked back at Ben, who started laughing hysterically.

I wanted to crawl in a deep, dark hole and never come out. How could I possibly explain to these beloved people what "P-ness" meant—that it referred to Myers-Briggs and the way our marriage worked despite our personality differences?

Laughing, Ben took out his phone and started to dial his beloved cousin, Jon.

"Don't tell Jon!" I pleaded. Of course that didn't stop him, and you can hear me begging on Jon's voicemail, "Don't tell Jon!" as Ben is divulging every last inappropriate detail. By then we were both laughing.

When everyone sat down for dinner in the Olive Garden, no one said anything about Ben's P-ness.

3

Double Cousins

WHEN I MET JONATHAN Larson, his hair was longer than mine: thick, curly, and blond, enough to make any hockey or soccer player jealous. Jon's laugh was infectious, a wide-open-mouth laugh that revealed his very straight, white teeth.

I met Ben and Jon in the Wartburg Seminary chapel after a worship service in which Jon played guitar, Ben played mandolin, and a woman I had met the week before named Elly played violin. When the service ended, I approached Elly to thank her for helping me move into my apartment when I arrived on campus. She said, "You're welcome. Have you met Ben and Jon yet?" I had not. They were chuckling together about some joke as they greeted me.

"Are you just visiting campus or are you a student here?" Ben asked.

"I'm a student," I said.

"Great!" Ben and Jon chimed at the same time. Then Ben asked, "Do you happen to play piano?"

Surprised at how quickly that question came out, I said, "Actually, I do."

"Would you like to play with us in chapel tomorrow?" Elly inquired.

"Um . . . sure." From that day on, Elly, Ben, Jon, and I hung out often. We played music together when we were not playing card games or studying.

It quickly became clear that Benjamin Judd Ulring Larson and Jonathan David Ulring Larson had a very special relationship. First of all, Ben and Jon's humor stood out. They fed off one another and understood each other's jokes instantly while the rest of us stared blankly. Ben and Jon simply laughed together, all the time, and it was a beautiful thing.

Each morning before Greek class, Jon—who woke long before Ben—would knock on Ben's dorm room door to make sure he was up. I would always see them sitting together in the refectory at breakfast as I walked to class, Jon bright-eyed and awake, coffee in hand, smiling at his half-asleep cousin.

They were so close, and there was enough family resemblance, that many people assumed Ben and Jon were brothers. When asked, they would say, "No, but we are three-fourths the same person," or "No, but we're double cousins."

This was true. Their dads were brothers and their moms were favorite first cousins. Jon's parents, David and Miriam, met at Ben's parents' wedding, but went on their first date a number of years later when April's sister, Janet, set them up. They were both so shy that their friends and family wondered if they would ever have gone on their first date without Janet's help.

Dave and Mim were married two years later. They didn't expect to have children because in her late teens Mim had been diagnosed with a brain tumor that affected her pituitary gland. She had surgery to remove the tumor, but was told that conceiving someday would be difficult if not impossible. And yet, at the age of thirty-four, Miriam gave birth to Jonathan, two months after her cousin, April (also thirty-four), gave birth to Ben. Four years later, Mim and Dave had a daughter, whom they named Elizabeth. Jon loved being her big brother, and the two are still very active in each other's lives. The double cousins—Katie, Amy, Ben, Jon, and Liz—formed the closest of relationships.

Until Jon was in eighth grade, his family lived in Apple Valley, Minnesota, a suburb of the twin cities, and then they moved about an hour south to Red Wing, Minnesota. Jon's dad went through law school and became a lawyer after working for many years selling quality windows. His mom was a special education teacher, working with junior and senior high school youth who had developmental challenges.

In high school Jon worked at a small grocery store while he was involved in many school activities. He was a co-captain for the new high school soccer team. He was in choir and helped choreograph their spring concerts. He attended school dances in a borrowed powder-blue suit from the 1970s. As a good community member, his senior year, Jon started going to his friends' school organizational meetings, including becoming an honorary student council member. Who even does that sort of thing? Jon truly enjoyed seeing community at work and his leadership skills were emerging in serving others.

Jon played clarinet and violin growing up, but much of his musical instrument formation began when "Cheepo Weepo" entered his life in the eighth grade. "Cheepo Weepo" was Jon's first guitar, a gift from Ben.

Jon was not officially a part of the pep band at Red Wing High School, but a number of his friends were, including his good friend Matt, who played tuba in the very back. Tuba players rotated to play the giant cowbell, and once when it was Matt's turn, he waved Jon over and gave it to him to play as a joke. Soon the joke was happening every time the pep band played, and Jon become the honorary cowbell player. There he was on the basketball floor his senior year—long locks, aviators, and a giant cowbell keeping the beat to "Low Rider." The band director finally became aware of the new addition to the band when one of the junior high band directors approached him and said, "You know what makes this band really good? Jon Larson on the cowbell. He keeps a great rhythm and he really seems to enjoy himself."

This experience sparked Jon's love for hand percussion and drumming. He later became skilled at playing the djembe and congas.

Jon loved music, and he entered Augustana College in Sioux Falls, South Dakota, with a music scholarship, so a music major would have been natural. Instead, he chose to major in religion, and fostered his love for music by singing in the choir and taking voice lessons.

Jon didn't go into college specifically planning to be a pastor; he simply loved God, loved theology, and loved the church. Jon had been nurtured in faith by a number of pastors and people in his life. His godparents were Ben's parents, Judd and April, who were ordained as the first husband and wife to go through candidacy and the master of divinity degree program together in seminary. I have often heard Judd and April call Jon "godson" or "beloved godson."

Jon's grandfather, Morris (Morrie) Ulring, also served as a pastor for many decades. One cannot speak with Morrie without hearing about Jesus and how the Lord has blessed his life. Whenever Jon spoke with his grandfather, it was less than a minute before Morrie witnessed to Christ crucified and raised. This was not aggressive proselytizing, but a genuine, heartfelt witness of the love between a human being and his Creator, Redeemer, and Sustainer. When Jon was eventually ordained, Morrie gave him the cross he had worn throughout his ministry. Now at the age of ninety-five (as of this writing), Morrie still "cruises" around with his walker, declaring that whenever the Lord is ready to take him, he is ready to go. Until then, he talks about Jesus to everyone he encounters.

Jon thrived at Augustana College. He joined the choir and campus ministry; he became a community service coordinator, a co-chapel musician coordinator, chapel president, and a peer advisor in his dorm. Jon also worked at Okoboji Lutheran Bible Camp in Iowa, where he served as a counselor for two summers and a worship director for a third summer.

Years later, I would occasionally hear Ben call Jon "Your Majesty." Jon's cheeks would instantly turn red and he would become very embarrassed. When I asked Ben about it, I found out Jon had been Augustana's Homecoming King.

Every year at Augustana, five "Covenant Awards," which were origi-nally developed by students, are given to five different seniors who model five core values of the college: Christian, liberal arts, excellence, community, and service. Jon was awarded the "Christian" award, which states:

> I recognize that dialogue centered on the Christian faith is es-sential to an Augustana education. We encourage the search for religious faith by learning through open dialogue within our own faith and with those of other faiths. We understand the importance of relating Christian virtue and ethics to every facet of life.

Jon was humbled and also quite uncomfortable with the idea of receiv-ing an award for modeling Christian values. As a Lutheran Christian, Jon thought such an award—earned by merit—seemed contrary to grace. (As a boy, he had left Boy Scouts partly because he was uncomfortable earning "merit" badges.) Nevertheless, it spoke to Jon's character and how others perceived him.

Like most college graduates, Jon was faced with choices: get a job, vol-unteer, attend more school, and so on. He chose more school and to become a pastor. He knew that ordination would empower him to live out his voca-tion more fully in the world—his passion for the global church, the outsider, issues of hunger and poverty, simplicity, music, worship, and community.

It amazed me that Jon and Ben enrolled at Wartburg independently of one another. When I asked them why they both chose to attend Wartburg, they had the same answer: "I loved that worship and community were cen-tral to learning, that after worshiping together, students, faculty, and staff would flow into the refectory to have coffee and conversation."

Shaping

Jon's first exposure to diverse cultures came in his senior year in high school when he took two service-learning trips with his church youth group to inner-city Chicago, where he spent time in African American and Puerto Rican communities and helped to lead vacation Bible school for the chil-dren there.

Before his first trip, his mom wrote him this little note and sent it with him:

Jonathan,

How special you are—and how wonderful of you to share with
the children of Chicago. God's PEACE!

As your Mom, I will name you by name in my prayers. You
are named and called in baptism—now you are sharing with
many special children in Chicago.

We trust God for your every need.

Love,
Mom

P.S. Oh, remember to eat your fruits and vegetables.

Jon was further shaped by three significant international trips during
and after college. The first two were with the Augustana Choir; he traveled
to Ireland in 2004 and Tanzania in 2006. Jon loved the hospitality of the
people of Tanzania, who lined the streets with welcome. People dressed in
bright colors danced, sang, and welcomed the visitors into their villages.
In return, the Augustana Choir sang "Neno lake Mungu" ("Listen, God Is
Calling") and the Tanzania national anthem in Kiswahili. In Ireland the
Augustana Choir sang "Danny Boy" and an Irish blessing in Gaelic. In both
countries the people were touched that these guests had learned some of
their language and the songs they held dear.

Jon's third trip was the "January term" for his first year at Wartburg
Seminary. He went to Guyana in South America, where he practiced his
pastoral skills, mostly learning from and listening to the fascinating, unique,
and diverse people in the small northern coastal country of South America.

When I met Jon in seminary, I could immediately see his enthusiasm
and how ready he was to engage with people from different cultures and
learn from brothers and sisters in Christ from around the world. Jon served
as the student assistant for the Center for Global Theologies at Wartburg,
helping to provide opportunities for seminary students and the people of
Dubuque to hear theologians, ambassadors, and others from around the
globe. Jon knew that entering into conversation with others provided valu-
able opportunities to learn and be changed.

Jon also served as a co–senior class president, which meant—among
other things—that he sat in on the faculty meetings when our instructors
determined whether or not each of us was ready to become a pastor in the
ELCA. Everyone in our class knew we had a good advocate and a deep and
compassionate thinker representing us.

On the Myers-Briggs scale, Jon is an INFP, which matches Ben's type
except that Jon is introverted instead of extroverted. Jon loves being around

people and in group settings, but he primarily processes his decisions and his learning internally. As I was getting to know Jon, I often had to ask him about himself or what he thought about something.

It wasn't that Jon never shared what he was thinking; instead, he was more of a listener, and very humble. If there was ever a decision to be made, Jon would say, "I need to think about it for a while." All of us who knew Jon understood the careful thought and intentional prayer behind whatever he did, decided, and committed himself to. He certainly loved spontaneity and enjoyed changing plans to make life more fun, but you could also sense Jon's groundedness and deep faith.

Jon completed his seminary internship in Portland, Oregon, part of the so-called "none zone," [1] at a redevelopment church. This was essentially a larger church that had lost much of its membership and was trying to reestablish itself. Along with his pastoral responsibilities, Jon was involved with campus ministry and an ecumenical group at Portland State University. He was part of a Christian/Jewish group that focused on peace issues and a "reconciling in Christ" group, which worked to welcome those who identified as lesbian, gay, bisexual, or transgender. He enjoyed biking everywhere, playing pickup soccer games, and hanging around in local coffee shops and pubs.

Unfortunately, early in his internship, Jon's supervisor's wife was diagnosed with terminal cancer. Her condition was challenging for the ministry, devastating for Jon's colleague, and required Jon to navigate with a supervisor who was unable to be fully present. More than halfway through the year, Jon was given a secondary supervisor, whom he deeply appreciated. Shortly after Jon left his internship site and returned to seminary, his supervisor's wife died.

Loss and Grief

Death was no stranger to Jon. It first visited his family when his grandmother was killed in the fall of 1999, when she was struck by a pickup while she was out taking a walk. It then hung around, like a despised and unwanted guest.

In the fall of 2002, during Jon's first semester of college at Augustana, his mother fell ill while participating in a teacher's strike in Red Wing, Minnesota, where she marched with her fellow teachers for more equitable and just pay. The only thing that would prevent her from continuing that fight

---

1. The "none zone" is an area of the country in which the majority of people, when filling out forms and asked to identify a religious preference, check the box "none."

was a fight for her life. Mim was diagnosed with scleroderma, an autoimmune disease that built up scar tissue on her skin.

In late November, Jon's father, Dave, lost his own father suddenly to a heart attack. Mim was unable to attend the funeral because she was in the hospital. While the Ulring/Larson family was still grieving, Miriam Joy Ulring Larson died on December 1, 2002, less than a month after her diagnosis.

Jonathan came home from college and was in the room with Mim when she died. He saw his mother struggle for breath and die in agony. To this day Jon is uncertain whether he regrets having witnessed her death because of her suffering. His only consolation was a trip he and his mother had taken together to Augustana earlier that fall, when she had seen him sing in the Augustana Choir—the choir she sang in while attending Augustana herself.

The rest of that semester and the second semester of college were incredibly difficult for Jon as he tried to process his life without the presence of his mother. Forced to drop some classes, Jon made them up through independent study while working at Bible camp the following summer. Dave and Liz tried to cope with Mim's death in their own ways. Dave remodeled their home, something he and Mim had always wanted to do. Liz, on the other hand, was only a freshman in high school. She does not even remember whole sections of her life after her mom died. She says it was like living in a daze.

To remember her mom, Liz photocopied her own birth certificate, where Mim had written the middle name they shared—Joy—and took it to a tattoo shop. A guy named Yedi, at Electric Dragonland, tattooed "Joy" in her mother's handwriting onto Elizabeth Joy's skin to help her carry Miriam Joy wherever she walked.

Mim's death was devastating for Jon's family as well as Ben's family and everyone else who loved her. After Mim died, the two Ulring/Larson families became closer than ever. April and Judd started to include Dave, Jon, and Liz in their prayers as they prayed for their own children every night. Jon and Ben relied on each other and grew to care for and love one another on an extraordinarily deep level.

There are countless Ben and Jon stories. Most of them are goofy and fun, but there are also many that display their great love and respect for one another. Of course, Jon stood as Ben's best man in our wedding. When I think of Ben and Jon's relationship, a few words come to mind: joy, mischief, hospitality, loyalty, music, play, bond, and love. Even though they were born just two months apart, grew up together, and shared many similar characteristics, Ben and Jon were each their own unique person: gifted and wonderful.

Many people do not realize or do not remember that there were three of us in Haiti, not just two. It is also hard to understand the deep bond Ben and Jon had without meeting them or knowing some of their history together. People understand the depth of the loss when a husband is killed; it can be harder to appreciate the depth of the loss when a cousin is killed— even a "double cousin."

As difficult as Mim's death was for him, Jon has told me more than once: "Ben's death is harder for me than my own mother's death." I weep for Jon and his loss of his brother and best friend.

4

Arrival in Haiti

THE FIRST TIME HAITI registered on my consciousness was in 2002. I was a sophomore at Concordia College in Moorhead, Minnesota, and had decided to join a small group of six students and three professors on a trip to Nicaragua. The trip was sponsored through campus ministry, and we planned to spend our "May term" building two houses with Habitat for Humanity International.

When we landed in Nicaragua's capital city, Managua, we piled our bags into the back of a pickup and sat on them as we were driven to our hotel for the night. I closed my eyes in the cool evening air, my hair whipping behind me. Damaged roads paved the way for vehicles, carts, people, oxen, and other animals. I realized the depressions and upturned chunks of concrete were left from a major 1972 earthquake in Managua that killed 5,000 people. When I asked one of our hosts why the damage hadn't been repaired thirty years later, she said, "The government did not use money for earthquake relief."

I loved Nicaragua and its people, culture, food, and music. I felt so free and full of joy there because of the people's hospitality, gorgeous landscape, and new learning opportunities.

Our group worked with local male Nicaraguan volunteers to build two homes in a "small" city of 70,000 called Diriamba. We built the homes out of concrete that we mixed by hand. I loved the hard physical work, as well as the much-needed, two-hour daily siesta (nap). Women and children stood around the periphery of the work area, smiling as they watched us "white people," and especially those of us who were female, hauling buckets of concrete and digging septic tank holes. One woman gave me a little flower in appreciation for what we were doing in her community.

Before we traveled to Nicaragua, our professors gave us materials to read about the country so that we would not be totally ignorant when we touched down in Managua. I kept reading, "Nicaragua is the second poorest country in the western hemisphere, right behind Haiti." This didn't mean much to me until I actually arrived in Nicaragua. In addition to wonderful people and a beautiful landscape, there was also incredible poverty. We walked garbage-filled streets and saw undernourished children, mangy dogs, pieces of tin propped up to serve as family dwellings, and children as young as seven or eight lying dazed in the streets as they sniffed glue in glass jars. I thought, *If this is the second poorest country in the western hemisphere, then what is Haiti like?* I would find out just a few years later.

Internship and Haiti

From August 2008 to August 2009, Ben and I served as pastoral interns in Lincoln, Nebraska. Wartburg Seminary assigned our internships, so when I opened my envelope and saw *Lutheran Student Center, Campus Ministry University of Nebraska, Lincoln,* I was surprised and excited. "I'm going to be in campus ministry!" I exclaimed to Ben. "Where are you going to be?"

"Our Saviour's Lutheran Church. It looks awesome! It has a prison ministry and everything. How exciting!"

We had an incredibly rich internship experience between our two ministry contexts, often spending time at each other's sites. The Lutheran Center was a wonderful ministry for me to be involved in, providing opportunities to walk with college students in their faith life. Rich theological conversation, training for a half marathon, pancakes and morning book studies, and worship with students greatly enriched my life and shaped me into a more competent pastoral leader.

I think of our internship year with fondness and gratitude. One of the many reasons our internship experience was so rich was because Ben and I had the opportunity to travel to Haiti.

People become introduced to Haiti in all kinds of ways, but for Americans who are not in government or the military, it's usually indirect: they know someone who knows someone, or they become connected with an organization that has a presence in Haiti. Haiti is close to the U.S. (less than 700 miles or an hour and a half flight from Florida), making it a "convenient" and exotic travel destination for missionary folk to visit a nearby developing country.

The "someone" I knew who had a heart for Haiti was my internship supervisor, Eric Bostrom. He and his wife Rhonda had been introduced to Haiti through their internship congregation, Abiding Hope Lutheran Church in Littleton, Colorado, which founded an organization called the Haitian Timoun Foundation (HTF). *Timoun* is a Creole word for children, and the foundation's mission is to raise up and empower young people "by identifying visionary Haitian-led organizations in the areas of education, poverty eradication, and leadership development."

In 2008 HTF became a national organization, sustaining under its umbrella organizations such as Pazapa, a school for deaf students in Jacmel; Chemen Lavi Miyò ("the pathway to a better life") through Haiti's largest micro-finance bank, Fonkoze; Tèt Kole, an open center for street children in Jacmel; and St. Joseph's Home for Boys in Pétionville (part of Port-au-Prince), Wings of Hope in Fermathe, and Trinity House in Jacmel. In May 2009 my internship supervisor Eric, Ben, myself, and six University of Nebraska–Lincoln college students decided to travel to Haiti to visit HTF organizations and develop relationships with the people living on the western half of the island of Hispaniola.[1]

It is a challenge for me to travel long distances, whether by car, train, plane, or boat. As much as I love to see new places, meet new people, and be exposed to different cultures, food, and music, it is difficult for me to travel because I have terrible motion sickness. I have to carry Dramamine with me everywhere I go. I also fear for my father's health, because he frets so much when any of his children venture outside of North Dakota. Finally, I hesitate to travel to developing countries in particular because I know my life will change and I will possibly never be the same.

When I was trying to decide whether to go to Haiti for the first time, I remembered the challenges of visiting Nicaragua. I knew Haiti would expose me once again to the wretched reality of extreme and systemic poverty. You cannot leave places like Nicaragua or Haiti without permanent images stamped in your mind of what a human being looks like who is starving to death, or the deplorable feeling of saying "No" to an outstretched hand, knowing that you have more than a month's wages in your pocket. But when I asked Ben whether we should go on our first trip to Haiti, he responded, "Yes, of course, Renee. It will make us better pastors." That was all that needed to be said, so we bought our plane tickets.

Raising money to go to Haiti with six college students was its own adventure. We gathered our courage two by two at the Lutheran Center on the university campus. We had our list of donors, and our plan was simply to call these unsuspecting people and ask them for money. Now, requesting donations to do concrete things like building houses, taking care of orphans, cleaning streets, and painting is hard enough; asking for money to simply learn and build relationships turned out to be even harder. Here is how many of the conversations went:

1. The eastern half of the island is the Dominican Republic.

"Hello, my name is Renee, and I'm serving as the Lutheran Center's pastoral intern. We are taking a group of college students to Haiti this spring and are in need of donations to help us get there."

"What are you going to do there?"

"We are in the academic world, so learning is very important. We plan to build relationships with the Haitian people and learn about what life is like in Haiti."

"Hmmmm. Yes, well, what are you going to *do*?"

"We are going to build relationships and learn."

"Um, are you going to build something?"

"Yes, relationships." *Long pause . . .*

One of two responses usually followed: "Not right now," or "You can put me down for $50."

I am not exposing these conversations to make fun of people; I mention this because we live in a culture that values "doing" and measures success by tangible results. The U.S. sends group after group to developing countries to build things as though the people living in those places cannot build for themselves. I am not saying that good does not come from this or that transformation does not happen (I was undoubtedly shaped by my service trip to Nicaragua), but it is not a sustainable or empowering practice and way of doing mission.

The people who said, "Put me down for $50," planted a seed. They invested in our education and empowered us to accompany the people of Haiti.

Arriving in Haiti

In Haiti we spent time in all three homes of the St. Joseph Family, which is specifically supported by Hearts with Haiti, a nonprofit organization based out of Raleigh, North Carolina. The organization was formed in 2001 to support the mission of the St. Joseph Family by walking with its Haitian leaders to raise the next generation of children out of slavery and poverty through education, self-worth, family, and faith.

The three homes are St. Joseph's Home for Boys in Pétionville; Wings of Hope in Fermathe; and Trinity House in Jacmel. All three served as guesthouses for travelers like us, yet each was also home to Haitian children. St. Joseph's and Trinity House were home to young boys who used to be "restaveks" (street or slave children). We heard story after story from children who were once forced into slavery. They described how they were now experiencing resurrection and new life by living as a family who cared about one another.

Wings of Hope is a home for severely disabled children. We helped the staff feed, play with, and educate the kids. We learned about the social stigmas in Haiti around disabilities. Many disabled children were abandoned on the street and left to die. I witnessed small miracles each day at Wings of Hope as the staff worked with minimal resources. Despite physically painful disabilities and a society that did not want them, the children smiled, laughed, lived, and thrived thanks to the care and love given to them every day.

I particularly remember a young girl named Belinda. She was the size of an eighteen-month-old toddler, yet she was three years old. I did not know the diagnosis or extent of her illness; all I knew was her eyes and her smile. Ben took an interest in Belinda, holding her and making up songs with her name in them. She would look up at Ben and smile a big smile. She moved me.

Little did I know that within two years both of them would be dead: Ben killed by the earthquake, and Belinda killed by injustice and prejudice. When Belinda fell seriously ill, the staff at Wings of Hope took her to hospital after hospital, but one by one they turned her away because of her deformities. Belinda died in the arms of a Wings of Hope staff person on the street in front of a hospital that refused to give her medical care.

Tourists and Soccer Games

It was fascinating to see how Haitians perceived the United Nations soldiers, better known as "MINUSTAH,"[2] who were occupying their country. Some Haitians were very happy the soldiers were there; others were definitely not. Some people called the soldiers "tourists" because they did not feel they were doing anything for the people—just carrying their cameras around and taking photos.

I saw this firsthand when we all went with our guide, Verbo, a lawyer and activist in Haiti, to the large soccer field in Jacmel (a field that would later become a tent city after the earthquake). In an effort to bring the community together, he had helped start a soccer league for the local people. He had reserved the field for a game of men versus women (yes, all men versus all women!). When we arrived at the field, a team of U.N. soldiers was also there, as well as a group from the Haitian government. The U.N. and government personnel had not "reserved" the field, and it created a big problem

2. *Mission des Nations Unies pour la stabilisation en Haïti.*

that four teams were now at the field expecting to play. Verbo pointed out that this type of situation occurred often and that unfortunately the soldiers were causing more problems than solutions for the community.

We watched as Verbo diplomatically went to work convincing the government and U.N. workers to leave the field. While he did this, other U.N. soldiers kept pointing at us white people in fascination. A few of them took out their cameras and started taking photos of us. I was terribly uncomfortable and felt on display, like an animal at the zoo. I realized that this is probably how the Haitians feel when we take pictures of them without their permission. The soldiers eventually came up and asked us if we were from the U.S. and if they could take a photo with us. A couple of the guys adjusted their guns and came over to have their buddy take their picture with us Americans. *Tourists,* I thought.

As soon as there were only two teams left on the field, things became even more interesting, at least for me. Verbo asked me, "Renee, do you like soccer?"

"Yes, I like soccer."

"Do you play?"

"Yes, I like to play."

"Well, here's a T-shirt. You're on the women's team." He handed me an oversize blue T-shirt and I stood there with it in my hand, not knowing what to do. I truly enjoyed soccer, but I had never actually played an official game in my life and I knew for certain that I did not know all the rules, let alone the positions. I looked at Ben and exclaimed, "What should I do?"

He laughed in a way that said, *This is going to be great,* and replied, "Hand me your purse!" Men evidently never carried purses in Haiti—people pointed and laughed—but Ben walked confidently. He was much more interested in watching his terrified wife step onto the field. Luckily, two others from our group played on the men's team, so I was not the only pale person out there.

I have to say that this soccer game was the most challenging cross-cultural experience I have ever had. I did not know the language, I hardly knew the game, and I was playing with a bunch of strong women whom I deeply respected. The coach invited me to play center, a sign of Haitian hospitality.

The women wanted to win, and so did I. Although I hardly had a clue what to do, I did have a couple of things going for me: I could run and handle the ball decently, and I was in shape. I did the best I could, but I still felt terribly inadequate. I marveled at the hundreds of people from the community who came to watch the game. We "blans" (white people) received a lot of pointing and laughter, as well as cheers and excitement. There were lines painted on the field, but the crowd was the real boundary. They kept creeping onto the field with anticipation, so that whenever the ball rolled by, they all had to backpedal quickly to get out of the way. I had never seen anything like it, nor had I ever been part of such a celebration as the women outscored the men, one to zero!

A Young Church and an Old Friend

Before we left on our trip, I had called the ELCA Global Mission office in Chicago to let them know we were taking a group of ELCA college students to Haiti. I wanted to learn what relationship the ELCA had with Haiti and the people there, and discover any contacts. I was excited to learn that there was a brand-new evangelical Lutheran church called Eglise Lutherienne d'Haiti. It had just been officially recognized by the Haitian government in January 2009 and had four pastors. I tried calling the U.S. contact, Dr. Patricia Hansen from the ELCA Florida-Bahamas Synod, but was unable to reach her.

Ben and I hoped to meet at least one of the pastors and learn how an evangelical Lutheran church came to be in Haiti and about their experience starting this new body of faith. By the time we left for Haiti, though, we had given up on contacting anyone with Eglise Lutherienne d'Haiti. We focused instead on the people and organizations we knew we would be visiting.

On the day the church celebrates Pentecost, our group of ten traveled from Jacmel back to St. Joseph's Home for Boys in Pétionville. We arrived about an hour before dinner and were going to spend just one night there before heading back to the U.S. in the morning. Ben decided to go upstairs and visit the chapel on the sixth floor before dinner. On his way up, he needed to cross an open space on the fifth floor, where the Resurrection Dance Theater of Haiti performs. There he found four male Haitians and an older white American woman seated on chairs in a circle. Ben didn't wish to disturb them, so he tried to sneak up another flight of stairs to the chapel, but then he heard, "Ben! Ben! What are you doing here?" He turned to see a familiar face: Joseph Livenson Lauvanus, who had studied for one semester with us at Wartburg Seminary, was walking toward him with a joyous laugh and his arms wide.

Ben could hardly believe it. "What are you doing here?" he exclaimed as he embraced Livenson.

"I live here! I am Haitian, remember?" Ben learned that Livenson had become the president (bishop) of the new Eglise Lutherienne d'Haiti, and he was sitting there with the three other pastors of the church, as well as Dr.

Patricia Hansen! Pat often stayed at St. Joseph's as a guest when she traveled to Haiti, and the pastors were meeting her there.

"I need to tell Renee you are here!" Ben said. "Will you join us for dinner so we can catch up?"

"Yes, of course," Livenson accepted. "I can't wait to talk with you!"

Ben came bursting into our room and told me everything. We had worked so hard to try and connect with Pat Hansen and the four "unknown" pastors, and the night before we were to leave Haiti, there they were—all five of them in the same building with us. Soon we sat down to dinner with Livenson, who was already a friend but also now both pastor and bishop of this fledgling church in one of the poorest nations in the world. He kept smiling and laughing because we were all together in his home country. "The Holy Spirit has brought you here on this day of Pentecost," he said with certainty.

We asked, "Livenson, how can we accompany you and this new church?"

He thought about this for a moment and said, "We really need Lutheran theologians to come and teach Lutheran theology to the people. We do not have the resources to send our lay leaders and potential seminary students to the U.S. or Jamaica for school, so we need people to come here and teach in our lay schools."

Ben and I looked at one another and said, "When would you like us to come?"

"January!" he replied.

"We'll be here."

5

Before the Earthquake

AFTER OUR INTERNSHIP IN Nebraska ended, Ben and I returned to Wartburg Theological Seminary for our senior year. We made plans to travel to Haiti in January as we had promised Livenson. Naturally, we asked Jon if there were any J-term classes or trips he wanted to take in 2010. He didn't have anything particular in mind, so we invited him to come with us to Haiti. He jumped at the chance.

The three of us left for Haiti on January 4, 2010, and planned to stay until January 19. We were excited to spend the first whole week living with and learning from the people of a young church.

We stayed at Villa Ormiso in Carrefour (a community near Port-au-Prince) to join in teaching a lay school of about thirty people from all over Haiti. The school was led by the four ordained pastors of Eglise Lutherienne d'Haiti, along with Dr. Pat Hansen and Rev. Dr. Marcia Cox (also from Florida), who had been invited as the head theologian for the lay school.

I was particularly excited because I was writing my master's thesis on what Lutheran mission looked like in the context of Haiti, as well as the history of Eglise Lutherienne d'Haiti. I planned to base my research on first-hand interviews and observations.

The Lutheran Church in Haiti

Essentially, Eglise Lutherienne d' Haiti began because of pigs, or rather the lack of them. In 1978 there was a swine flu epidemic in the Dominican Republic, Haiti's neighboring country. In 1982, fearing the epidemic would eventually spread north to the U.S., the United States Agency for International Development (USAID) condemned Haiti's 1.3 million pig population, promising to replace Haitian pigs with "better" ones. In a little over a year all of Haiti's pigs were slaughtered by the Duvalier militia.[1] The extinction of

---

1. See chapter 21 for more information about the Duvalier influence on Haiti.

the Haitian pig especially impacted rural farmers who were no longer able to make a living or send their children to school. UsAID tried replacing the Creole pigs with pigs from Iowa, but the imported pigs could not cope in the Haitian environment. They needed special feed, vaccinations, clean water (which is often not available even for humans in Haiti), and roofed pigpens. Haitian farmers simply could not afford to raise and keep them. The effort was a disaster, and the extinction of the Creole pig has had irrevocable negative effects even today.

The ELCA Florida-Bahamas Synod wanted to help its neighbors in the Caribbean. They asked the Lutheran World Federation (LWF) in Port-au-Prince, an international organization that had been in Haiti for decades, what they could do. LWF decided to take on an appropriate pig repopulation project in Haiti and asked the synod for support, which they gladly provided.[2]

In 1998, two Lutheran missionaries from the Florida-Bahamas Synod, Luther and Dottie Kistler, went to Haiti to help with the pig project. As they sought Lutheran congregations in Haiti to work with, they spoke with Tomas Jonsen, who was then director for LWF Haiti. The Kistlers soon discovered that there was no formal evangelical Lutheran church, but that a number of self-declared pastors were calling themselves Lutheran.[3]

In fact, Haiti has a history of self-declared pastors. Men would simply say, "I'm a pastor." They would use their house or their land as the gathering place for the community's worship. This all worked fine until the "pastor" left or died. Then the community no longer had its house of worship, nor a shepherd, and the congregation simply disbanded. The missionaries and LWF wanted to prevent this from continuing to happen to these communities, so they worked to bring the self-declared Lutheran pastors together for conversation.

It didn't take long to find out that almost none of the pastors had connections to each other, formal theological or pastoral training, or much specific knowledge about what it meant to be a Lutheran Christian. LWF workers, together with Luther and Dottie Kistler, gathered all the pastors and some laypeople together and held a Lutheran communion worship service. Afterward they encouraged the Haitian leaders to talk and discern their future together as Lutherans.

2. "Report on Haiti," unpublished document by Luther Kistler. The pig repopulation effort had its challenges, but it opened the door for future accompaniment, the relationship between the ELCA and the Haitian church, and eventually helped lead to the formation of Eglise Lutherienne d'Haiti.

3. The Lutheran Church–Missouri Synod has had a presence in Haiti since 1978. For more information, visit http://lcms.org/haiti.

They did and decided they were going to raise up young leaders in Haiti who were steeped in Lutheran theology. They wanted an evangelical Lutheran presence in Haiti, and a church that was formed and led by Haitians. The group chose one young Haitian man to attend seminary in Jamaica as well as Wartburg Theological Seminary in Iowa. His name was Joseph Livenson Lauvanus, and his father was one of the self-declared pastors (as well as an outspoken journalist). Once Livenson[4] completed his seminary education and was ordained, the church voted to call him as the first president (bishop) of Eglise Lutherienne d'Haiti in 2009.

During the church's early years in the late 1990s, it was known as the Federation Evangelique Lutherienne d'Haiti (the Evangelical Lutheran Federation of Haiti or FELD'HA). The Haitian leadership, in partnership with the Florida-Bahamas Synod, invited Lutheran theologians every year for at least a decade to teach Lutheran theology to its lay and pastoral leaders. Every year Dr. Pat Hansen, the Florida-Bahamas Synod member known as the "mother of the church" by the Haitian leadership, attended the lay school and did whatever she could to accompany the fledgling church. On January 30, 2009, Livenson and two others (Ezekiel Elma and Alfred Eniel) were ordained in the Lutheran Church of Haiti at the Episcopal Holy Trinity Cathedral in Port-au-Prince. A fourth pastor, Denis DuClair, was ordained a short while later. Eglise Lutherienne D'Haiti was given its formal certificate of authorization by the Minister of Cults in Haiti on October 22, 2009; it was now fully recognized by the Haitian government as an organized church.

Lay School in Haiti

During that week with the lay school, I conducted interviews and taught with Ben and Jon when Rev. Dr. Marcia Cox was not teaching. We ate all our meals together with our Haitian brothers and sisters and had hours of sessions on Christology, resurrection, communion, and baptism. The liveliest conversation was spurred by a discussion on baptism: infant baptism or believer's baptism? For some Haitians, infant baptism seemed too Roman Catholic, which was also strongly associated with the culture and religion of Vodou.[5] For others, believer's baptism seemed to be too Pentecostal, which

---

4. As mentioned in the previous chapter, Livenson studied at Wartburg for one semester with us, but I knew little of his story at the time. I had no idea that our futures would be so closely connected.

5. Vodou has been spelled many ways: Vodou, Voodoo, Vodoun, Vodun, Vaudou, Vodu, and Vaudoux. I have chosen the spelling "Vodou" here.

reminded them of many outsiders who were coming in and starting new churches all over Haiti.

What was the Haitian Lutheran voice concerning baptism? I sat back and observed a heated discussion with Bibles being pulled out and confident arguments. I was getting uncomfortable with the heightened emotions at certain points, but after it was all over, the debaters put their arms around one another, laughed, and ate together.

In my conversations with the pastors, I found that all of them held other jobs as they worked on mission development and building the church. Because Bishop Livenson was the only pastor who had attended seminary, other credentials needed to be developed for the ordination process for the other pastors. The lay school served as the formal education piece. The Florida-Bahamas Synod developed a board to serve alongside the developing church, always in communication and relationship with the leaders undergoing pastoral formation. Still, with only four pastors—all also working other jobs—and one of them already near retirement age, the new church certainly faced significant challenges.

Every Lutheran church that was started in Haiti was linked with education, whether that meant a formal school or other ways of teaching people, such as helping them earn sustainable income by raising chickens. The leaders asked Pat Hansen to help establish a teacher training program, which she did. The church wanted to focus on empowering people through education. And that education wasn't free; parents had to pay for their children to attend school with the Lutheran church. As Bishop Livenson explained:

> If we have a school and it is free and parents send their children to the school, there might be a day where they don't make the children go or other things become more important. But, if we charge even one dollar for their child's education, they become invested. If we have a day we don't have school, then the parents are at the doors saying, "I paid for this! This education is important for my child." So, we have a philosophy of charging a very minimal fee so that the community is invested in the education of all our children. Our first poverty is the poverty of the mind. We must help the people understand that they can build up their future. It is not hopeless.

My favorite conversations that week were with the women leaders. A question was always in the back of my mind: "How is this new Lutheran church going to raise up women in leadership—particularly pastoral and ordained leadership?" A Haitian woman named Marie Anne, who served as the church accountant and secretary, acted as translator as I met in a circle with eight other women. I asked them to tell me their stories, how they understood their relationship with God, and their hopes for this new Lutheran church and their involvement in it.

The word that came over and over again from the mouths of the women was *grace*. Clearly, they already had a deep understanding of what it meant to be Lutheran. Grace was the foundation of the church and its people, its unique voice in Haiti. When I asked them what helped them persevere in hard times, such as when some of them had lost children, they answered, "We sing and pray and God helps us." The majority of the women had traveled for many days to be at the lay school, leaving behind their duties at home and their children.

One of the church ministries the women had developed was a wedding dress ministry. In their communities there were a number of unmarried women who were living with men. Often it wasn't because they did not wish to get married; it was because they could not afford a wedding dress. The women of Eglise Lutherienne d'Haiti worked with the Florida-Bahamas Synod of the ELCA to provide wedding dresses for the women of the church. Then they would tell other women in their community that if and when they wanted to be married, they would provide a dress to wear.

It was clear to me that the women served in important roles in the church, but there was a long road ahead before they would serve as pastors. It would be counter-cultural for any of the Haitian women to be ordained, and even if they were, it would take a long time and work from the Spirit of God for the people to see them as ministers of Word and Sacrament.[6] However, there was one young woman named Naomi who expressed her desire to become a pastor, and she seemed to believe it was possible for her in Eglise Lutherienne d'Haiti.

I also learned that the partnership with the Florida-Bahamas Synod opened up the doors for villagers in Thiotte to market their coffee through Equal Exchange under the name "Kafe Haiti." The coffee project was started through LWF in order to create sustainable work, especially for women, in rural communities.

Language

The language of the church was intriguing. Few Haitians speak English, and if they do, it is usually their third language. Everyone speaks Creole, which is a unique language created by enslaved Africans who needed to

6. Even in the U.S., many people challenge my call as a pastor because I am a woman.

communicate with one another to unite and overthrow their captors.[7] At first the language sounds a little like French, but it quickly becomes apparent that it is not. Creole is a combination of French, Spanish, English, and several tribal African languages. The highly educated speak French as well as Creole, and the universities teach in French.

Because French is the language of the Haitians' oppressors, it has a perceived stigma. Sometimes when a Haitian is speaking French, they will throw in a Creole word at the end of the sentence to make it "better." They might speak French, but they are Haitian, and most believe Creole is the best language.

I discovered all this when I asked the pastors what language their worship services would be conducted in. They had said they wanted to speak in the language of the people (Creole), but I noticed that they were using the French Canadian Lutheran hymnal from the Evangelical Lutheran Church in Canada. I received a confusing answer. "Both Creole and French," they said. They were such a new church that they needed to use an existing resource (the French Canadian hymnal), but they desired a liturgy that was in the vernacular of the people. The church's leaders would also need to know French in order to study at universities or seminaries.

Holding the worship service in Creole had its own pitfalls. The Roman Catholic churches said mass in Creole, and as mentioned earlier, Vodou was highly syncretic with Roman Catholicism, which had been the religion of the slaveholders. Many of the enslaved Haitians suffered forced baptisms and were made to attend mass. The African people continued some of their tribal rituals and spirituality as they were able, and eventually developed the Vodou religion under the guise of the Roman Catholic mass. The full historical context, of course, is too complex to relate here.

Eglise Lutherienne wanted a new liturgy in Creole, but for now, they needed to conduct the liturgy in French, which many people did not fully understand. Because Ben and Jon were musicians, they offered to write a liturgy for the church the following week. This offer was accepted with excitement, but the liturgy was never written because of the earthquake.

We loved our time with the church and learned so much about its history, its people, and life in Haiti in general. As a gift and thanks, we taught them a French song from Cameroon called "Louez Le Seigneur" (known in English as "Praise, Praise, Praise the Lord"). They loved it, and some went on to teach their congregations the song.

---

7. For an account of the slave trade and history of occupation in Haiti, read *The Black Jacobins* by C.L.R. James.

Jon, Ben, and I spent the last evening learning the four verses of "Lord Jesus, You Shall Be My Song" in French so we could sing it for them the next day. We were sad to be leaving, but anticipated future visits.

Building on Relationships

We could have left Haiti after our time with Eglise Lutherienne, but we wanted to continue to build on the relationships we had formed the first time Ben and I were there. We also wanted to learn more about the work of the Lutheran World Federation over the next week and a half. Finally, of course, we also wanted to leave some room for spontaneity.

On Friday, January 8, after saying goodbye to the people of Eglise Lutherienne, we took a tap tap (the public mode of transportation in Haiti) to St. Joseph's Home for Boys in Pétionville. It's called a tap tap because when you arrive at your destination, you "tap tap" on the side of the vehicle to signal the driver to stop. Tap taps are usually very full, with people standing or sitting shoulder to shoulder, and even on top of the vehicle. A common, fervent prayer is: "Lord, let not these brakes fail!" I rode on the back of the tap tap while hanging onto the side. Ben said, "Renee, I don't like you so close to the edge. Be careful and come inside a little more."

I smiled and said, "I'll be just fine. I'm loving this!"

One of the first people we met when we entered St. Joseph's was a young woman named Keziah Furth. Kez was originally from Boston and had been living in Haiti for a couple of years. She had a tiny, single-level house (nicknamed the "Shoebox") right next to St. Joseph's. She did all kinds of things in Haiti, but was trained as a nurse and her passion was caring for children in the ravine in Port-au-Prince. We hit it off immediately and spent quite a bit of time together playing cards and sharing stories. We were curious about Kez's work, so she invited us to join her for a day on her rounds in the ravine.

A few people came into St. Joseph's to sell handmade items. Roxanne was one of these. She was an older woman who sold dresses made by the women in her community, along with cards and other things. I bought a number of cards, and as a gift, she gave me a small painted butterfly cut out of an oil drum. I was touched, and the next time I saw Ben, I said, "Look, Ben! Look what Roxanne gave me!"

He immediately and joyfully exclaimed, "Resurrection!"[8]

Ever since we arrived in Haiti, Ben and I had been telling Jon about the great coffee St. Joseph's roasted themselves that we would get to drink every

8. The butterfly is a common symbol of resurrection and new life.

morning and evening. (Ben had roasted some at the Trinity House in Jacmel six months earlier.) That evening, Jon and Ben proceeded to drink four cups of coffee each and didn't sleep at all that night.

On Saturday we went with Pat Hansen, who was also staying at St. Joseph's, to the Lutheran World Federation office a couple of miles away. There we met a Finnish woman named Sylvia Raulo who described the LWF's many current projects. She invited us to go on a road trip for a couple of days with three of the Haitian staff members. We would go to Thiotte and other places in the countryside to learn about water projects and other things the LWF was doing in the communities. We were excited to go, but the trip was canceled when the LWF vehicle broke down and needed major maintenance. Still, we were okay with the change of plans because it meant we could join Kez for a day instead.

On Sunday, we stayed "home" at St. Joseph's. Ben and Jon were headed to one of the top levels of the home when they were stopped by about fifty Pentecostals on the Resurrection Dance Theater floor, which St. Joseph's let them use for worship every Sunday. Ben and Jon were quickly identified as honored guests. These Haitian Christians expressed their hospitality by inviting them to sit with the elders, an offer they couldn't refuse. This was no short service; they were there for hours. When I went looking for them, I found them right up front, honorary flowers pinned to their shirts. They were made to speak in front of everyone. When the leaders of the church found out that they were studying to be pastors, they said they would come back later in the week to talk through the details of starting a new church with them in Port-au-Prince.

We also had some free time on Sunday, which Jon and Ben spent doing one of their favorite things: making up songs, jingles, and new versions of existing songs. They made up their own rendition of "The Rose" by Bette Midler, as well as theme songs for the hats they had brought to Haiti. Ben's hat resembled Indiana Jones's, so he and Jon sang the *Indiana Jones* theme song as Ben looked around for danger and jumped on and off things. Jon's theme song was "Down Under," since his hat looked more Australian.

On Monday we went to the nearby Caribbean Market and exchanged U.S. currency for Haitian gourdes. We also met with Pastor Denis DuClair and his daughter Naomi from Eglise Lutherienne at St. Joseph's. There were other groups and guests staying at St. Joseph's, and we were sometimes invited to join them in the evenings. That night we joined a group that was part of the Methodist church. Later in the evening all the guests in the home attended a Resurrection Dance Theater performance. St. Joseph's was getting ready to celebrate their twenty-fifth anniversary in a couple of weeks. That day, the words "Celebrating 25 Years" were painted on the top beam of the floor. The dance show was amazing. At the end, the dancers pulled everyone out onto the floor to dance and sing together. We did! We danced and danced and sang and sang.

That night before bed, Ben, Jon, and I did evening vespers, sang hymns, and prayed, just as we had done many other nights in Haiti. We prayed for God's protection and for growth during our time in Haiti. We asked to be open to the Spirit in whatever our purpose was in that place.

The Day of the Earthquake

I awoke on Tuesday morning, January 12, greatly disturbed because of a distressing dream. I dreamed that all three of us were in the room that Ben and I shared at St. Joseph's. I felt very anxious and knew something was wrong. Ben looked at me and smiled gently. With a very serious and solemn expression, Jon reached his hand out to mine, indicating that I was to take it. Taken aback, I looked at Ben again, but he was motioning for me to take Jon's hand and go with him. I didn't know what to do, but in my dream I took Jon's hand and we started walking away from Ben. My heart and everything in me screamed, "No!" I continued looking back at Ben as Jon and I walked forward, and Ben kept gently smiling and telling me that it was okay. Then I woke up.

I didn't know what to do with this dream. I was so disturbed that I didn't feel ready to talk to Ben about it, nor did we have time as we hurried to join Kez and three others on her rounds in the ravine. All of us were way out of our comfort zone as we walked through the narrow ravine with its rusted metal shacks on both sides. There were so many people it was hard to pass through. We went inside some of the homes with Kez, where we visited numerous people in the tiny spaces and found malnourished children with lice, scabies, and other skin diseases. Kez gave us treated shampoo to rub on their heads.

At one point a woman came up to me with a baby whom she said was a month old, but was just four or five pounds and looked deathly ill. She asked me if I would be her "godmother" and take the child. I said I could not. Kez spoke with her and found out that the woman was anemic and thought she could not breastfeed her baby because of it. Kez urgently tried to convince her that it was okay and that she needed to feed her baby, but the mother would not listen to Kez because she was a woman. Kez convinced Ben to play the "doctor" and tell the woman she needed to feed her child or she would die.

One of the others who joined us had brought along balls to give away to children. I knew this was a bad idea. We soon had a whole village of children following us, and not enough balls to give away. Those who had balls started hoarding and fighting over them. It was a challenging situation that we created and could not resolve, and I was embarrassed.

I was thankful to see a makeshift clinic where parents were bringing their children to be checked and weighed. I also saw a group of men playing dominoes, a popular game in Haiti. The loser had clothespins clipped on his ears and he had to shove his face in a bowl of flour. The men were clearly enjoying themselves, as were those watching. We experienced so much that day that we could not have seen if we had stayed inside the walls of St. Joseph's.

By the time we made our way back up the mountain, it was mid-afternoon and we were ravenously hungry. Kez suggested we eat at a Chinese restaurant that was less than a mile away. When we arrived, I deeply regretted that I hadn't changed clothes first. I felt disgusting. I had a white bandana on my head and had been sweating all morning. To make matters worse, it turned out this was no ordinary Chinese restaurant. There were a few Chinese men in very nice suits reclining in the middle of the restaurant. Jon, Ben, Kez, and I each had our own waiter. I ordered a small bowl of soup and it was nine U.S. dollars! I couldn't believe how expensive the meal was in a country where you could buy a pineapple off the street for a nickel. Ben had kung pao chicken, his favorite. We laughed together at the situation and how awkward we all felt to be in such a nice place and feel so dirty. We went that morning from the ravine to "China."

On our walk back to St. Joseph's, I had hardly ever felt so free. I loved being on the street in the hustle and bustle of everyday life in Haiti. Ben tried to make sure I was paying attention and not getting hit by a tap tap or other moving vehicle. I had a few close calls, but I just loved taking it all in and chatting with Kez.

I also loved walking through the streets with Ben. Every time he would pass someone and make eye contact, he would smile, wave, and say, "Ça va!" People would give him a surprised and curious look, but would eventually wave and say it back.

I said to Ben, "Do you even know what that means?"

He said, "No, but everyone sure seems to like it!"

I found out later that "Ça va" basically means "I'm fine." It still cracks me up to think about Ben in his Indiana Jones hat walking the streets of Haiti, waving and smiling at everyone and saying, "I'm fine!"

As we walked down the narrow street to St. Joseph's, I looked up at our temporary home and was thankful to be where we were and doing what we were doing. For the first time I noticed the iron cross that stood on top of the building, which declared by its presence, "Christ dwells here." We thanked Kez for the great morning and said we would see her later that night. I anticipated a shower and some rest.

PART II

The Earth Moves

Concerning Great Chasms and Friendship
Kalen Barkholtz

It feels like
you all are over there
and we are here
with no idea
how you must feel.

Your story world
has been shaken
and the contents are swirling
like water and sediment in a jar.
Pictures, voices, sounds,
Haiti, a cloud of dust and crying,
receiving awful, dreaded news,
everything breaking inside and outside,
wrenching and coming apart.

And now it is like
we are over here
on this side of a chasm.
We hold a piece of the story.
It hurts in our hand.
And you are over there,
holding the rest of it,
not just in your hand, but everywhere,
and oh, how much it all must hurt.

We ache to come and be with you
but we can't jump this one—
the drop is too great.
We are learning to be friends in a new way,
shouting across, singing across,
telling you about the prayers we have been praying,
saying: we love you.

It feels desperate sometimes, this friendship,
but we know God is over there, really, really over there.
God has set up a tent.
God is building a fire and making you food.
God is feeding you, knowing you,
understanding deeply.
And God is here too, and God is in Haiti.
God is building warm fires everywhere,
glowing and red, crackling with hope and life.

6

The Earthquake

I WHIPPED THE FILTHY bandana off my head and enjoyed my cold bucket shower more than I ever had before. Finally clean and feeling refreshed, I returned to the room I shared with Ben, but he wasn't there. I wondered briefly where he was, but I was tired. I dressed and laid down on the bed to close my eyes for a few minutes.

A little later, Ben came in with a handful of wet clothes and a smile on his face. He and Jon had been washing their clothes together. Ben draped his laundry neatly on the backs of chairs and bedposts to dry. He looked at me and addressed me as he often did: "Cutie!"

We hugged. His hair was still wet from his bucket shower, and I remember thinking how handsome he was. I often told him that I thought he was handsome, but I regret to this day that I did not tell him in that moment. I also wanted to tell him about my dream from the night before, as well as process our morning in the ravine, but I thought we could talk about these things after dinner. Ben told me he was going to find Jon and hang out with him until chapel. It was about 4:45 p.m.

Ben started making his way up the stairs to the floor where the Resurrection Dance Theater of Haiti performs. We liked spending time on that level of the home because of its open floor plan. There were no walls; instead, spaced pillars held up the floor and open roof above, creating what felt like an outdoor space. St. Joseph's Home for Boys was located a few miles up a mountain, and so there was a spectacular view of the neighboring mountains and the city of Port-au-Prince.

I called after Ben. "Hey! Should I bring cribbage or the cards so we can play with Jon?" He didn't hear me, so I grabbed both, along with the book about Haiti I was reading, *The Black Jacobins* by C.L.R. James. I climbed the stairs to the dance theater floor and found Jon, Ben, and another guest named Al sitting at a table together, chatting.

Ben and I had met Al and his wife, Gail, the previous May in Jacmel at Trinity House. They were from North Carolina, were in their seventies, and had great Southern accents. I went to join the three at the table. Not wanting to interrupt their conversation, I sat and admired the incredible view. I was so happy to be in Haiti and to feel the breeze drying my damp hair. I felt content. I smiled.

There is no adequate language to describe 4:53 p.m., January 12, 2010. Terror, shock, disbelief, adrenaline, outcry, concrete, crumbling, shaking, dust, fear, screaming, car horns, deep rumblings of the earth. No words can capture my experience and the experience of the millions of people who felt the earth writhe beneath their feet and the world come crashing down around them.

The earth started to shake. It began as a low rumble from below, and everything around us started vibrating. My heart pounded. I had never experienced an earthquake, but I recognized what was happening immediately. Wide-eyed, Jon, Ben, and I looked at one another. Al said, "Oh, don't worry, we have these in North Carolina all the time." I hoped that the shaking would stop quickly. It did not.

I found myself up on my feet and running, but running where? There was nowhere to go. *Find a doorway, Renee,* I thought as I remembered some elementary school lesson about what to do in an earthquake. I looked around frantically. There were no doorways, only pillars and the ceiling. The whole floor and building began to sway as the shaking became more violent. I found myself in the center of the dance floor, not knowing how I arrived there. I looked up. *In case the ceiling comes down, I should stand between these sets of lights.*

For the first time I noticed Jon's silhouette out of the corner of my eye. *Ben . . . no, that's Jon. Oh God! Where's Ben?* I turned to look for him and realized that I had somehow run right past him. He was clinging to one of the pillars closer to the table where we had been sitting. *That's smart. I need to get to that pillar.*

No sooner did that thought come into my head than the ceiling started coming down. At first I saw only dust and small pieces of concrete start to fall. They were not falling on me; they were falling on Ben. His eyes were closed.

"Ben! Ben!" I yelled. He didn't hear me. *God, everything is falling on Ben and he doesn't hear me!* I decided to run to him and pull him to where I was, but a split second later the two floors above us came crashing down with a force and sound that were indescribable. I screamed and put my arms up to protect my head as the ceiling rushed downward. I felt like a rag doll, tossed around, not knowing when the earth would finally settle. Everything seemed to be happening in slow motion. With the ceiling now directly above my back, I lay facedown on the floor with my hands under my chest. I screamed through the thunderous noise, a plea to God for the shaking to stop. The building swayed beneath my body and the floor continued to shake.

My family, I thought. *I am going to die and I will never see them again. They do not even know I am dying. I love you Mom and Dad, Eric, Jessie, and Janessa. I love you all so much. God, watch over my family. Don't let my death destroy them. Help them through their loss. How will they retrieve my body? God, be merciful and let my family lay me to rest.*

With everything still in slow motion, the shaking seemed to go on for an eternity. Then it stopped as suddenly as it had begun. I felt as if I was waking up, but to a new reality I had never known before, a world of death, pain, loss, and uncertainty. I could feel with both hands that the floor beneath me was still intact. I opened my eyes and saw darkness and thick dust. My hearing was muted from the crash of concrete, but not enough to silence the screams of a woman nearby and a car horn somewhere below on the street. The earth started shaking again. *No, no, no, God.*

It stopped. I tried to move my limbs. *I'm not hurt.* Choking on concrete dust, I coughed. I wiped the dust from my eyes and realized there was a pocket of space around me. With the ceiling tight against my back, I crawled on my belly out of the area I was in. In the small space I could see and hear someone on my left. "Jon! Jon, are you okay?"

"Yes, I'm okay." *Oh, thank God. But what about Ben?*

"Ben! Ben! Are you okay? Where are you?" No response. "Jon, have you seen Ben?"

"No." Another aftershock as Jon and I tried to make our way to one another.

"We've got to try and get out of here and look for Ben," Jon said softly. "There will be more aftershocks and it's not safe where we are." We noticed that two beams—those supporting our floor and the ceiling—had compacted on one another when the floors above us collapsed. Fortunately they held, and created the few feet of space that Jon and I were in when everything came crashing down. The ceiling angled down to where it met the floor, right at the spot where I had last seen Ben. We began to search for him.

"I'll try over here," I said. I made my way to the step where the Resurrection Dance Theater drummers played. There was a small opening up above. I tried to crawl up and out, but my hips were trapped by rebar and I couldn't fit. "Ah!" I screamed as I tried with all my might to get out, but I could not. *If there's another aftershock I may be crushed. I've got to go back down.* I crawled back down into the confinement of our pocket and saw Jon a few feet away. He was motionless next to a larger hole in the side of the building. "Can we get out that way?" I asked him.

"No. There is a beehive with a ton of bees. We can't go this way," he said. *Great! We'll get out of this building only to get stung and who knows what will happen next.* We kept searching for options and for Ben as the aftershocks, car horns, and screams of people persisted. I saw that the stairs to the lower level were blocked, filled in with broken concrete. *There is no way out and I can't find Ben. No one will be able to get us out and we are going to die because the building will eventually collapse.*

I had almost given up hope when I saw a small opening about the size of a softball where the beams held. I could tell it was getting darker outside, but a little light was coming through the hole, so the sun must still be up. "Jon! Let's try this!" I pulled at the concrete. It was weakened by the earthquake and began to give way. I kicked at it with my feet and tore at it with my fingers until they were raw, all the while saying, "Ben . . . Ben . . . Ben." The hole was eventually big enough for Jon and me to crawl out onto an extended part of the floor. By now the sun was setting. We were stranded on top of the swaying building with no way to get down.

I scrambled up to the very top of the roof that had collapsed on us and desperately searched for Ben or another way in. I knew that he could not be reached from where we had been before, so I needed another entry point. I moved cautiously to the very edge of the other side of the roof just as there was another aftershock. I screamed as I crawled quickly back to the center of the roof. There I clung for my life. I knew the building would crumble beneath me. I screamed at the top of my lungs. The whole building swayed back and forth. I clung to the roof on my hands and knees begging God for mercy. When the earth settled once again, I gazed out over the city of Port-au-Prince from that rooftop on the side of a mountain. *God . . . God . . . God!*

The world ended. A haze of concrete dust blanketed the city. As far as my eyes could see, buildings lay in rubble. I heard the screams of mothers and the sound of buildings continuing to fall. I looked up and saw a helicopter above me. *How can you keep flying above us all and leave us here!* I thought angrily. Then I wondered if there was a TV camera and if they were filming me, vulnerable, helpless, and devastated on the rooftop with my husband surely broken-bodied beneath me. I started to rip off the roof tiles with my bare hands. *If I cannot get around I will go through!* I let the tiles go and realized that they were sliding off the roof. There were people on the ground, and I might be hurting them. I stopped. I stopped and cried. Crushed by the weight of what was settling in my soul, I gave up.

A Song

Then I heard Al's voice. "I hear him!" he cried. "I can hear him singing!" My spirit lifted and a new burst of energy returned to me. There was hope! I ran past Jon, who stood motionless, clinging with one hand to the iron cross that was still fastened to the roof. I kept going past Al, whom I noticed had a bloodied head and arms. I made it back to the hole we had crawled out of and started to go in.

"No, Renee! No, don't go in there!" Michael[1] and Walnes, two members of the St. Joseph Family, called from the adjacent roof of the art center *Ah! God!* Frustration welled up inside of me, but it soon passed because I could hear the sweet voice of my Ben. I started to yell and call out for him, but I didn't want to interrupt his song. It was so sweet, so in tune, and sad. His voice was strong enough for me to hear even through the layers of concrete between us. He was not just singing for me. He was singing for his Lord, for Jon, for the Haitians, and for each one of us. I knew I had missed part of what he sang, but I heard this whole verse of his witness:

> O Lamb of God, you bear the sin of all the world away;
> Eternal peace with God you made, God's peace to us we pray.

When he finished his song, I held my breath and strained to hear more. There was nothing. No more song. "Ben!" I cried. "Ben! Keep singing, sweetheart! I will find you." My own breath quickened as I felt in my being that I had heard Ben's last, singing breaths. I wanted to ask him again to keep singing, but I knew he would want to know that Jon and I were okay. "Jon and I are okay, Ben. We're okay." I strained to hear a pin drop, anything from my love. Nothing. There was only one thing left to say: "I love you, Ben! I love you."

I wanted so desperately to crawl back into that hole, find Ben, and lie down with him as he died, but I knew there was no way to get to him and it was now dark. I could hear voices behind me. "Renee, Renee, you must get off this roof." I turned around. Someone had found a ladder and created a bridge from the roof of Kez's house onto what was left standing of St. Joseph's.

"Renee," Jon said gently, "we have to get down."

"I can't," I said. "I can't leave Ben."

"We have to. Just for the night. We'll come back as soon as it's light."

---

1. Michael Geilenfeld is the founder of the St. Joseph's Family. Originally from Iowa and a member of the order "Missionaries of Charity," Michael moved permanently to Haiti to work with street children.

My whole body shook as I traversed the twenty-five-foot drop over a rubble-filled alleyway. Crawling on my hands and knees from ladder rung to ladder rung, I made my way from the roof of St. Joseph's to the roof of Kez's house. Al, Jon, and I eventually made it down onto the street. Walnes was there at the bottom of the ladder. I fell into his arms and wept. "My husband!" I cried. "My Ben."

"I know," Walnes said, and he hugged me tight. I did not know it at the time, but Walnes had just lost his best friend in the entryway of the home. Walnes had been right behind him when concrete came crashing down, and his friend died there in front of him.

Michael approached us. "Have any of you seen Bill?[2] Was he on the roof with you?"

"No," I replied. "We haven't seen him."

"TiPatrick[3] is buried and some guys are getting him out. As soon as they get him out, we'll keep looking for Bill."

I looked down and noticed an electrical line that was snapped but not active. I realized we were still in danger. Just then there was another aftershock, and the wall on our side of the street began to collapse. "Run!" someone yelled. Jon and I grabbed hands and ran up the street as concrete crumbled down around us. I had only flip-flops on and Jon had no shoes at all. "Ah!" I heard Jon cry as we both stumbled over concrete in the road. We finally made it up to the open lot at the top of the street, where we found a few hundred Haitians sitting on the ground. Some were silent and staring into the distance with hollow eyes, some were crying, and some were carrying injured family and friends. Others were singing hymns or praying aloud.

Jon and I found the boys from St. Joseph's and sank to the ground among them. We were the only non-Haitians in the lot besides Michael, Gail, and Al. It was the beginning of the longest night of my life.

---

2. Bill Nathan was a restavek (slave child) who found his way as a young boy to St. Joseph's Home for Boys and was raised in the St. Joseph Family. Bill was one of the leaders and staff in the home and one of the main drummers for the Resurrection Dance Theater of Haiti. To read more about his story, see *A Crime So Monstrous* by E. Benjamin Skinner.

3. A young boy living in the home.

7

The Longest Night

PEOPLE KEPT COMING INTO the open lot. Many of them were injured, and their friends carried them in on whatever was available.

Soon I recognized some people from St. Joseph's. They were carrying Bill into the lot on a mattress. He writhed in agony. I could not see his injuries, but from the look on his face, I worried he was going to die.

I learned later that Bill had been one floor above us, in the chapel, when the earthquake hit. Right before the floors pancaked, Bill jumped. His body was battered by broken concrete as he fell. He landed in the neighbor's yard, and looking up, he saw another large piece of concrete coming toward him. A tree stopped it long enough for him to roll out of the way. He was able to call Michael on his cell phone and let him know where he was, and then he lost consciousness.

Bill lay limp all night on the mattress as all the boys from St. Joseph's crowded around him. They tried to get comfortable in the midst of death and the destruction of their home. Looking at them, I remembered that the night before, during the Resurrection Dance Theater performance, I had thought about how devastating it would be for this family to lose Bill. *How ironic and terrible.* I sat next to him and wished I could ease his suffering. His face was contorted with pain. All I could do was sit there, and sometimes pray when I could find the words.

At one point during the night a boy who did not speak any English came up to me and pointed to the large tree in the lot. I noticed that most people were a little farther away from the tree than I was. Recognizing that the tree might topple at any point during an aftershock, they had settled at a safe distance. I appreciated the care the boy was showing me, but I honestly didn't care whether the tree fell on me or not. Still, I tried to give him the best "thank you" smile I could muster and made an effort to move further away.

A boy from the home named Emerson came up behind Jon and hugged him for a long time. Even after he let go, he stayed right by Jon for much of the night.

One of my most vivid memories of that night was of a young girl, probably around ten years old, who was carried into the lot on some boards. My heart ached for her. I could tell she was in great pain, but I saw no injuries. I sat down next to her and touched her hand. She flinched, and I let go. I sat next to her for a while. Finally I got up and went back over to Bill.

I was a little thirsty and my mouth was caked with concrete dust. There was a five-gallon water cooler at the foot of Bill's mattress with about a quart of water in it. One of the guards for St. Joseph's looked at Jon and me and offered us some water. I took a small drink to wash out my mouth, and so did Jon. The guard said to us, "If either of you needs anything at all, just ask. I will do anything for you." I looked at what was left in the cooler. Not one of the Haitians made a move to hoard it.

Ironically, despite the scarcity of water, nature called. I went off by myself into a dark corner near a one-story house, but then I found that I didn't care who might see: I just dropped my pants and peed.

As I made my way back, I saw Al sitting next to his wife, Gail. They told me how sorry they were. Al said, "I am old. I should have died instead of Ben." Al had been sitting with us at the table when the earthquake hit, and he somehow ended up with us on the roof. How had he survived? I still don't know.

I looked up and saw Renee Dietrich, an American staff member of the St. Joseph Family, who had just arrived from Wings of Hope. She came straight up and embraced me. "I am so sorry, Renee. I am just so sorry." I wept and laid my head on her shoulder. Another American arrived named Troy Livesay. I had not met him before, but he locked eyes with me and said, "I am so sorry for your loss."

Renee asked me if Jon and I wanted to go to Wings of Hope for the night. One room of the building was still standing, and all the kids and staff were okay. "No, thank you," I said. "We don't want to leave Ben." She understood and took Gail and Al with her.

I finally saw Kez arrive in the lot. *Thank you, God, Kez is alive!* We hugged, but did not say much to one another. She had plenty of work to do tending to Bill, stitching people up, and deciding whom she should try to save and who was beyond saving. She was the only medical worker in the whole lot.

Later, Kez approached me again. I have no memory of what she said; I only recall her sadness over the loss of Ben.

"Kez," I said. "Do you know what happened to the young girl who was lying over there earlier tonight?"

"Yes. She died."

She had her whole life in front of her, I thought. *I don't understand what is happening here, God. How is it that the lives of so many innocent people are ending this night? Aren't you holding the world in your hands? Aren't you a God who cares about what is happening right here, right now, when children die and families and homes are destroyed? I don't understand, God. Where are you?*

The lot quickly became a makeshift medical treatment area and eventually a small morgue, with the living still there, still singing, still praying.

Some men took a headlight and battery out of a nearby car and rigged them together somehow. They put the makeshift lamp in the one standing tree so it would give light to all. That was when I realized I could not see very well. I put my hands up to my face and found that my glasses were missing. *They must have fallen off when the ceiling came down,* I thought. *How will I see when we look for Ben in the morning? Ben picked out those glasses for me. Ben. Oh, Ben.*

"Do you think Ben is alive, Jon?" I asked through my tears.

"I don't know, Renee." He paused for a long while. "I don't think he is."

"The one thing I cannot bear is if he is still alive, alone, and slowly dying."

"I really don't think he is alive, Renee. I think he sang and he died."

It was then I prayed the strangest and most difficult prayer of my life. *God, I pray that Ben is dead. Please, God. I know I cannot reach him and I cannot bear it if he is still alive and dying alone. Please, God, have mercy.*

When I finished this prayer, the Word from Romans 14:7–9 came breaking into my mind and heart:

> We do not live to ourselves, and we do not die to ourselves. If we live, we live to the Lord, and if we die, we die to the Lord; so then, whether we live or whether we die, we are the Lord's. For to this end Christ died and lived again, so that he might be Lord of both the dead and the living.

Never in my life have I "heard" Scripture so clearly. A wave of peace and sorrow spread over me. With this Word, I knew Ben was dead. I was still breathing, but somehow we were still connected in Christ, who is Lord of both the dead and the living. I clung to this promise and Word from the Spirit in my deepest need throughout that night.

So that I would not forget Ben's dying song, I hummed the melody as often as I could. My body began to shake violently. So did Jon's. We were in shock. We were trying to sleep on the cold ground, and our bodies were having none of it. A group of women right next to us had three sheets. Someone had undoubtedly risked their life to retrieve them from a teetering house. Without a word, a woman handed me one of those precious sheets. "Merci," I said, and took it with overwhelming thankfulness for this gift of grace that would provide a layer between us and the cold earth. Jon and I laid down on the sheet and used the corners to wrap up as best we could. *Thank you, God, that Jon is alive.*

I turned my back to Jon and came face to face with a young boy who was lying on the ground next to me. His eyes were wide and stared back into mine. He closed them and tried to sleep. I felt tears run down my face and splash onto the trash-covered ground.

I could not sleep. Buildings continued to fall in the distance as the aftershocks continued, and I kept waiting for St. Joseph's to collapse completely. Whenever the ground started shaking, women would cry out with their hands lifted to the sky. "Jezi, Jezi!" "Merci, Seigneur!" I just curled up in a ball and felt the strangeness and terror of the earth shifting beneath my body. Even when the earth was not moving, my body felt as though it still was.

Among the aftershocks, buildings falling, the cries of parents losing children and husbands losing wives and wives losing husbands, I could hear one powerful voice that carried over all else. It was the voice of one woman singing. She was at the center of the lot. Many other women were gathered around her, like Mary sitting at the feet of Christ. This woman sang hymn after hymn after hymn all night long. Sometimes others would join her, and the whole lot would become a chorus of saints raising our voices to our Creator. I could feel the music deep in my chest welling up into my throat as I hummed along to the hymns I recognized. Occasionally the singing would stop, but only so that people could pray out loud. This singer, a daughter of God most high, my sister in Christ, carried me through the night with her song that joined Ben's dying song.

Sometimes I could hear other groups singing in the distance. It was truly a glimpse of beauty and resurrection in the midst of disheveled and broken bodies and hearts. The Haitian people, even as they lost everything, turned to God for strength, courage, hope, healing, and life.

In the middle of the night I rose and sat by Michael for a while. He was by himself on the outside of the lot. The St. Joseph Family was less than one week away from celebrating its twenty-fifth anniversary. A quarter of a century of hard work on a place to really call home, and now it was a pile of rubble. I don't remember much of our conversation, but I do remember Michael looking down the street at the collapsed home and saying, "We will rebuild and there will be resurrection." I wondered whether there would be resurrection for me. What would life be like without Ben?

I longed for daylight, but I also dreaded it. I did not want the day to come and reveal the reality that Ben was dead.

8

Dawn

WHEN THE WORLD YOU know comes to an end, it seems like creation itself should stop along with your heart. But it doesn't. The earth keeps spinning on its axis, people get up and have their morning coffee, and time marches forward. The sun rose on January 13 in Haiti just as it had any other morning, but nothing was the same.

Jon and I negotiated our way among pieces of broken concrete down the alleyway to St. Joseph's. It was still standing! Michael was there at the entrance. He said, "We have been going in and getting pieces of art and other important things."

"We need to get to the level of our rooms and see if Ben came through the ceiling," I said. "While we are there, we can try to get our passports."

Jon looked at me reluctantly, but followed. We stumbled over boulders of concrete in what used to be the entryway, right where Walnes's friend died. We made our way into what was still standing of the swaying house. Water pipes were exposed and leaking in every direction. It was eerily quiet except for the *drip, drip, drip* of water. We climbed the stairs to our rooms. My glasses still missing, I looked up with my blurry vision at every square inch of the ceiling, searching for some part of Ben: a hand, a foot . . . anything. Most of the ceiling was still intact, and I could not see him.

The stairs that led up to the Resurrection Dance Theater floor were blocked with rubble. I squeezed between pieces of concrete and the broken railing, climbing up what used to be the stairs. When I could go no further, I strained my neck and eyes to see if I could enter the floor we had been on. I was so frustrated with my inability to see clearly! It was impossible to go any further.

I shimmied my way back down and went around to the balcony to try to get a look from there. "Ben!" I yelled. Silence. "Ben!" I called again. Nothing. *He could be right above me and I cannot get to him!* More frustration.

As I looked for Ben, Jon and one of the boys from the home worked on breaking down our doors to retrieve our passports. The doors were jammed by the weight of the collapsed floors above. Once they were forced open, we grabbed our passports and a few other things, including the resurrection butterfly, which I found on the desk. Then we ran out of the room, down the stairs, and out of the house as quickly as we could. My whole body was shaking.

When we made it outside, I turned the corner and climbed over huge pieces of concrete in my flip-flops down the alleyway between Kez's house and St. Joseph's. I wanted to see if Ben's body was accessible from the other side of the building. Again, I found nothing but piles of rubble.

There was only one more thing to do: ask for the ladder. "What are you going to do with that, Renee?" someone said.

"I'm going back on the roof to crawl in the hole we came out of and look for Ben."

"It's really dangerous," people pleaded.

"Give me the ladder." They did.

Jon and I and a man whose name I do not remember set up the ladder to climb onto Kez's roof. Then we made a bridge with it to the roof of St. Joseph's. Rung by rung, Jon and I crawled our way back up to the place of death. Approaching the escape hole, I took a deep breath and crawled back in. It was still fairly dark in the space, and there was not much room to move. Things had shifted during the night. I headed toward the place where Ben had been standing at the time of the earthquake, only to be stopped by a part of the ceiling that had come down. I called out, "Ben! Ben, can you hear me?"

No answer. I hated the silence because it told me what I did not want to believe. I kept calling his name and crawling around on my belly, all the while feeling around for my glasses. I did not find them, nor did I find Ben. There was no way to get to him, not from the inside or outside, above or below.

"Renee," I could hear Jon. "You need to come out of there. It isn't safe."

I was defeated. I came out. We crossed back over the ladder bridge and descended to the ground empty-handed. Once down, I heard someone say, "Renee, Ben might have fallen off the roof and landed in the neighbor's yard! He may have been taken to a hospital!" When I heard this, I knew it was too good to be true, but I began to hope anyway.

I had grabbed some of Ben's things from our room, and I started to pack a small bag. I put in a few snacks, a hymnal, a Bible, and Ben's deodorant. Irrationally, I thought, *Yes, he might want that.* Michael came up to me and said, "Renee, he might not be okay. He is probably very hurt."

"I don't care! I will take him however he is. I just need to be with him."

"I don't know, Renee. I don't know how he would have fallen off the roof," Jon said gently.

"We need to find out. Let's go to the neighbor's and ask." On the way, I asked people, "Ki kote myri m'?" meaning, "Have you seen my husband?" Everyone shook their heads.

We knocked at the gate of the neighbor's house and a woman answered. Through a translator we asked, "Did someone fall into your yard last night?"

"Yes," she said. "I told the people to take him out of my yard because I didn't want him dying in it."[1]

"Where did they take him?"

"I don't know . . . to a hospital, I think."

"Which one?"

"I don't know."

Then I asked the most difficult question. "Was the man who fell in your yard American or Haitian?"

"Haitian."

My heart sank as I felt the life drain out of me. My eyes showed the agony I already knew, that Ben was dead and still trapped on top of a crumbling building. The woman looked at me and boldly said, "Kouraj" (courage).

I turned to Jon and said, "Jon, it's Bill. Bill is the one who fell in her yard."

"I know," Jon said sadly.

We finally realized that there was nothing left to do but to go to the U.S. embassy. We needed to see if they could help us, and to try and contact our families to let them know Ben was dead and we were alive.

"Michael," I said. "How do you get to the embassy from here?"

"It's down the mountain about seven miles away." He described how we could get there on foot.

To the U.S. Embassy

We said our goodbyes to the people who survived with us through the nightmare of the earthquake. I said to the boys of St. Joseph's, "I am so sorry about your home. Will you please care for Ben's body?"

"We will," they promised.

---

1. In Haitian culture it is bad luck to have someone die on your property, especially someone you don't know. It is believed that their spirit would then be present in that place and might cause problems for the living.

Jon and I checked on Bill one more time. He was being loaded on a mattress into the bed of a pickup truck to be driven to a hospital. He was still in incredible pain. I wondered if he would make it.

"We will be back tonight," we told Michael and Walnes, and we made our way up to the main road. Buildings were crumpled on top of one another everywhere. Vehicles had been crushed by falling concrete. *No wonder I heard so many car horns.* We saw the Caribbean Market now a pile of rubble. We knew people were trapped underneath. So many people needed help, but it was overwhelming, and Jon and I knew we needed to get to the embassy. We kept going.

Following closely behind us was a young man I recognized. His name was Ronald, and he used to come to St. Joseph's and sell his homemade shoes and jewelry. He waved us over to a motorcycle driver and asked us how much money we had. Luckily, we had some of the Haitian gourdes we had exchanged a few days earlier at the Caribbean Market. Ronald began to bargain with the motorcycle driver. It was clear that the driver wanted nothing to do with taking us down the mountain. Ronald pleaded on our behalf until the driver gave in.

All three of us got onto the motorcycle, me right behind the driver, Jon behind me, and Ronald all the way in the back. It was not a big motorcycle. The four of us barreled down the mountain, dodging piles of concrete, crushed cars, collapsed buildings, and people in the street who were wandering helplessly. I remember seeing a young man and woman side by side on the street. I was jealous. *You both lived and are together.* Then I saw that the woman had a huge gash taken out of her ankle, exposing the bone. *If she doesn't get help, she might die or lose her leg.* I felt guilty for being jealous and not realizing the severity of their situation. For the first time, I recognized and was thankful that Jon and I were not injured.

We had made it only a couple of miles when the motorcycle ran out of gas. We thanked and paid the driver. *No wonder he didn't want to take us,* I thought. *Now he has to get back up the mountain somehow with no gas.* Once again, we were recipients of the incredible grace and hospitality of the Haitian people.

We continued our journey on foot, which further exposed us to the widespread devastation of the earthquake. There were people everywhere, both alive and dead. All kinds of buildings and homes had collapsed into the street. Cars were crushed, and those that weren't were lined up at the gas pumps. No fuel was forthcoming.

One woman walked down the street toward us with her hands flailing. She was crying and speaking as she walked, and she had a look of disbelief and horror on her face. I wondered where she was coming from and where she was going. Whom she lost. Whom she was journeying to find, hopefully alive. There was no way for her to know who among her family was okay and who was not. She simply needed to walk the streets, seeing the reality around her.

Many people formed solemn circles around crumbled buildings and homes. There was nothing they could do but stare at the immovable concrete, knowing that family and friends lay beneath, dead or alive. My heart ached for them, yet we kept on walking.

We passed what appeared to be a hospital. Outside its gates, injured people lay limp on the ground. I saw a white girl with red hair. Her eyes were closed and her limbs wrapped, but much of her skin was exposed as she lay in the heat. No one was with her. I had nothing with which to cover her pale skin to protect it from the sun. I only wondered if she would live, and I kept walking.

We walked for a long time, until Ronald convinced another motorcyclist to take us the rest of the way to the embassy. Once again, all three of us piled on the motorcycle behind its driver. This time we made it to our destination.

We were some of the first U.S. citizens to arrive at the embassy. A small crowd was gathered outside the doors. I noticed one man in particular and wondered about his story. His eyes were red from crying as he stood there waiting.

Jon and I went inside. It was much quieter than I expected. Apparently the embassy was short on help because some workers had died. We went up to one of the windows where a woman was at work behind the glass. "What can I do for you?" she asked.

I did not know what to say. *Give me a miracle, some workers, and heavy equipment to get my husband out.* "Is there any help coming?" I asked.

"None right now," she replied. "Internet and phones are down and there are no medical workers to help the injured. There may be some planes later today to evacuate, but we are waiting to hear word."

"My husband is buried in a building. Is there any way to get him out?"

"Is he alive?" she asked.

Is he alive? I hope so . . . I hope not. "I don't know. I don't think he is."

"I'm so sorry," she said with genuine sympathy. "Do you have identification for him?"

"Yes, I have his passport. It's right here." I opened Ben's passport and saw his photo. The tears welled up in my eyes. I handed it to her. She filled out a piece of paper and said they would do the best they could to get him out when help arrived.

She handed Ben's passport back and asked Jon and me to fill out some paperwork. "Is there any way for us to reach our family to let them know we are all right?" I asked.

"Not at the moment, but as soon as the lines open up, you will be first on the list." This was the best we could hope for. Jon and I began to fill out the paperwork. Soon I came to the question: "Married, single, widowed?" I put down the pen and wept. *What the hell am I? I am married. I feel married and I am married to Ben Splichal Larson and he is currently underneath some concrete.* It was the first time I felt myself shift into another category: Widowed. *I am a widow.* I wanted to tear out my hair and beat my chest. I wanted to put on sackcloth and ashes. *The earthquake took my husband and I am left with a damn box checked, "Widowed."*

Jon and I waited for hours outside the embassy, not knowing what else to do. After some time we went to check on Ronald, who had been waiting for us faithfully. We gave him some jerky and power bars. We needed to communicate, but he spoke little English. I looked around and saw the same teary-eyed man from when we first arrived at the embassy. I asked him, "Do you speak English?"

"Yes," he said. He helped us have a conversation with Ronald. We told him we wanted to go with him back up the mountain before dark, but we needed to make sure we could communicate with our family first. Ronald said: "Why would you go back up the mountain? There is no water and no food. What are you going to do, sleep in the street again? There is nothing you can do. You must stay here."

I knew he was right. We wrote a note to Michael, Walnes, Kez, and the boys telling them how sad we were that we were not returning to them. We thanked them for keeping watch over Ben and said that we would continue to pray for them. We gave Ronald some money and embraced him before he turned to make his way back.

I turned to the stranger. "Tell me, what happened to you?"

With tears in his eyes, he said, "My wife and two children were here from Florida for my father's funeral. When the earthquake hit, my wife and I were outside and my two children and mother were in the house. The house collapsed with them in it and I am here looking for help to get them out. There is no help."

"I am so sorry," I said. "Are they alive?"

"I am not sure." He looked hollow, drained of all life.

I did not know how to reconcile my demands and desperation for help to get Ben out with this father's loss. He needed to get his children out. *There are people who are buried alive and they need help before I do.* I let go of the possibility of people storming up the mountain to dig Ben out. I will never forget the look in the stranger's eyes as he told us about his children, of his helplessness in being unable to save them. All of us were linked in our loss, in our grief, and in our vulnerability in the face of such devastation.

9

Forty-Eight Hours

THROUGHOUT OUR FIRST DAY at the embassy on January 13, more and more people poured in, especially injured people. I noticed one man in particular. I am not sure where he was from, but he was not Haitian. He was large and strong, and had long, curly, blond hair. He carried in injured person after injured person. He dripped with sweat, and I wished I could be like him. I wished I could rush valiantly back into the streets and start saving people, but I could feel my energy and hope depleting with every passing hour.

As I wandered through the embassy, I heard the word "tsunami" echoing on the TV news. My chest clenched with fear, for I knew that tsunamis were possible after a massive earthquake. Devastating images of the great Indian Ocean tsunami of 2004 flooded my thoughts. *Oh God, a giant wave would wash us all away!* Videos of the earthquake and its aftermath played continuously on TV screens around the embassy. How strange it was to watch CNN's footage while still in Haiti. When I did not see the images on the screen, I saw them in my mind. We were all trapped in a horrible nightmare with no way to escape.

I felt so helpless and vulnerable, and my grief over Ben seemed too painful to bear. *Maybe it wouldn't be so bad to be swept away in a cleansing flood. Maybe it wouldn't be so bad to have this pain end, to give up my breath.* At that moment, I didn't care whether I lived or died. If there was going to be a tsunami, so be it. I had already lost Ben and I couldn't picture my life without him. It might be a pretty good deal to just get it all over with and die while I was still in Haiti.

But when I looked at Jon, I was snapped back to reality. I knew we needed to live (he needed to live!) and return to our families. As much as we wanted to be embraced by our loved ones, Jon and I had already decided not to board any of the evacuation planes. We had first priority to leave because we had arrived at the embassy early. But we could not bear to leave Haiti without Ben.

Finally the embassy's Internet started to work, but not its phones. It was decided that we would each be able to have one e-mail sent to one person, and we all received paper forms with boxes to check that said things like, "I am okay," or "I am okay, but _____ is dead." I checked the box that said, "I am okay, but Ben is missing." I could not bear to choose "dead" before I could tell our family myself. My e-mail would go to my dad, and Jon's would go to his sister, Liz. I had no capacity to think about what it would be like for my dad and Liz to receive these messages. Liz would only know that Jon was okay and Ben was missing, and my dad would only know that I was okay and Ben was missing. They would need to put the pieces of the puzzle together and figure it out.

Jon and I could hardly tolerate being inside a building, so we spent much of our time outside the embassy on the grass. I sat paging through the hymnal I had retrieved from our room, trying to find the song Ben sang as he died. I looked through the lyrics of every hymn without finding the words he sang, so I went through it again looking for the melody, which I had been humming over and over again so I could not forget. I came to hymn 359, "Where Charity and Love Prevail." There it was! "Here it is, Jon! Here is the melody Ben was singing, but not the words. Maybe he was making them up. That's like him, anyway. Beautiful . . ."

Jon was quiet for a while. Then he looked at me and said, "You are going to write about this someday, Renee."

Someday . . . I laid on my stomach and buried my face and hands in the green blades. I wept. My body heaved with sobs. It was all starting to sink in: Ben's death, what we had experienced, what we had seen, what lay ahead, the potential of a tsunami and more strong aftershocks. That I was a widow at age twenty-seven.

Finally, restless, I got up and said to Jon, "I'm going inside."

I opened the door and I must have looked pretty pathetic, because a woman whom I would come to know as Lori took one look at me and said, "Oh, my God . . . what happened to you?" She invited me to sit in a chair in front of her.

I choked out, "I cannot get to my husband. He died and I cannot get to his body."

"Are you alone?"

"No, my husband's cousin, Jon, is with me. A building collapsed on us. We lived, but Ben died."

"Where is Jon?"

"He is outside."

Lori turned to the woman next to her and said, "We are now a group of twenty-two, not twenty." Lori and nineteen others were part of a group of Presbyterians and Baptists from New Jersey who had landed in Haiti on the morning of the earthquake. They were a medical mission team. They made it to their destination right before the earthquake hit. Luckily, none of their buildings collapsed. They had struggled to decide whether to stay where they were or go to the embassy. In the end they chose the embassy to see if they could be of help. The embassy was desperate for them! There were no medical personnel to help the many injured people who were pouring in. The group set up shop and went to work immediately. Now part of the group, Jon and I cared for people with them.

It was good to keep busy and be helpful. We collected bandages, ointment, aspirin, and anything we could find to help the injured. People graciously gave whatever they had that might help. One of the doctors from the New Jersey group used sticks to make canes for people who were having trouble walking. Ibuprofen became a sedative when bones needed to be set.

Jon helped carry U.S. citizens who needed to be airlifted by helicopter for life-saving medical care. Jon had been barefoot at the time of the earthquake, but he had retrieved Ben's Keens from our room at St. Joseph's when we returned for our passports. Now Jon grabbed the shoes, put them on, and said, "Come on, Ben!"

Still, Jon felt guilty carrying people to the helicopters. So many Haitians surrounded the airfield, unable to leave. They could only watch other people being flown out of the devastation. Anyone who had a U.S. passport had reason to hope for survival and safety; for anyone who didn't, survival and safety were uncertain.

One Haitian girl who was about eight years old was brought in on a reclining lawn chair. Her left femur was fractured and she had a deep gash in her forehead. I do not remember her making any sound other than occasional low moans. She mostly held her head in her hand, but she smiled once. I stood next to her and hummed some hymns. Eventually she needed to urinate. There was no way for us to move her, so we told her to just go ahead. All the liquid came running down from the lawn chair onto the table. We simply wiped it up with towels and kept going.

A woman about my age was brought in and put on the next table. She was clearly in terrible pain. She was a dual citizen of Haiti and the U.S., and she and her husband were here visiting family. Her husband was killed in the earthquake and she was trapped for a while until someone dug her out. Her right foot and ankle were badly injured, including two broken bones.

I continued to hum and sing a little and the injured woman joined me. Some others joined in as well. Slowly, a whole day passed. I noticed people were starting to wear masks because of the stench of rotting bodies in the streets. People tried to persuade me to eat, but I was not hungry. Jon brought me a tortilla with peanut butter on it. He said, "I know you aren't hungry and you don't want to eat, but will you please eat this for me? Just try. Think of our families. You have to eat something."

I took the food reluctantly and tried to choke it down. My mouth was so dry. Someone was passing out instant coffee, and Jon and I took some. Just holding those cups of coffee made us so sad. Hardly anyone loved coffee as much as Ben did. We both thought of him as we drank it, tears running down our cheeks.

I tried to sleep that night, but could not. Jon and I lay in the grass with others scattered around, and shook from grief and shock.

Psalm 46 and Forty-Eight Hours

The next day I noticed a beautiful flower growing up through the dirt. I took a photo of it, thinking, *One day new life will come, but not today for me.* A butterfly came and landed on the flower. Such beauty in such devastation; a small sign of resurrection in the midst of death.

I looked up. No one was around. I let go. I screamed and screamed and wept. I was so angry! I wanted to punch and throw something. I kicked a rock wall and screamed to the heavens. One of the team members from New Jersey, named Joan, came outside, but I did not see her because my eyes were closed. She came up to me, reached out her arms, and embraced me gently. At first I was startled and a little embarrassed that someone had seen me in that state, but then I fell into her arms and let her hold me. All she said was, "It's okay. Let it out."

Gradually, I calmed down. By that time Jon was looking for me. He came over to us and Joan took out her Bible and read Psalm 46. As she read it, I looked up to the mountains surrounding Port-au-Prince.

> God is our refuge and strength,
> a very present help in trouble.
> Therefore we will not fear, though the earth should change,
> though the mountains shake in the heart of the sea;
> though its waters roar and foam,
> though the mountains tremble with its tumult.
> There is a river whose streams make glad the city of God,
> the holy habitation of the Most High.
> God is in the midst of the city; it shall not be moved;
> God will help it when the morning dawns.
> The nations are in an uproar, the kingdoms totter;
> he utters his voice, the earth melts.

The LORD of hosts is with us;
the God of Jacob is our refuge.

Come, behold the works of the LORD;
see what desolations he has brought on the earth.
He makes wars cease to the end of the earth;
he breaks the bow, and shatters the spear;
he burns the shields with fire.
"Be still, and know that I am God!
I am exalted among the nations, I am exalted in the earth."
The LORD of hosts is with us;
the God of Jacob is our refuge.

The indispensable Word had come to us once again.

After the reading I recognized some people coming into the gate of the embassy. One of them was Troy Livesay, who had come to the open lot the night of the earthquake. I barely knew him, but I was so glad to see him again. He was checking on a few individuals to make sure they made it to the embassy, and then he was going to go back up the mountain to help care for people. We asked him to carry another note for us to let the people of St. Joseph's know we were thinking of them.

The next people to come in were the Williams family. Trevor, who had spent time with us in the ravine on the morning of the earthquake, was carrying his mother, June, whose leg was injured. They were so sad for us and gave us their sympathies. They did not stay long because they needed to evacuate so Trevor's mom could receive medical attention.

More and more people were coming to the embassy. Many walked in with huge suitcases packed full. Some of them became angry when they were told they would not be allowed to take their possessions with them when they evacuated. The embassy became crowded with people. Many of those who were taken to the airport had to wait there for hours on the hot tarmac without water. The evacuation planes were not cleared to land because of political and other issues. They just circled overhead while the people waited below. I was thankful that I was still at the embassy helping out where I could.

I remember when Jon looked at me and said, "Forty-eight hours, Renee. Even if Ben lived for a while, there is no way for him to survive any longer." I realized that Jon was still hoping Ben was alive and that we could get to him. But any hope Jon still had died at that forty-eight-hour mark.

As the second day at the embassy came to a close, the U.S. military and medical team arrived! We all cheered. We were so happy to have help and be relieved of the strain of caring for injuries. Just before the medical team fully took over, all twenty-two of us, plus the injured woman and little girl, formed a circle and prayed together. We prayed for God's mercy and presence, for help, healing, strength, and courage. It felt good to pray together, and I found that I still could pray and have confidence that God heard.

After the prayer the American Baptist pastor, Marlene, came up to me and said, "Someday you will be a healing balm." I wanted so badly to believe her. I felt deflated and empty, but somehow she still saw life in me. It was a great gift to me for her to say such a thing. She also said: "The Holy Spirit is alive and active, and the gospel story is still being written. It's time for the third testament and it is being written by women, women like you."

"I hope so." I knew that I would be called to witness to what had happened. I was amazed that she was able to see me as a minister even in my deepest sorrow.

As we left the medical area of the embassy, I heard one of the military men say to the woman with the broken ankle, "Brace yourself!" I heard bones cracking and the woman's piercing screams. Her ankle was set.

Evacuation

Once again we were out on the grass, except this time the group was larger because we were no longer needed inside to care for the injured. Lori gave me one of her sweatshirts to help me keep warm. Suddenly she exclaimed, "Hey! My phone is working! I can't call out, but I can send and receive text messages." Jon and I looked at one another hopefully.

"Do you think we could try and text our family, Lori?" I asked.

"Of course you can." She gave me the phone, and I texted my dad.

"Dad, Ben is dead. What should we do?" I guessed it was around 1 a.m. for my parents, but I heard back from him immediately.

"Who is this?"

"This is Renee. Ben is dead. Call Judd and April and ask them what we should do."

Jon then texted his sister. "Liz, this is Jon. Ben is dead. Please tell Judd and April and ask them what we should do." Liz called Judd and April and tried to tell them, but she could not do it. She just cried and said, "I will e-mail you." She sent an e-mail to tell them their only son was dead.

Less than five minutes later I received a text from my dad: "April and Judd and all of us want you to evacuate as soon as you can."

"What about Ben, Jon? How can we leave him?" I moaned.

"I don't know, Renee," Jon replied.

Just then another text came in: "Where is Ben?"

"Who is this?" I responded.

"Rafael Malpica. Where is Ben located, Renee? I will send Lutheran World Federation staff over in the morning." Rev. Rafael Malpica-Padilla was serving as the executive director of the ELCA Division for Global Mission. He was a longtime friend of Ben's family, and April and Judd had called him immediately after finding out about Ben.

"The address is 91 Delmas, Rue Herne #48, at St. Joseph's Home for Boys. He is buried on the top standing floor of the home."

"We will take care of him, Renee. It is okay to evacuate. You must leave Haiti." With this last text a huge weight lifted off my shoulders. I knew I could entrust Ben's body to the St. Joseph Family and the church. Those were the words I needed in order to let go and evacuate.

It had been so long since Jon and I had slept, and we had hardly eaten. Our new friends from New Jersey said, "Take these sleeping pills. You need to rest. We will wake you if anything happens. There is nothing left to do now but rest." Jon and I each took a sleeping pill and lay down. It was dark.

Our sleep was short-lived. "Wake up, Renee and Jon!" Lori said as she shook us awake less than half an hour later. A man I had never seen before was standing at our feet.

"Okay, there are twenty-two of you on this list," the man said. "I will read your names. If I call your name, you will not go and get bags or anything else. You will get in these vehicles and you will be taken to the airport. This is a secret. Tell no one. From there you will get on a plane and be evacuated."

Fighting the sleeping pill, I tried to regain consciousness as the man read the names. I looked at Jon and saw that he was really out of it, too. "Renee . . . Jon . . ." Our names were read! We were allowed to evacuate.

"We are very grateful for your service in caring for the injured people until we arrived. Now you can get in the vehicles." All twenty-two of us piled in.

My eyes kept rolling into the back of my head on the way to the airport. I fought to stay awake. When we arrived, we all stepped onto the runway and were shuffled onto a small plane. A man at the front said, "Welcome, everyone. This is a military plane and has never carried civilians. We thank you for your service at the embassy. Buckle up . . . we're going to Puerto Rico."

I watched Haiti disappear as the plane ascended. *I'm sorry, Ben. I'm so sorry we're leaving you. I'm sorry . . .*

Before I knew it I was out cold.

10

Returning Home

I woke just in time to see the lights of Puerto Rico. It was early in the morning on Friday, January 15. Because we were on a military plane, we had access to a different part of the airport not available to the general public. There we used a phone to book tickets to the mainland of the U.S. and eventually home. Jon negotiated the tickets, explaining that we had been in the earthquake in Haiti and were now in the U.S. on the island of Puerto Rico, but needed to get to Minneapolis, Minnesota. American Airlines was very understanding and booked us free flights via a connection in Dallas.

We traveled to Dallas with the group from New Jersey and waited there with them for connecting flights. I was sitting on the floor with my shoes off when one of the women from the group looked at my feet, gasped, and asked me to come with her to the bathroom. I followed. She invited me to sit up on the counter by the sink.

I noticed my feet for the first time. They were almost black, covered in dirt and concrete dust. There were scrapes, abrasions, and dried blood on them. I was too exhausted and overwhelmed to be embarrassed. I just let her take my feet in her hands as she gently scrubbed my wounds and washed the filth away.

I don't remember a single word she said (or even if she said any words) while she washed my feet. Tears rolled off my cheeks, and the ache in my heart was mended a little by this incredible and simple act of love. "Wash one another's feet," Jesus says.[1]

Once my feet were clean, it was time to say goodbye to the dear group of people who were responsible for getting us back to our families so quickly, people who had been Christ to us. I hugged Lori as she said, "I will remember you forever." We parted and Jon and I boarded the plane to Minneapolis.

1. John 13:14.

Jon and I had tears running down our faces that entire flight. I heard Jon sigh deeply over and over. "I can't believe he's dead, Renee," Jon wept. "I don't know how I can face our family."

Our hearts descended with the plane. We walked silently up the jet bridge, heads bowed. Unexpectedly, as we exited the gate, our three immediate families were right there waiting for us. Jon was a little ahead of me and I saw him collapse into everyone's arms, as if he was just barely holding on until that moment. I quickly followed. I fell into my father's arms first and I heard him sob as I had never heard him cry before. Everyone huddled around Jon and me and we all wept together loudly. The airport was silent except for our wails of grief and gratitude. All eyes were on us.

All Jon and I could say was, "I'm sorry! I'm sorry!" We were so sorry to leave Ben and so devastated that he had died. Our family kept hugging us, kissing us, and crying. I hugged Ben's parents and his sisters. They all said, "We are so happy you are here and are alive." This was the first time since the earthquake I truly felt thankful for my life and relieved I had lived—not for myself, but for my family and for Ben and Jon's families.

I finally noticed how weak I was. My brother and dad must have noticed, too, because they moved to either side of me. With my arms around their shoulders, they walked me to a restaurant near one of the airport exits. At least fifty of our family and closest friends were there waiting for us. Ben's parents had gathered this group of people, saying, "We need to support Renee and Jon."

Although I was deeply moved by their presence, I did not feel ready to face so many people. I buried my face in my dad's chest as he sat on a chair and held me. Everyone gathered around Jon and me with tears in their eyes. I felt like crying again, but I had no more tears. We started to tell what happened. Everyone strained to hear every detail of the story. When we came to the part where Ben sang, April grabbed her chest and said, "He sang! Oh!" and began to cry.

Judd's humor did not desert him even now. "Don't expect me to sing when I'm dying!" he told her.

"Oh, Judd," April said through her tears.

When we finished our story, everyone simply surrounded us with their silent presence. There was nothing to say. Bishop Peter Rogness was there, and April asked him if he would pray. He was a pastor we all needed in our time of reuniting and grief, someone who reminded us of Christ and God's love and care for us and for Ben. Close to the end of his prayer, Jon said, "Please pray for the people of Haiti," and he did.

After the prayer we left the airport. I shivered from the January cold as my mom and sister tried to get a scarf and jacket on me. We made our way to Ben's aunt and uncle's house, where there was food waiting for sixty people. We all stood wherever we could and held a hand next to us. We sang a Taizé song Ben's family loved called "Jubilate Deo" in a six-part round. I held my father's hand and partway through the song he started to weep again. His tears ran down his face and onto my pant leg. I felt such compassion for my father, who had lost so many of his family members to cancer and Alzheimer's. Now he had lost a son-in-law.[2]

We finished singing. I didn't feel like eating, but everyone looked so worried about Jon and me that I took some food and tried to eat it. Later I would hear April say that she had never seen anyone look the way I looked when I came off the plane who would not be dead within a few hours. I am sure we scared her and everyone half to death, and that was why they were trying urgently to get some water and food in us.

Jon and I were totally exhausted. It felt so good to be with our family and out of the devastation of the earthquake, but we knew that millions were still trapped in that nightmare. Our white skin and U.S. passports had allowed us to leave, but we left so many behind who lacked safe buildings to sleep in and proper medical care. The Haitians had the loving arms of their families, just as we did, they had faith, they had each other, but that night I would have a bed to sleep in and most people in or near Port-au-Prince would not.

I needed to sleep, but I heard that our friend Elly had taken a flight from Egypt and would be arriving soon. We waited for her and she came. We hugged and cried.

My immediate family and I, along with Elly, stayed with Irish friends of Ben's aunt and uncle, Sean O'Driscoll and Trisha Barry. They were so kind and gave us the space we needed. My sister, Jessie, prepared a warm bath for me, and she and Elly helped bathe my body of sorrow. They listened to me say things like, "I don't know how I'm going to live without Ben." The water felt good on my skin and so did the presence of my baby sister and a good friend.

I still couldn't sleep. I rose in the middle of the night and crawled in bed between my parents. My mom ran her fingers through my hair. Every once in a while my dad said, "Don't worry, honey. It will be all right." The hours passed slowly.

Eventually the sun rose, as it always does, and there I was with no clean clothes and a haggard face. Luckily my dear sister brought plenty of her own

---

2. Even though he had lost so many family members, Ben's death changed my father like none other. He began to sing. Not just little jingles; he really began to sing and let music touch his heart and soul, and it made me happy.

clothes for me to wear and put some makeup on me so I would not look so pale.

I will never forget coming down the stairs in the morning and smelling my favorite food, oatmeal, and my favorite thing to drink, coffee. I felt hungry for the first time. It was the best bowl of oatmeal and best cup of coffee I have ever had. I don't think it was just because I had barely eaten for days; it really was amazing, thick-cut rolled oats and dark, fair-trade coffee with real cream. As I ate and drank and sat with my family, I felt life begin to awaken in me again.

That day a Lutheran Social Service worker came to visit Jon and me. We sat at a table with her and answered her questions. We both looked at her as if she could give us a magic pill to make the pain go away and bring Ben back to life. We were desperate for anything she might offer. She looked at us compassionately and said, "There is nothing I can do to help you other than listen. You are both suffering some post-traumatic stress disorder, which is to be expected, but you are thinking clearly, making good decisions, and are physically okay. I am so impressed with both of you."

My heart sank. *There's nothing she can do! We're okay? I don't feel okay. I feel like I am in a nightmare and cannot wake up.* But although we had extreme sleep deprivation, Jon and I were thinking clearly and could already talk in detail about what had happened. We simply needed to be with family, cry, make some decisions, and let God begin the healing process.

Planning the Funeral

On Saturday, January 16, Ben's parents and sisters, my mother, and Jon, with other family, all sat at a table and started to plan Ben's funeral for Friday, January 22, 2010. There would need to be a funeral service with no body to bury. We decided to hold it at Luther College in the Center for Faith and Life (CFL). The CFL had a lot of meaning for Ben, as he had sung in many Nordic Choir concerts there and led a worship band for Sunday night services.

I poured out my life that week in planning the funeral for Ben. Judd, April, my mom, and Elly stayed by my side and helped me make the necessary decisions. In the early planning stages of Ben's funeral, I kept wondering: *What hymns and Scripture might Ben want?* Then I started to ask: What hymns give me strength? Which ones would give comfort to our family and friends? Which speak Christ crucified and raised? We all needed to hear the gospel and be reminded of the hope of the resurrection. We needed to sing, to be together, to share in Holy Communion, to thank God for Ben's life, and to entrust him to the care of our Maker. Once I let go of the pressure to identify things Ben would want, I was able to open up and ask the Spirit for guidance in choosing what was needed for those who were still living.

Elly helped me put together the twenty-four-page bulletin full of music and liturgy. I did not care how long the funeral would be. Whether to have communion was not even a question. We would have communion because the gathered community needed it. I needed to come to the table where I knew I could meet Ben and share in the foretaste of the feast to come.

The only other memory I have of the week leading up to Ben's funeral was going to a shoe store with my mom to buy black high heels, and Ben's aunt Nancy taking me to a tailor to have my suit hemmed. This suit had been purchased two months earlier by April, Judd, Katie, Amy, and Nancy in preparation for my pastoral call interviews after seminary graduation in the spring. It was an all-wool, three-piece suit with a purple silk shirt. I had been so excited to wear it to my first interview. Never could I have guessed I would wear it to my husband's funeral.

The Funeral

I woke up incredibly sad on the day of Ben's funeral. I felt as if I were living in another world. My mind was somewhere else and my body was just going through the motions. After showering, I lay down on the bed in the hotel room in my towel. My step-grandma, Arlene, came into the room. She hugged me and with tears in my eyes I said, "I can't do this, Grandma."

She who had buried two husbands rubbed my back and said, "I know it's hard, Renee, but you can do it. We are all here with you."

I put on my suit. It was strange to hear from various people throughout the day, "You look good, Renee." What did people expect, for me to look like I just went through an earthquake and lost my husband? I did not know how to reply. I felt anything but good or even alive. I wanted to go into a room and shut the door and wait until it was all over. I deeply appreciated everyone coming, but I did not want to face anyone and I did not want to say goodbye to Ben. What saved the day for me at Ben's funeral was the music.

Right before the service, about one hundred of us gathered in a choir room to pray. When it was time to walk out, I felt once again that I could not do it. People waited patiently for me to gather my courage. Finally, I took a breath and said, "It's time to sing," and we all walked out together singing "I Want Jesus to Walk with Me."

More than 1,000 people came to the funeral. The service lasted two and a half hours, and we had a committal ritual at the end even though we did not have a body. Rev. Susan Briehl, our presider, wrote lovely and appropriate words for our situation, never knowing whether we would ever retrieve Ben's body in order to bury him.

When I was out in the entryway afterward greeting people, I spotted my college roommate of four years, Emilie. Her presence was so important for me that day, along with so many others who traveled so far in the winter to grieve with us. I was deeply honored that four members of the group from New Jersey came to Ben's funeral. They came, even though they had returned home to their own families only the week before. How I wished that they had known Ben! I do think they received a glimpse of who he was by attending the funeral.

I was exhausted when the day finally ended. That night, by the mercy of God, I slept.

Time to Get to Work

When I went looking for Jon and Ben's family the next morning, I found everyone gathered in a conference room at the Hotel Winneshiek in Decorah, where we were staying. I felt as if I had just walked into a top-secret headquarters. Jon and Ben's parents, sisters, aunts, uncles, and others were all sitting at a massive table. There must have been ten computers on the table, with papers spread out all over the place. Some of the family were on their phones with politicians, governors, and military personnel. The list of officials seemed endless, and they were all doing their best to try and help us. I could hear Rev. Rafael Malpica-Padilla on his phone: "So there is a possibility of getting a small plane to fly into Haiti . . ."

Everyone paused and looked up at me when I walked in. "We're going to get Ben's body back, Renee," someone said. It was time for mission impossible. We pulled up Google Earth and amazingly, we could see from a bird's eye view the hole near the roof of St. Joseph's where Jon and I had crawled out. I was able to point out the place in the building where I believed Ben was buried.

We tried to stay in contact with the St. Joseph Family and the Lutheran World Federation as best as we could, but the Internet in Haiti was sparse and the people there were concerned with basic survival. Renee Dietrich at Wings of Hope and Michael at St. Joseph's Home for Boys assured me that they were watching over Ben's body. Michael even said he would go daily to where he believed Ben's body was and pray. This was a great comfort to me.

We heard from the U.S. embassy, who sent people from the U.S. military and workers from the United Nations to evaluate the situation where Ben was buried. They told us that the building was much too dangerous to enter and that they could potentially get Ben out in two months' time—or maybe not. This was hard to hear, but I understood. They needed to focus on survivors and many other immediate needs.

That meant it was up to us and to the Haitians. The original plan we came up with was that Rafael, Jon, and I would fly to Haiti in a private plane, gather a team, and dig Ben out. That idea didn't last long because there was no way for us to obtain clearance to land anywhere. We formed a new plan.

Through Rafael we learned that Louis Dorvilier, who was head of the ELCA's International Lutheran Disaster Response, and his wife Mytch had decided to travel to Haiti via the Dominican Republic to check on their families. Louis and Mytch were Haitian and they, along with their children, had been forced to flee Haiti ten years before because of political death threats. They had not been back since. Rafael asked if they would stop at St. Joseph's Home for Boys and see what possibilities there were to get Ben's body out.

During all this planning, an important question came up. Was it right for us to go into Haiti and dig out one body when so many other people were still buried? What might that look like from a Haitian perspective?

Our friends from different developing countries offered helpful wisdom and clarity. It was a question of accompaniment. They asked us: What would it look like for the ELCA, the church, to leave one of their pastors buried in the rubble? What kind of hospitality would the Haitians be able to show if we did not allow them to aid in getting their guest out? Friends from the "global south" said that people would think something was wrong with us if we did not try to get Ben out.

April had traveled to Africa a number of times while she was serving as bishop. Once in Tanzania her hosts insisted she sleep in the bishop's suite, which had a perfect view of Mount Kilimanjaro. She felt that they were going to too much trouble for her and wanted to stay in a more humble place. She tried to talk them into moving her, until the Tanzanian woman who was hosting her spoke up: "Bishop, what would it look like to our people if we did not take care of you and give you this particular place to stay?" We needed a lesson in what accompaniment meant, versus what we assumed. We needed to listen to our friends.

Once Mytch and Louis agreed to assess the situation and gather a Haitian team to dig Ben out, all we could do was wait. Meanwhile, I received word that Bill had been flown out of Haiti for medical care and was going to live, thanks be to God.

PART III

The Body

Knowing the Names
Kalen Barkholtz

Because of Ben
we are buying a globe.
He taught us
the world ought to be in our living room.
On a rainy January night we decided
we needed all the places on earth
in a way that we can touch them.
We needed to know the names
of nations and cities,
of islands and mountains
where brothers and sisters in Christ live
so we can say the names
and pray them.

11

Excavation

I WAS DESPERATE TO hear any word from Haiti as I waited with Judd and April in wintry Duluth, Minnesota. I will never know the physical difficulty and emotional strain of digging Ben's body out of a pile of rubble on top of a swaying, unsteady building. I was not there. The aftershocks continued in Haiti, and there was little food or water for earthquake survivors. People continued to die daily from their injuries. Most people were afraid to sleep in their homes—even if they were still standing—so there were many sleepless nights. This was the situation Louis and Mytch found when they arrived in Haiti. Had their own family members survived?

Thankfully, their immediate families did survive, but to their deep grief, Louis and Mytch each lost other family members and friends, and their country was in ruins. Several of their lost friends had been educators. Many of Haiti's academics, teachers, and artists died in the earthquake, which would make the nation's recovery and rehabilitation that much more complex and difficult.

Soon Louis stood on the roof of St. Joseph's Home for Boys, and he prayed there for an hour and a half. When he finished his prayer, he decided that he and Mytch would not leave Haiti without getting their friend Ben out.

Mytch and Louis went to the Port-au-Prince airport to ensure that once Ben's body was free he could be flown back to the U.S. Unfortunately, no Haitians were being allowed into their own airport, so Mytch and Louis had a very difficult time trying to communicate with the workers. After much frustrating conversation, they were finally let in and assured that Ben's body would be taken care of and flown back to the U.S.

One of Mytch's relatives was a structural engineer, and they also hired a second engineer to help ensure the building could be shored up in order to dig safely. Once the building was safe enough to stand on, Mytch and Louis gathered a team of four Haitians from the community. We had sent them our sketches using Google Earth to pinpoint exactly where we thought they would find Ben. They began to dig on January 26 from the very top of the roof using their bare hands and small tools. After a full day of digging, they could see part of Ben's leg.

When I received the call from Louis that they had found Ben, something unexpected happened: I slipped into a depression. I was thankful they had found Ben's body, but there was some small part of me that had still hoped he was alive, that he had indeed fallen off the roof and had been taken to a hospital, where he was recovering. Now Ben's death became more real for me than ever before. I was so unsettled. I moved from chair to chair and window to window at Judd and April's, staring out with hollow eyes.

Louis instructed the workers that they were to give Ben's wedding ring to him so that he could give it to me. Either Mytch or Louis was on the roof at all times during the excavation. Louis found Jon's camera. He also found the book I had with me at the time of the earthquake, *The Black Jacobins* by C.L.R. James. In fact, it had been Louis who had originally recommended the book to me, saying it would give me the most honest and accurate picture of the history of Haiti. He made sure to return it to me complete with torn pages and rubble nestled in the binding.

It took two more long days to release Ben's body from its concrete tomb. After the first day, the number of people on the roof began to grow. People in the community were interested in what was going on atop the roof of St. Joseph's. Still, the morale of the diggers waned because the work was so difficult. A negotiation and increased pay became necessary. I didn't know it at the time, but to encourage the workers and the community, Louis translated and read aloud an e-mail I had sent him and a few others the week before:

Dear Friends,

I think Louis's wisdom in putting together a team of locals is a great option. What an important witness of the Haitian people to the U.S. and the church as a whole with the intentional removal of Ben's body, who was a guest of St. Joseph's, who in turn is considered part of that family. Louis, thank you so much for all you have been doing to walk with us in our grief over Ben's death and your dedication to recovering his body. Your people are suffering so much and we all continue to hold them in prayer.

Accompaniment with the Haitian people has been a priority for us, along with the recovery of Ben's body. How do we move forward together in accompaniment with the Haitian people and St. Joseph's, while still having a goal of the retrieval of Ben's body? The night of the earthquake, Michael was already

envisioning many people coming together to help rebuild St. Joseph's. How can we empower the Haitians to aid in the rebuilding of St. Joseph's and recover Ben's body? It seems to me that it
gives people hope to be working toward a goal together.

Louis, I'm so thankful that you are working so hard on the
recovery of Ben's body, while at the same time providing work
for people in Haiti who need income to provide for their families. How can we continue to accompany you in these things?

Yours in Christ,
Renee

Many Haitians gathered to hear Louis translate this message. He told
me later that there was a renewed spirit among the community as they
learned we were praying for them and encouraging them in the nearly
impossible work. Mytch and Louis also told them that the Evangelical Lutheran Church in America—more than four million people—were praying
for them and grieved with them. He told them how grateful and honored
the people of the ELCA were that Haitians would be freeing Ben's body from
the rubble. Led by one local man in particular, named Pierre, they all kept
digging.

In the meantime, Rafael and I were corresponding with Terry Krinvic,
an employee of the Clinton Foundation, who was working with the U.S.
embassy to be ready to receive Ben's body.

It took three whole days to dig Ben out because the pillar he was clinging to during the earthquake had fallen on him and crushed his upper body.
He was facing up, and rebar from the pillar made it difficult to fully remove
his body. Some of the tired workers thought removing the pillar would put
them all at risk, so they suggested just pulling, but Louis and Mytch insisted
that they keep his body intact. It took a full day to carefully cut through all
the rebar and gently remove Ben's head and arm from beneath the pillar.

Ben's body was freed on January 28, the evening of the third day. Michael from St. Joseph's witnessed the removal and described it to me in an
e-mail:

> The night that Ben's body was removed from the roof the moon
> was full. When the bag holding the body of Ben emerged from
> the rubble, one of the men . . . carried three lit candles in front
> of the procession down the roof to the waiting ambulance. I was
> up on the roof of the art center prayerfully being a part of it and
> [was] moved by the reverence and dignity of the removal.

The workers carefully placed Ben's body into an ambulance that took him to the only standing morgue in the region of Port-au-Prince.

I was so relieved to hear that Ben's body was out, but the relief was short-lived. Louis and Mytch had now left Haiti, and Ben's body, as far as I knew, was at the morgue. But because of a miscommunication, Ben's body was left there when it should have been taken to the U.S. embassy. The staff at the embassy waited at the gates for Ben's body, but it never came. I was told that Ben's body was lost.

Lost! I thought. *Ben's body is lost in a city of three million people that is in chaos.* Suddenly all of my grief and frustration built up into an explosion in my body and soul. I needed to go for a walk. I stumbled my way through the January snow in Duluth. I did not know where I was going, so I just kept walking until I reached the shores of Lake Superior. The moon was full and bright. The dark blue waters lapped on the shore. Ben and I had been at this spot less than a month before during our second anniversary. Ben took beautiful photos of the ice on the rocks of the beach. He said, "I just love this place, Renee."

I fell to my knees and let out a sound like nothing I had heard before. I turned my face to the heavens and wailed. I did not recognize my own voice. From the depths of despair and loss the sound of agony poured out of me. It came from the hidden places in me that felt the sting and finality of death. It came from the helplessness I felt in being unable to care for Ben's body or bring him home and bury him. Exhausted and spent, I lay facedown in the snow on the shores of the great lake.

I do not know how long I was there. I eventually forced myself to get up and walk back, thinking that Judd and April would be worried about me. As soon as I walked in the door, Judd and April said I had a phone call.

"Hello, Renee. My name is Paul. I work for the U.S. embassy in Haiti, and we are trying to get your husband's body here. I found out that his body is at the morgue in Pétionville, but they won't release it until they are paid $950. I will go and pay the money myself and personally see that his body gets to the embassy. You can wire me $950 into my account to reimburse me. I think this is the best plan to get your husband's body back to you."

I could not believe what I was hearing. Pure grace from God! This Paul, whom I had never met, had been copied on the series of e-mails between Terry Krinvic (from the Clinton Foundation) and me. I am forever grateful to him and to God for what he did for us. I considered his intervention nothing less than a miracle, and the ways we were taken care of by our country, sheer gift.

Paul called me once more to tell me that Ben's body was safely at the embassy and would be flown along with two other bodies to Dover,

Delaware, via military plane as soon as possible. The "as soon as possible" took a few more days because of a blizzard on the east coast. Then the people in Dover needed dental records so they could properly identify Ben's body during the autopsy. They also asked me questions, such as: Did he have any identifying scars or other markings on his body? It was agonizing to intimately recall my husband's body so that strangers could tell whether or not it was really him after being crushed, hauled around Port-au-Prince, and flown to a military base.

The medical examiners in Dover confirmed Ben's identity and prepared his body to be flown to Minneapolis in a casket. We started making preparations for his burial service in Decorah, Iowa.

When I finally had the opportunity to thank Mytch and Louis for all they had done for us, they said, "We were meant to do what we did. It was a gesture of love."

12

Burial

WHEN BEN'S BODY ARRIVED in Minneapolis, his mother April, needing to be as near as possible to her dead son, rode in the hearse to the funeral home in Decorah, Iowa. When they arrived, April asked the funeral director to open the casket. She needed to see and touch Ben. She needed to know it was really him. But the funeral director had been given strict instructions not to open the casket under any circumstance.

What should she do now? April contacted some of her friends from the global south, seeking counsel. She knew they had an entirely different perspective on mourning and the importance of caring personally for a loved one's body. The president of the Evangelical Lutheran Church in Peru told April that in his culture when a loved one dies, their family collects and cares for the body however they can. "It is so important for the family to be able to touch and be with their deceased loved one," he said. "We mourn as we wash their body and prepare them for burial. If they are killed in a way that their body is not intact, like in war, we gather every piece of their body we can ourselves and bury them."

April spoke next with her friend Musimbi from Kenya, who happened to be in the London airport on the way to her beloved brother's funeral. She listened compassionately and helped give April the confidence she needed to proceed. April also called her cousin Paul Ulring, a pastor in Ohio who had worked for a mortician while in seminary. He said, "Tell the mortician that you need to cover your son."

Everyone was afraid to open the casket. The body inside had been dead for three weeks. No one knew its condition or what being confronted with Ben's body would do to us emotionally. Would we be able to see his face? Would his body be crushed? Would nightmarish images be imprinted permanently in our minds?

Despite these questions, the alternative seemed worse: to bury the casket unopened. Would we be able to live with the regret? Would we ever find closure? Would we always wonder if the body in the casket was really Ben's?

Finally, against all logic and social pressure, April persuaded the funeral director to open the casket. It was the most difficult thing she had ever done.

I arrived at the funeral home shortly after the casket was opened. I was terrified. The last time I had seen Ben he was alive, eyes closed, and bracing for the impact of concrete. Now I was finally going to reach him once again. There was no longer a concrete barrier between us, just the thin veil of death. As I walked alone into the room with the open casket, I relived the determination I had felt in ripping the roof tiles off St. Joseph's. I needed that same determination, that courage, now in order to move forward and look into the casket.

My whole body shook just as it had following the earthquake. I approached the coffin, put my hands on its edges, and looked inside. I did not see Ben, but rather a body that was carefully and tightly wrapped in white linen from head to toe. Yet, I knew with every ounce of me that my husband's body lay within this cocoon of cloth. I touched Ben's head and chest first. I ran my hands down the sides of his arms to find his hands placed comfortably on his abdomen. I put my right hand on his and imagined his beautiful, guitar-playing fingers that fit so perfectly into mine. I laid my head on his chest and remembered how we used to fall asleep at night. I wept, knowing that this was the last time our bodies would touch, even though we had been one flesh. I wanted to crawl into the casket and lie down beside him one last time, but refrained. I kept my head on his chest as long as I could. The smell of formaldehyde wafted into my nostrils. It was the most intimate and heartbreaking moment of my life.

Ben's left shoulder was clearly dislocated, perhaps even partially severed. His head seemed to have the most damage. The left side felt as though it was pieced together and held by the cloth. I pictured the concrete coming down and crushing his skull immediately. I marveled that Ben had been able to sing as he died, and thanked God for the mystery of it.

Finally, I felt that I could justify no more time alone with Ben. I invited others to join me with him.

The scene was gut-wrenching. Ben's older twin sisters sobbed and stroked his hands and head. They wanted to be as near to him as I did. April kept lifting up Ben's legs to feel his weight in her arms. She, too, knew that it was Ben. Judd wept quietly nearby. Jon stayed next to Ben. He kept shaking his head, tears running down his face, not wanting it to be real. Everyone grieved as they needed to, some close, some at a distance.

The funeral director gave us as much time as we needed, but we could tell he would be relieved when the casket was closed once again. We said our goodbyes as best we could and covered Ben's body with a white family blanket. It felt good to do something useful and tender for Ben and for one another.

Now closed, the casket was moved to the sanctuary of First Lutheran Church in Decorah. We gathered our strength for the worship service and burial that would be held the next day.

One Last Night Together

That evening, Elly, Jon, my sister Jessie, and I stayed with the coffin in the sanctuary as long as we could. We played cards, told stories, cried, and sang hymns, including "What Wondrous Love Is This." Never have the words of the fourth verse illumined my heart as they did that night:

> And when from death I'm free, I'll sing on, I'll sing on;
> and when from death I'm free, I'll sing on;
> and when from death I'm free, I'll sing God's love for me,
> and through eternity I'll sing on, I'll sing on;
> and through eternity I'll sing on.

I also wrote my first journal entry since the earthquake. The life before me was fraught with uncertainty and many unanswered questions. Here is part of what I wrote as I lay on the floor by Ben's coffin:

> I have been told that if I would have died and Ben lived, that Ben wouldn't have "made it." Tonight I am with Ben's body sealed in a casket for the last time and I wonder if I am going to make it. My beautiful, shining, starry-eyed lover . . . gone. What am I to do? What am I to say? I look at our wedding photos and I ache so badly in places I have never felt. I can't cry hard enough. I can't yell loud enough. I can't breathe deep enough for my pain to be softened. My breathing, life-filled husband, my Ben . . . lifeless, unmoving, wrapped in cloth . . . dead.
>
> Are you with our Shepherd, my Ben? Are you at peace? Are you joyful? Are you singing? Are you with me? Where are the dead?

The next morning I woke up with a dream of Ben. I dreamed of Ben almost every night, but the dreams were never good. I was plagued with dreams of searching for Ben, but never finding him. Sometimes I would glimpse him or have brief conversations, but I would always know he that would die soon, or sometimes he would just disappear. I always woke up sad and frustrated.

The morning of Ben's burial was different. In my vivid dream, Ben was wearing his gray suit with his classy, long winter dress coat over it and his leather winter gloves. He was standing in the snow by himself under the maple tree by his grave. He was radiant. His green eyes sparkled as he sang "The King of Love My Shepherd Is." He was so alive. It gave me a sense of peace in what would be one of the most difficult days of my life.

It was uncertain whether we would be able to bury Ben in February in Iowa because the ground was frozen. People often waited to bury their loved ones until the ground thawed. Once again, my mother-in-law April was on the case. She told the gravediggers what the Haitians went through to dig Ben out and return him to us so we could bury him. The gravedigger said, "Well, if the Haitians can do that, I suppose we can cut through the frozen ground of Northeast Iowa." They did.

On February 6, we lowered Ben's body into the ground in its final resting place at Phelps Cemetery while the Luther College Nordic Choir sang "Hymn to the Eternal Flame" by Stephen Paulus. We all knew very well what a miracle it was to have the privilege of burying Ben's body, of knowing where he lay. So many people who died in the Haiti earthquake were lost or in mass graves, leaving their families wondering which grave they might be in, or where their bodies remained buried under the rubble. What a strange feeling it was to be so thankful and so devastated at the same time.

I watched the casket that held my husband as it was lowered into the earth. My body trembled with cold, fear, and grief. Somehow I brought myself to grab a shovel like everyone else and throw dirt on the casket at the bottom of the grave. It was awful and sacred. Many of us grabbed pieces of rock from the hole for memory's sake, and called them "Ben rocks." Ben's body was taken out of the ruined concrete in Haiti and embraced by the rocky ground of the hills of Decorah.

Ben's body had been cared for by the military, which was ironic because Ben was a pacifist. I, as his widow, received his dog tags from the funeral director at the graveside. I held on to them as any widow might and sat beside the hole in the earth for as long as my body could stand it. It was dreadfully cold.

Those of us who remained in Decorah that night went to Mabe's and had pizza and root beer in memory of Ben.

13

A Birth

BEN AND I NEVER had children, which was another source of incredible grief to me. As I grieved Ben's death, I also grieved our unborn children. Ben and I were very close to being ready to try to conceive. We had been married for two years, were finishing seminary, and were preparing to move into our first call. Ben wasn't as ready as I was since he was two years younger than me, but he told me that when I said the word, it would be time. He followed that up with, "I'll have nine months to get ready."

Never did I desire to be pregnant more than the day before the earthquake. I was reading Kent Annan's book *Following Jesus Through the Eye of the Needle*. I was lying in my bottom bunk in our room at St. Joseph's and reading about when Kent and his wife, Shelly, found out she was pregnant. They were living in Haiti at the time. I came across this paragraph right after they had their sonogram and found out their "li" (girl or boy) was six weeks and five days old in the womb:

> After paying the receptionist twenty-five dollars, Shelly swings up onto the motorcycle and settles in behind Emmanuel. I get on behind her. As we wind through the busy streets, I feel a surge of panic. I feel more protective of her than ever before. In my mind I scream, "Stop the motorcycle! Where is the nearest Volvo dealer? We'll walk. Stop now!" (No, not one of us is wearing a helmet.) But it also feels wonderful, the wind rushing past. Our secret. Nobody else knows about this new, tiny life. My arms around Shelly, on her stomach, as we slice through the city chaos on the back of the bike. I feel like a fool for having her—them—exposed like this. Yet for a moment my arms feel almost strong enough to keep her and *li* safe.[1]

I pictured the same scene for Ben and me, his arms wrapped around my waist to protect our own "li." I knew right then and there that it was

---

1. Annan, *Following Jesus*, 185–86.

time. I almost told him that night as we were about to go to sleep, me on the bottom bunk and Ben on the top one, but we were both very tired. I decided to wait and discuss it with him when we were back at home. He stretched his arm down over the side of his bunk, and I reached up and placed my hand in his. We held hands briefly, sad that we could not share a bed, then let go and drifted off to sleep. I felt happy and had a longing deep within me for this next step in our marriage.

This "next step" would never happen for Ben and me. The next day he died in the earthquake and I was never able to tell him that I was ready to have a baby with him. I have had to live with this regret. I longed for Ben to be a dad and for him to live on through our child. Instead, he died at age twenty-five, a month and a half before his birthday on February 27.

At the time Ben died, his sister Katie was nearly seven and a half months pregnant. The fall before, Katie and her husband Seth had asked Ben and me to be their daughter's godparents. We were so excited! They were going to name her Rebekah. All throughout Katie's pregnancy Ben would lean over her stomach and say, "Rebekah, remember, be born on February 27! I want to share my birthday with you." Rebekah's due date was March 1, so it was a real possibility.

After the earthquake in Haiti and Ben's death, we all anticipated Rebekah's birth in the midst of our deep sadness and grief. When Katie sobbed, her belly would heave up and down, and I knew this child would be born into our family's heartache. I wondered whether I wanted Rebekah to be born on Ben's birthday after all. That day would hold such sadness for us all. What would that be like for Rebekah? How would the rest of us handle it as we celebrated her life each year and mourned Ben's death?

On February 26, Katie said, "There is no way this baby is coming tomorrow. She is somersaulting around and not in position to be born." I still wasn't sure I wanted her to be born on Ben's birthday, but I leaned over Katie's belly anyway and said, "Okay, Rebekah, Ben wanted to share his birthday with you, so February 27 is the day. Get to it girl!" Three hours later Katie went into labor and Rebekah Renee, my namesake, was born on February 27, 2010.

Less than half an hour after Rebekah entered the world, I held her tiny body in my arms. Rebekah's eyes were open, looking up at me and around her birthing room. I marveled at her as tears ran down my face. I pictured Ben holding her and singing to her. How happy he would have been that she was born on his birthday. I held this miracle of life in my arms and wondered at the joy, mystery, and vulnerability in it all.

Jon held Rebekah next. Katie and Seth asked Jon to help raise her in faith as her godfather. He accepted with tears in his eyes as he held her small body.

I was so happy, but I also felt incredible loss. As I stood there in the birthing room, I knew that the gift of motherhood would never be mine.

Sometimes it is good that we don't have a choice about certain things, like when babies decide to enter the world. Rebekah's birth held all kinds of confusion and mystery, along with pain and joy, for me. I could only wonder at what her birth on Ben's birthday could mean for us, and what in the world God was doing in the midst of it all.

I tried to ponder, or throw together, all that had happened, what was happening, and what would happen. I wanted to understand or make sense of it all, death and life. Whether I liked it or not, Rebekah was already involved in the mess of hardship and death. I could not protect her from the future any more than I could control the day she was born. All I knew was that she was a great gift to our family that would continue to unfold.

The next day Katie and Seth's pastor came and led worship with the whole extended family there in the hospital room. We had a full service complete with communion. At one point I could "feel" Ben standing behind me with his hands on my shoulders. I told no one, but just closed my eyes and felt his presence among us.

Rebekah Renee was baptized on April 3, 2010. As her godparents, Jon and I gave her the resurrection butterfly that survived the Haiti earthquake.

PART IV

Grief and Healing

Prayers
Kalen Barkholtz

Somewhere in the sea of words
we all have been reading
and hearing
as we try and stay connected to you these days,
Renee, you said about prayers—*I feel them.*

May prayers continue to wrap you,
hold you.

May prayers be solid ground
under your feet.

May prayers soothe
like a cool cloth
when you are feverish with grief.

May prayers pulse and hover
the way stars sometimes do—
shimmering, close, and all around.

14

Raging at God

THERE WERE ALL KINDS of firsts for me after Ben died. First night going to bed without him, first meal, first shopping trip, first worship, first birthday, first holiday, first bill pay, first everything. Every first was hard as I tried to orient myself to my "new normal." The first time I went shopping, I kept noticing clothing that I knew would look great on Ben. I wanted to keep buying him things as if he were alive. I wanted to keep cooking meals I knew he loved, and make frozen lemon pie on his birthday. The reality of Ben's death was that there was never a point when things would just go back to the way they were. My life was changed and I would never be the same. I needed to walk the painful road of firsts. Each day was a struggle for a long, long time.

After burying Ben in early February, Jon and I returned to Wartburg Seminary to finish our final semester. The community received us with a worship service. I felt Ben's profound absence as we walked into the midst of the community gathered in the chapel, the same place where I first laid eyes on him. After worship we had a time of sharing with everyone, and then I made my way back to our apartment for the first time since leaving for Haiti.

I stood facing the door alone. I unlocked it and stepped into what had been *our* home. I looked around. A pair of Ben's shoes lay to the right of the door; our table was to my left. Some dishes were still by the sink. A blanket we used to wrap up in was draped across the couch. Books were stacked everywhere from finishing up papers. It looked exactly as we left it.

I went down the hallway and entered our spare bedroom, which we had made into a music room. All our instruments were lying out; music was scattered everywhere. I looked at the piano and there on the stand our *Evangelical Lutheran Worship* book was open to hymn 359, "Where Charity and Love Prevail." I stared, dumbfounded. I could not remember Ben singing this hymn before we left for Haiti, or even mentioning it. It was the hymn I found while paging through the hymnal at the U.S. embassy in Haiti—the melody Ben sang in his dying song.

I stepped out of the room and continued down the hallway to our bedroom. I could smell Ben, but he was not there. Clean and dirty clothes littered the room. I felt hollow. *This is now my life.*

Life after the earthquake felt like one long season of Lent. Even though I had an incredible community at Wartburg Seminary, and family and friends who would drop anything to be with me, I still felt alone. Never in my life did I experience so much loneliness and silence. I wrote this in my journal more than a year after the earthquake:

> Silence, again, is my constant companion. Bone of my bone,
> flesh of my flesh . . .
> Where are you?
> Hollowed out and empty I lie in bed like a corpse
> With tears running down my face blankly staring at my past
> and future.
> In the present I know absence . . . silence . . .
> How is it I can be so cared for, loved, and affirmed, yet feel so
> worthless and unworthy of my life?
> Why this plague of self-blame?
> Why this feeling of unworthiness to have been your wife?
> What a job death does on us!
> It can make the best of loves seem false and tainted.
> I am so tired of being tired.
> I have nothing left for today . . .
> Nothing.

Both Jon and I struggled intensely with survivor's guilt, as did many Haitians we knew. Jon and I kept trying to convince ourselves that we could have done something to save Ben, finding ways to blame ourselves for something as uncontrollable as an earthquake. *Why was it Ben who died? Why not me? Why so many?* Both Jon and I could have died just as easily as everyone else who was crushed by concrete on January 12, 2010.

The most helpful thing in our struggle with survivor's guilt was that we had one another. I reminded Jon how important his life was, and he reminded me how important my life was, both to the church and to our family and friends. We each knew there was nothing the other could have done to save Ben. We reminded each other often.

I have asked every theological question I could think of as a result of the earthquake and Ben's untimely and tragic death. Ben's death rocked so many people's worlds, as well as my own. Often in our marriage I had looked at Ben and thought about how devastated I would be if he died. What had always given me comfort was trust in God's protection. I truly believed that Ben's life was so special that he might be exempt from death until at least his eighties. God could not afford to not have Ben using his gifts on this earth because he carried the love of Christ and the Kingdom wherever he went, to whomever he met. He was a worker for the harvest.

Once when Jon and I were sitting at Ben's grave, Jon said to me, "You know what was special about Ben? It was that when people think about Ben, they think about God; they think about faith. I want my life to be like that."

People would meet Ben one time and consider him a good friend; that was just how Ben made them feel. Ben's most obvious gift was his music, but I believe his strongest gifts were inclusivity and love. Like no one else I had ever met, Ben had the ability to sense who in a room was being left out, or who was on the margins, and he would bring them into the center with everyone else. He had a way of talking with all different kinds of people and making everyone feel special and loved. I saw it happen over and over again. If someone had never felt the love of Christ before, they did when they met Ben. He had the gift of joy in the Lord, and he shared it freely with everyone around him. It was infectious.

Ben's death challenged the idea that somehow the righteous, or those who are actively following the call of God, might be protected. Ben's death was so wrong, as were the hundreds of thousands of other deaths in the earthquake. I heard the story of a little girl who was crushed by concrete, but was still alive. Her mother dug her out with the help of some others and she held her little girl close to her. The little girl said, "Don't let me die, Mommy." A few moments later she breathed her last and was left limp in her mother's arms. Where was God in that? What was just or right about the little girl's death and a mother being left childless and helpless to do anything to save the one she birthed?

The earthquake and Ben's death intensely challenged how I had come to know God in Jesus Christ. Before the earthquake, I believed God was just and present in this world through the Holy Spirit. I trusted that God was guiding and leading us to Haiti. I believed God saved and cared for all people, especially those who loved God. I believed God had a future with hope planned for me and for Ben and our life together. I believed God showed preference for the poor. I believed God could create new life out of dreadful circumstances. I believed God raised the dead to eternal life. I believed in the power of Christ to heal and transform.

On January 12, 2010, everything I believed about God, life, death, and love was thrust into uncertainty and suspicion. I had no idea what to believe anymore, and I did not know if I could trust God any longer. This was especially distressing because I was in my last semester of seminary and already approved for ordination. I did not know if I could be a pastor; I did not know if I could love God.

I needed serious help and pastoral care. I asked two of my seminary professors, who were also pastors, to meet individually with me once a week. Rev. Dr. Duane Priebe and Rev. Dr. Thomas Schattauer agreed to walk with me.

My time with them was essential to my healing and who I am today. They listened to me even when I was irrational. They did not try to minimize how I was feeling. They prayed with and for me, they absolved me of any weight or guilt I was feeling, they laid hands on me, they announced the gospel to me, and they assured me of Ben's place in the resurrection as well as my own. They cried with me and they questioned with me. When they did not have answers for my questions, they did not make answers up, but rather sat in the uncertainty with me.

Lamentation

I talked to, yelled at, and cried to God. I gave God the silent treatment. I could never settle for "Everything happens for a reason," and luckily no one dared to say that to me, at least not to my face. I needed to arrive at a place in which I felt I could love and trust God again. The alternative—perpetual, lifelong anger and resentment—did not sit well with me. I didn't want to give in to that way of being without a fight.

I found South African theologian Denise Ackermann's words to be true: "Lament is the sound suffering makes when it recovers its voice."[1] She also said: "Lament . . . is our way of bearing the unbearable. It is a wailing of the human soul, a barrage of tears, wails, reproaches, petitions, praise and hopes which beat against the heart of God."[2]

I asked: "God, where are you in all of this? Where is Ben? How could you let the earthquake happen? Don't you hold the earth and all things in your hands? How could you allow so many to die? How could you allow even more suffering in Haiti? Don't you care about your creation? Are you with me? What do you want of me now? Will I ever feel joy again? Did you cause the earthquake?"

I knew if the answer to that last question was "yes," I could no longer love or trust God. God would be a vengeful, evil tyrant who did not care about the suffering of the world and its people.

For months I wrestled with these questions (and still some of them today). I needed space to work out the turmoil in me, so the week before Easter 2010, I went by myself to Ben's family cordwood cabin on Juggler

---

1. Plantinga, "Living By the Word," 20.
2. Ackermann, "Lamenting Tragedy," 221.

Lake in northern Minnesota. It was a natural break in my last semester of seminary, and I packed up all kinds of notebooks and papers of Ben's until I had a huge stack. I brought anything that had his handwriting on it. Most of the papers contained lyrics to Ben's songs, both finished and unfinished. He would start a verse or two of a song on whatever scrap of paper he could find with the onset of creativity. I gathered the pieces of paper from all corners of our apartment and carried them with me to the cabin. I was going to go through it all and allow myself to feel the knife of loss. I made the ten-hour trip from Dubuque, Iowa, to the cabin.

The little cabin in the woods by the lake is called Tømmerhytte, which means *log cabin* in Norwegian. It was built by Ben's parents, Judd and April, along with a number of family members in 1982. Ben and I spent time there often in our life together. It was one of my favorite places in the world.

It was late March and chilly when I arrived at the cabin. I lit a fire in the woodstove, settled down at a table, and started to go through the papers. Soon I picked up a torn sheet of paper with these handwritten words:

> The pages of my life
> Turn steadily every day
> While poor ignorant me
> Forgets to read the story
>
> Until a paper cut comes to my skin
> And reminds me of the grand story I'm in
> And I'm thankful for the pain
> Because it's better to be awake

I do not know what it was about these particular words Ben wrote, but I needed to stop and rage at God for a while for allowing this creative and beautiful mind to die.

"Did you cause the earthquake?" I asked God. Nothing.

"Did you cause the earthquake?" I asked more forcefully. Silence.

"Did you cause it!" I yelled at the top of my lungs.

I sat in silence for a long, long time. Even though I was terrified of what the answer might be, I was going to sit there until I received one. I stared out the large picture window at the lake and waited for God. So much time passed that it became dark. God never came . . . or so I thought.

Giving up, I stood, turned on a light, and sighed deeply. I sat back down at the table with the stack of papers and thought I might as well keep reading. The next sheet of paper on the stack was strange because it did not have Ben's writing on it; the hand was someone else's I did not recognize. I started to read:

> We have to learn that the earthquake and accident, like murder, robbery, are not [the] will of God but stands independent of His will and angers and saddens God just as it does us.

I looked around. I could not believe what I was reading. *Is this a joke? Where did this come from?* I continued to read:

> God does not reach down to interrupt the workings of laws of nature to protect [the] righteous. A world in which good people were immune to these laws would cause even more problems. Earthquake not "act of God": Act of God is courage of people to rebuild lives after the earthquake.
>
> What do we do with pain so that it becomes meaningful and not just pointless empty suffering? What do I do now that it has happened[?] Better question[:] now that this has happened what am I going to do about it?
>
> God does not cause. Some by bad luck, bad people, some negative consequences of being human and mortal and living in a world of inflexible natural laws.

I read it over and over again. I kept thinking: *This has got to be some coincidence.* But eventually I had to admit that it was possible that these words were a direct answer to my question, mysterious as it all was. I was thankful and perplexed. I wanted to love God. I wanted to believe that God did not cause the earthquake. I found truth in what was written before me, and I let it settle into my heart and mend it a little. I thought of all the Haitians with their incredible courage who were already rebuilding their lives and homes as best they could. Ask almost any Haitian, and they will tell you that their courage and ability to rebuild comes only from the grace of God.

Later, I showed the paper to Judd and April. April recognized the handwriting immediately; it was that of her mother, Aleta, who had died several years before. For some reason Ben had this note his grandmother had written and it just happened to be mixed up among all the things I grabbed and took to the cabin. There it was, then, on top of the pile after I asked God, "Did you cause the earthquake?"

In one of my sessions with Dr. Schattauer, he said, "The hidden God is not the God we can trust, but only the revealed God in the cross of Christ." In my questioning and searching, I discovered that there was so much I could not know and would never know about God. I could not fully know God's involvement (or lack of involvement) in the Haiti earthquake, but I believed what was revealed to me from that note. I continued to believe in the love of God for the world that was revealed in Christ dying on the cross.

Dr. Priebe once said to me, "The cross makes it possible for us to forgive God. It also makes it possible for those who have died to be taken up into God and transformed. Joy is eschatological, but not the depth of consuming pain." When he said this to me, I realized I needed to forgive God for the earthquake and Ben's death in order to continue to love God, even though I believed God did not cause the earthquake.

Still, I struggled with the knowledge that God had *allowed* the earthquake. I believed in a God who could and did intervene in time; the incarnation was the prime example of this. *Do I believe God could have prevented or stopped the earthquake? Yes. Do I believe God caused the earthquake? No.* This might seem confusing, but there was an important difference for me.

Does God cause everything that happens in the world, like a puppeteer conducting a play? Or did God create the world and then sit back and watch it all unfold? For me, the answer to both of these questions is "no." Sometimes I think it would be easier if I believed that everything happens for a reason, if I could blindly trust that the earthquake and Ben's death were all according to God's plan. Luther's concept of *Deus absconditus,* the hiddenness of God, reminds us that there is always profound mystery with God. I have to admit that it is possible that Ben's death and the earthquake could have been God's plan; however, I could not accept this in my theology. As Dr. Schattauer pointed out, we trust in the revealed God. In the incarnation, in Jesus Christ, God took on flesh to live among us and be crucified for our sake.

In other words, sometimes the worst happens. Being a Christian means believing that God is right there under the rubble with you.

Here is scientific logic: We live on tectonic plates and they move.

Here is acceptance: God allowed the earthquake to happen and Ben and so many others to die.

Here is reality: When many people live in cramped cities with little or no infrastructure, an earthquake means many deaths. Poverty is one reason so many people died, including Ben.

Here is sorrow: The finality of death and its severing of relationships.

Here is consciousness: I am still breathing.

Here is faith: Christ is God in the flesh and dwells in me through the Holy Spirit.

Here is hope: God has or will raise all who have died and we will be with them again in eternal life.

It was and is all as simple and as complex as that.

I don't remember where I read this, but in my grieving I came across someone's reflection on his walk with God in his own loss. The author spoke directly to God, saying that his whole life he had turned to the Ever-Present

One for help and guidance. Now he had lost and suffered. He was helpless and angry with God. He raged at God, wanting to turn away and never look back. In the end, however, he found that he needed to turn back to God, the source of all things, whether in joy or in sorrow. Finally he abandoned himself into God's hands, turning to God once again for healing and new life.

I, too, followed suit. I threw up my hands in acknowledgment and said with the disciples, "Lord, to whom can we go?"[3]

---

3. Peter says these words to Jesus in John 6:68 after many of Jesus' disciples "turned back and no longer went about with him." Jesus asks the twelve, "Do you also wish to go away?" Simon Peter answers him, "Lord, to whom can we go? You have the words of eternal life."

15

Dreams and Visions

IN ONE OF MY sessions with Dr. Schattauer, he said to me: "What we want and what we can trust are two different things. We cannot ultimately trust what comes to us in dreams or visions because they will fail us, although they may help us to have faith in the promises of God. In the end, we trust God, even though it is hard to do."

None of the following dreams or experiences are ultimate sources of faith for me. Scripture is foundational to my faith and is the primary way I know and understand God, especially the incarnation of the Word made flesh in Jesus Christ. However, the dreams and visions I had, and that other people had, helped me release Ben to God, aided me in the healing process, and encouraged me to look forward instead of back. I see them as ways God helped me by working in and through the body of Christ.

There was nothing extraordinary about Ben, or about me, that merited extraordinary dreams and visions. I truly believe God gave them to me simply because I needed them so badly in order to survive. These experiences were not just for me; they were for all of us who felt the pain of Ben's death deep within our chests.

It makes me feel particularly vulnerable and exposed to share these precious experiences, but I do so in order that others may find hope and reassurance in the extraordinary grace of God.

Ben's Presence

One experience I had of Ben was three months after his death. It was quite unexpected and unlike anything I had experienced before. I was sitting up in my bed at night. Suddenly I felt a presence near me, and I felt sure that it was Ben. We had a silent "conversation" together:

Me: What do I do now?

Ben: Trust.

Me: Where is my comfort?

Ben: Read Scripture . . . John 11.

Me: What about the Haitians?

Ben: They are in God's care.

Me: My heart hurts so much.

Ben: Let Jesus in . . . You can release me; it is okay. I am okay and you are okay.

Me: The suffering of the world is so great . . . What happened to you?

Ben: I was not afraid.

Me: How do I know?

Ben: My song. Thank you for honoring and loving me. I love you. I am so proud of you. I will help you.

Me: What now?

Ben: Care for the people.

Me: Was it "your time"?

Ben: [No answer]

Ben: Our relationship will not be less than marriage. I live. We will dance again, my love. God will bring you new life.

During this conversation I kept imagining Ben running his fingers through my hair the way he used to and touching my cheek with his hand. I wrote the conversation down in my journal before going to sleep that night so I would not forget it, although a month later I wondered if it had been real. I opened the Bible to John 11 and read Jesus' words to a grieving Martha upon the death of her brother: "I am the resurrection and the life. Those who believe in me, even though they die, will live. . . ."

In a pastoral care session I told Dr. Priebe about this experience and tried to make sense of it. He told me: "Karl Barth said, 'Blessed is the one who receives a religious experience. Woe to the one who tries to make anything out of it.'" This took the pressure off and allowed me to simply accept the experience for what it was: a gift.

I had another gift, this time in a dream. In it, Ben and I were dressed up to go to a small dance. There were only a few people there, mostly seminary friends. A waltz came on. We started to dance, and it was if our bodies became one. Never had we moved so perfectly in step, so fluidly. It felt like stars. Ben was so much a part of me, and somehow we were still one.

Dr. Priebe also told me: "If God gives you a dream or vision, you might question your sanity. When God gives others dreams or visions to share with you, then you have to question their sanity or accept them as truth."

These were wise words, because in the following months other people began to share with me their dreams, visions, and experiences of Ben.

The Song of Benjamin

The vision that meant the most to me came from a man named Philip Moeller. I had never met Philip, and neither had Ben. When I was in Duluth in January, working as hard as I could to retrieve Ben's body from Haiti, a stranger who lived in Washington, D.C., called Judd and April and asked for my mailing address. He said he needed to send me something. I had completely forgotten about this by the time I arrived back at Wartburg in February after we buried Ben, but that month I received a letter in the mail from Philip Moeller.

In the weeks leading up to receiving that letter, one of the questions in the forefront of my mind was, "What was the earthquake like for Ben?" I had begun to realize that I was projecting my experience of the earthquake onto him. For me, it was absolute terror and chaos. But when I thought about Ben's singing, I realized that his experience of the earthquake was probably totally different from mine. I started to ask God what it had been like for Ben. It tormented me to imagine him coming to and realizing that he was trapped and dying.

When I received Philip's letter, I knew it was something important. I took it to my apartment and sat down to read it immediately. The first page was a letter of explanation dated February 8, 2010.

> To the Larson family and all who knew Benjamin:
>
> I know that you have received many expressions of sympathy concerning the loss of Benjamin. . . . The initial news . . . seized my heart, but further news fully bound me to the event. I was compelled to write down what seemed more than a creative endeavor. I am a firm believer in the power of the "Spirit," and it is only in that power that I can explain my need to write down what seemed to flood into my head and heart. I could not sleep well, and even my days bore this need. I offer this to you most certainly as a creative work, but I do hope there is some form of spiritual comfort, whatever its source, in it that can lead to the joy to which the words refer. . . .
>
> In Christ we are one,
> Philip

I trembled with the letter in my hand. I turned to the second page and quickly found that this stranger who never met Ben in this life certainly "knew" him in what he wrote. The first line is Ben's speech, which then alternates with the words of God.

The Song of Benjamin

Lord, hear me.
I hear you, Benjamin, I have always heard you.

Lord, hear my singing.
I hear your singing, Benjamin, I have always heard your singing.

Lord, I am not afraid.
Of course not, Benjamin, you never have needed to have fear.

Lord, I have more to give.
You have given, Benjamin, you have given greatly.

Lord, there is more to do.
Always, Benjamin, always, there is more to do.

Lord, I love them all.
Yes, Benjamin, you love them all, for you love greatly.

Lord, if I go they will know sorrow.
Yes, sorrow, Benjamin, but it will turn to joy.

Lord, comfort them.
Yes, Benjamin, their comfort, in me, will bring the joy.

Lord, I feel weak.
No, not weak, Benjamin, you are my strongest lamb.

Lord, I am yours.
Yes, Benjamin, you are sealed to me with the sign of the cross.

Lord, one more song.
Yes, sing, Benjamin, sing one more song.

Lord, I am ready.
*Come, Benjamin, come, and, with me, become even more . . .
come.*

Lord, lift me up.
Lifted, yes, Benjamin, I lift you up into eternal being.

Lord, I hear singing!
Yes, Benjamin, it is now our turn to sing for you.

When I called Philip, the first thing he said was, "I did not mean to cause you pain."

I told him that "The Song of Benjamin" was what I had been fervently praying for. When he heard that, he breathed a sigh of relief and said that made sense. He saw himself as a receiver of the Holy Spirit. He had had some other experiences with people who had died, but not with people he had never met. He described his vision of actually being in the rubble with Ben and hearing a conversation between Ben and God. The experience both surprised and challenged Philip, who felt moved to pass it along to me, although not without trepidation, not knowing how I might react.

Certainly, it made me weep, but it also gave me profound peace. I finally knew with confidence that Ben was not alone when he died. The Lord was with him, and he was well.

Some time after the earthquake, Walnes, a member of the St. Joseph Family, sent Ben's parents a number of photos of the excavation of Ben's body. He warned us that they were graphic. None of us wanted to see them, fearing what it would do to us, so April asked a church member who was a physician to look at them. The doctor looked through the photos and informed us that Ben's body suffered "massive trauma," particularly his head. He concluded that Ben would either have died instantly, or after having been unconscious for a while, might have been able to wake up and sing and then die shortly afterward.

"Lord, one more song.

Yes, sing, Benjamin, sing one more song . . ."

The doctor's analysis gave us some peace and reassurance that Ben likely did not suffer. I did not hear pain or struggle in Ben's voice when he sang "Lamb of God." During the earthquake, I was in the same space as Ben and felt the force of the ceiling's collapse, and I knew it was very possible that he died instantly. However, I heard him singing more than thirty minutes later. A more mysterious explanation may be that the thin veil between heaven and earth is thinner than we realize.

Street Singers

Another dream came from a family friend of Ben's parents. Karl Knudsen of Decorah, Iowa, sent a handwritten letter to Judd and April a week or two after Ben's death:

> Dear April, Judd, and family,
>
> Clara and I have been keeping you all in our thoughts and prayers this past week. We cannot even begin to appreciate the pain of this loss which was so unexpected and which involved

such a wonderful child. In Ben, we could see the spark of God. His life was a light to those around him.

Several days after hearing the news of the earthquake and Ben's loss (or more accurately *our* loss), I had a dream in which I saw Ben. I normally do not remember my dreams, and when I do I rarely share them, because dreams can be so confusing, but I think I should share this and I hope it will somehow be a comfort, although hard to understand.

In my dream, I entered a church and sat in the front pew because I was supposed to say something. I had no idea what to say and really did not want to get up and speak. Then someone came and sat next to me and whispered that he could speak instead. He went up to the lectern to speak, and a cross started to fall toward him, and he caught it and kept it from falling.

Then I saw a young, bearded man appear in one of those raised places that someone can speak from in a church and begin speaking. . . . The person who had started speaking and who had caught the cross was also speaking the same words at the same time, but I could only hear one voice, and I could not tell which one was really speaking.

But I noticed that the speaker in the raised area was so full of joy and energy and warmth that he seemed to be glowing. He was a person who no longer had any doubts about the good news of which he spoke, a person transformed into a Christ-like figure.

Then later in my dream, someone called for everyone to remain silent. As this happened, I was no longer seeing anything but some rubble. But, as things quieted down, I could hear a calm voice singing. This is what I heard, and I woke up and wrote down the words. The words I heard make little sense, or maybe all the sense in the world:

"I can always hear the cross; the cross has stubborn street singers."

I got up while the song was in my mind and found the notes on our piano and played them. It was only then that I realized, after waking up, that it was Ben that I saw in my dream.

"Stubborn street singers."

It was only days later that I read news accounts that Ben literally did sing after the earthquake. Also, that the people in the street sang hymns. So, there are our stubborn street singers. In fact, we all who share these losses but still hold Christ dear, are stubborn street singers. . . .

By taking on Christ, Ben has become one with Christ, and transformed. When someone preaches Christ, Ben is preaching

Christ, but with more conviction than anyone can who has not been so transformed. I believe Ben is alive with Christ, and need to share that with you.

Karl Knudsen

It was amazing for me to read Karl's letter. I truly felt those who sang in open fields, in the streets and dying in the rubble, despite the devastation and death, were stubborn street singers. His dream spoke of the power of the cross of Christ and the good news that speaks life no matter what the circumstance. Karl's dream made me feel that Ben was alive, vibrant, and glowing with the truth that is Christ. His dream held the tenderness of Ben's person and yet also his boldness and conviction of the gospel. It gave me a sense of peace that Ben indeed was transformed as Jesus would have us all transformed, full of joy and love and living into the resurrected life.

Proud Love

After graduating from seminary I went to Holden Village in the summer of 2010. Holden Village is a Lutheran ministry and place of renewal high up in the Cascade Range of Washington State, and Ben and I had spent time there together during our marriage.

At Holden Village that summer I kept asking Ben, "Do you love me, Ben? Are you proud of me?" I know these seem like ridiculous questions, but I truly meant them. When a spouse dies, they can no longer tell you that they love you. Ben never missed a day without saying, "I love you." In fact, he said it multiple times a day, and when we were going to bed each night, he told me why he loved me or gave an example of something that happened that day that made him love me even more. Ben made me feel so loved.

Of course, there were also times in our marriage when I was frustrated with him and he with me. We got mad at one another. We needed to forgive one another. That face-to-face relationship was so important, and I did not have it anymore. Besides this, I felt like a different person, a sadder person. I wanted to know if Ben loved this new Renee, the Renee who survived the earthquake and was trying to endure life. At the end of the day I had to try and convince myself that Ben loved me. When I remembered who he was and his character, this was simple; when I was lost in grief and could not hear him say the words, I struggled.

Therefore, at Holden Village I kept asking Ben, "Do you still love me, Ben? Are you proud of me?" It was important for me to ask him if he was proud of me. I was trying awfully hard to live without him and to move into the next phase of my life in pastoral ministry after graduating seminary. I needed encouragement.

A week or two came and went at Holden Village, and when I descended back into cell phone range, I had a voicemail from my friend Corrine. She said she had to tell me about a dream she had that she believed was for me. Here is her account of the dream:

> Your mom and dad insist you talk with Ben. Your dad hands you the plastic white bowl of white daisies and says they are from Ben for you, and they are. Your parents send you to a nice bathroom near their bedroom, kind of prepare it for your talk with Ben, draw the blinds and make it nice. It's white and warm and welcoming, and there are flowers. The sun shines in softly and welcoming, warming. You go sit in the bathroom on the floor cross-legged, and there's Ben sitting cross-legged across from you, so close you are almost touching knees (maybe you are). He's smiling the whole time, but gentle, playful, love love love love love love love love emanating from him for you. Love.
>
> At one point you can touch him, and you just grab and hold onto him and sob. He is physical. But there is also stuff that comes off of him when you do this, like little white ash or snow or dust or something, and it's okay. But he needs to stop you for some reason, but he does this with a little laugh, gentle, and always smiling, and sits you up carefully. He tells you he's real, that it's okay, and it's him. And he laughs at how loud his voice sounds when he talks because he's so real.
>
> Then he is serious with you (still smiling) and tells you to be happy, to live, to follow the call, that he's proud of you, so proud of you and is happy and wants you to keep going and minister and he's just so proud of you. That's a word I couldn't come up with at first, and it just sort of came to me, and now I can't stop typing it . . . because he is so proud and happy and loves you. Yes. Proud and happy and love. And watching over. Always with you.

On the phone, Corrine said, "Renee, I felt Ben's proud love for you. It was so strong. He loves you so much, Renee. Oh my gosh he loves you." She said the night she had the dream she felt like waking up her husband, Robbie, and saying, "Ben is alive. Very much alive. More than I am alive." She felt a sense of peace she had not felt since his death. Ben's song "Hush" came into her head, with these words: "I will rise you up on wings like the eagles, you'll find strength in me and be renewed, but for now hush . . ."

I told her what had been weighing on me at Holden Village. She said to me, "There is still a lot of hurt, but Ben is alive. He is among the communion of saints and in the resurrection. I feel so certain of that."

Shorter Experiences

Others had brief dreams or visions they shared with me. In each case they brought me some comfort and made the thin veil between death and life seem that much more mysterious.

Jon loves to play guitar, and after Ben died, Jon played Ben's guitar often. One time when Jon was playing Ben's guitar he could "hear" a mandolin playing along with him so loudly that Jon had to stop and listen.

A mutual friend of Ben's and mine named Kim dreamed that she walked into the New London Café in Duluth and Ben and I were sitting at a table. In the dream I was crying as Ben looked compassionately at me. Kim asked Ben, "Are you going to see your parents soon?" He said, "Not right now. Renee needs me." He held my hand and we simply sat together.

One early morning, Ben's dad, Judd, awoke to the sound of what he described as angels singing. He walked out of his bedroom, still hearing the singing, and saw a beam of light coming through the room and resting on a photo of Ben on a shelf.

Another vision came a year later. It was Jon's ordination day, Sunday, January 30, 2011. Standing in the pulpit of her congregation, Ben's mom April read the gospel aloud from Matthew's Beatitudes, chapter 5. As she was reading verse 8, "Blessed are the pure in heart, for they shall see God," April had a vision of Ben and stopped reading. After church, Judd said to her, "What happened when you were reading the gospel?" She said, "I wasn't overcome with emotion—I had a vision." Judd said, "I could tell you were having a spiritual experience. That's why I didn't come up to help you read."

April described the vision to me later:

> For more than a year, every day I could never get Ben out of dying in that gray earthquake cement. I would try to picture Christ holding his hand as he died. I even tried to picture Christ lying beside Ben and dying with him, which helped a little, but no matter how I prayed and visualized, I could never get my son out of that dark, gray tomb of crushing cement.
>
> That Sunday as I was reading the gospel lesson to my congregation, God gave me a vision. Ben was in that same room where he died, but the room was completely transformed. He was lying on the floor dressed in white. The room was much

bigger and open. Nothing was closed in at all. The walls behind him were layers of stunningly gorgeous shades of gold. If I were an artist I could paint those rich, different shades, which I can still see. There was no roof. The room was just completely open with a bright, radiating light everywhere. Ben was finally out of the cement.

16

The Body of Christ

DURING MY FINAL SEMESTER of school, the Wartburg Theological Seminary community was the tangible body of Christ for me. New life came to me through classmates, professors, worship, prayer, learning, and commitment to vocation. The Wartburg community embraced Jon and me; they embraced Haiti as well.

Life at Wartburg had always been centered around the Word, worship, and community, but never had I felt it so profoundly. I found Paul's words in 1 Corinthians 12:26 to be true: "If one member suffers, all suffer together with it; if one member is honored, all rejoice together with it." Everyone was hurting, but they all gathered around Jon and me to be Christ for us.

Daily worship at Wartburg was essential for my healing. Most people on campus worshiped together every day. After chapel, we all moved into the refectory for coffee, community building, and conversation. I went to worship as often as I could muster my energy. I needed the body of Christ to confess, pray, and sing for me until I could confess, pray, and sing again. I needed to hear the Word of God read and proclaimed. I met Ben at Christ's table each week and asked Jesus to have mercy on me and heal me from the inside out.

The gospel I had heard my whole life filled my body and soul. The good news of Christ crucified and risen had mighty power in my life. It was the power of Christ to be present in any and every situation, the power to bring life in the midst of death. This gospel was everything to me, and I staked my life on it.

I am convinced that I could not have lived without the gospel and the church, my brothers and sisters in Christ. Yes, the road of healing was long and lonely, but I truly felt carried by the body of Christ, as if I were resting in the loving arms of Jesus himself. The outpouring of love through cards, e-mails, and phone calls was overwhelming in a good way (most of the time). It was particularly moving for me when terminally ill, frail, old, or widowed people would approach me with incredible compassion in their eyes, reach for my hand, and simply inform me that they were praying for me. I knew they were telling me the truth. My name and Jon's name breathed across their lips in prayer and were lifted before the Good Shepherd.

Faith communities around the world grieved in January 2010. In addition to those in the U.S., I learned about prayer services that had sprung up from Japan, to Palestine, to Peru, to Mexico, and more. Our family received letter after letter from church leaders across the globe, letting us know that faith communities in other nations were walking with us and praying for us. More than ever, our brothers and sisters around the world cried out, "Kyrie, eleison—Lord, have mercy!" with the people of Haiti and with our family.

Scripture and the church have language and ritual for earthquakes and other atrocities. What can we do when terrible things happen, when we know loss and grief, when we are lost and broken? We gather together in worship to sing, pray, and lament using the ancient words brothers and sisters in Christ have been saying for thousands of years.

The outpouring of unity and compassion gave flesh to Ben's song, "Brothers and Sisters":

> O imagine how life would be if we were like the wind
> Blowing over everybody coolin' their skin
> Rushing clouds across the sky
> Bringing weather and healing to all we see
> O I pray, I pray, I pray, I pray
> O dear God, let me be like the wind
>
> Brothers and sisters together
> Bringing worlds together
> One spirit together
> Cross the ocean together
> One spirit together
> One spirit together

The first time I listened to these lyrics after Ben died, it struck me that his prayer was answered. He was like the wind, continuing to blow the sails of people together. He wanted to "bring across the boats, bring worlds together," as he sang later in the song. "Let me be a place for others," he prayed. In Ben's life and in his death his arms were wide open, wide open to anyone who felt a connection to him whether they ever met him or not, to anyone who would grieve his loss, and to his Lord in his dying breath. "Brothers and Sisters" was Ben's way of describing the church universal, Christ's arms spread wide on the cross embracing all things, all people, making us all brothers and sisters in and through Him.

One day I received a phone call from Ben's mom, April. She said, "Renee, the musician at my congregation thinks that maybe Ben was singing 'Lamb of God' from setting ten in the *Evangelical Lutheran Worship* book. What do you think?"

I gasped. It took me all of one second to finally realize that was exactly what Ben was singing. I couldn't find it before because I didn't think to look in the worship settings, only in the hymn section. I whipped open my hymnal and turned to the liturgies. There were the words and melody Ben sang. I only heard him sing the final verse, but Al must have heard him singing parts of the first two.

Evangelical Lutheran Worship, 208. Courtesy of Augsburg Fortress.

I thought I had heard Ben sing, "God's peace to us we pray," but whether he sang that or "give us your peace, we pray," makes no difference to me. I am forever grateful for his courage to sing and for his dying proclamation.

Mail

Receiving the mail after Ben died was like being on a roller coaster with unexpected turns and flips. A little more than a month after Ben died, I received his approval letter for call and his seminary report card from his senior fall semester. I was shocked when I opened the report card. All As!

Now, Ben was not what one would call a straight A student. In fact, I don't believe he had ever received all As on a report card. I knew well the effort and determination behind those high grades. Ben had become very serious about learning during and after internship because he wanted to be a better pastor. His whole demeanor toward school changed in the fall of

2009, and the report card I received in February 2010 proved that his efforts paid off. I was so proud of him.[1]

I also received Ben's autopsy in the mail that spring. Afraid that I might read it in a moment of inconsolable grief, I gave it to my seminary advisor, sealed and unread, for safekeeping. I still have not read it to this day.

I did not always receive heart-wrenching mail. I received encouraging gifts and letters all the time. Two specific ones come to mind. One was a silver heart necklace with the silhouette of Haiti etched out of the middle. I added Ben's wedding ring to the necklace since it was too big for my fingers. I also received a silver bracelet with the word *Bambelela* etched on the front and Luke 1:37 etched on the back. *Bambelela* is a Zulu word that means "Never give up" or "Hold on." Luke 1:37 is the angel's comment to Mary after he announces the incarnation: "For nothing will be impossible with God."

For what would have been Ben's twenty-sixth birthday, February 27, 2010, a group of his college friends gave me the gift of a seaweed wrap and massage at a local spa in Dubuque, Iowa. I had never done anything like this and was a little apprehensive, but it turned out to be essential in my healing. The woman spread mud all over my body and then wrapped me in seaweed. As she was wrapping me, I couldn't help but think about how the mortician might have wrapped Ben's body in strips of linen. Swaddled in earth and seaweed, I felt a comfort and peace, and imagined the peace and comfort that Ben must profoundly know. When she unwrapped me slowly, piece by piece, I envisioned the resurrection of Ben's body and the cloth that enveloped him being unraveled and laid aside like Christ's linens in his empty tomb on the resurrection dawn. It renewed my hope in the promise of life in and after death.

In March, I received a handmade lap quilt from a seminary classmate who had moved to Florida. She said each of the knots were prayers for healing and new life for me. Even though I was agonizing over my call to continue to be a pastor, it was a defining moment. I felt greatly moved to give my life in ministry to the body of Christ, my sisters and brothers, who upheld me in prayer all the time. I felt as if the whole of the ELCA and more were praying for me. I remembered Ben telling me that when his grandmother, Aleta, was going through chemo treatment for brain cancer, she said, "I feel like I am walking in a field of prayer." At the time I wondered what that must have felt like. Lying on that blanket, I knew.

Because of the overwhelming number of letters and cards I received, I asked a few of my women seminary friends, along with my mother who was visiting me at the time, to help me write hundreds of thank-you notes.

---

1. See Appendix C to read Ben's final paper from his senior theology course.

We spread out on my huge dining room table (Ben and I had a table that could comfortably fit at least twelve people at any given time) to write them. Even Brett Favre was among the thank-yous that needed to be written. Yes, *the* Brett Favre, the NFL quarterback legend. One of Ben's neighbors in La Crosse, Wisconsin, had written to Brett to have an autographed photo sent to me in memory of Ben. But how should I address him? *Dear Football Legend . . . Dear Mr. Favre . . . Dear . . .* I started laughing. I said out loud: "Dear Brett . . ." We all laughed. Laughter with my sisters in Christ had an incredible ability to heal my soul.

One of my women seminary friends wrote this in a letter to me in the months after the earthquake:

> I am praying for you as you discover more about who you are now. You have said this semester that you don't know who you are now, that you are a different person. Let me share what I have noticed about you. You shine! Your spirit is bright and shimmering, full of love and light.

Small Things That Were Really Big Things

After settling into the groove of my final semester, Jon and I each met regularly with a man named Joe who was trained and qualified through the Red Cross to help trauma victims. It was not unlike pastoral care, as he was a devout Catholic, but he focused more on our mental and emotional state rather than the spiritual. Joe gave us tools to help us cope when our minds and bodies were troubled by post-traumatic stress disorder.

My apartment building at seminary was right by some train tracks. Whenever the train went by and rattled the building, my heart nearly stopped with fear. I clutched the mattress, the table, or the couch, and waited for the shaking to stop. I knew it was just a train going by, but my whole body screamed "earthquake!" In every building I was in, I always looked around for my escape route. I knew I was not crazy, just traumatized.

Joe told me that the process of grief was like the stretching and working of muscles: at first, they rip and tear a bit and break down, but then they heal and get stronger. As a collegiate athlete, this was easy for me to understand. He also quoted Richard Rohr in one of our meetings: "If we do not transform our pain, we will most assuredly transmit it."[2] I did not want to be one who transmitted suffering. I needed God to transform it in me.

In our last session, I asked him, "What more do I need, Joe?"

2. Rohr, *Things Hidden*, 25.

He said, "There is no more I can do for you, Renee. I am now retiring, and in all of my decades of counseling, never have I met anyone who has gone through what you and Jon have gone through and come out as healthy as both of you are. There is nothing more I can do for you, and probably nothing more continued counseling can do for you at this time. You just need time and God to bring you to a place of new life."

I stared at him. I wanted him to fix all of it. Mostly I wanted him to bring Ben back from the dead. I wanted the pain to end, but I also wanted it to continue. I sensed that if the pain went away, then somehow I would be "over it" or "moving on," as if Ben did not mean as much to me as I thought. I hated the concept and language of "moving on," and yet I knew that at some point there needed to be a shift in my energy from existing and surviving to living again.

I have been a runner since the seventh grade, and when Ben died, I stopped running and exercising altogether. It took me two months to attempt my first run. As I jogged back to the seminary campus, I ran into Rev. Dr. Winston Persaud. Unlike me, he did not underestimate what it meant in my healing to be out running for the first time. He graciously shared how happy he was to see me running again and the sign of healing it was in my life. I was starting to reclaim a piece of who I was before the earthquake, and it was good for me.

One of my Hebrew Bible professors, Rev. Dr. Gwen Sayler, gifted me with ten yoga sessions. I had never done yoga regularly before, and it was so helpful throughout the spring to breathe in and out and stretch my body. It reminded me that I was still alive. I also continued to play table tennis over lunch with professors and classmates. Even though I was exhausted all the time, the movement and fellowship were good for me.

I cleaned our apartment for the first time on March 7 to reclaim my living space. This was a good step, and I felt relieved when I finished. But despite my relief, I still had all of Ben's things, and I did not know what to do with them. I knew the fateful day of moving out of my apartment was just around the corner and I'd be forced to drag it all with me. I decided that I would rather give people the opportunity to wear Ben's clothes rather than have them rot in a box. I also wanted people to have something of Ben's so they could carry him with them in a new, tangible way.

In the middle of the floor, I carefully and painfully laid out the clothing that once covered Ben's body. All of Ben's family members and Jon reverently offered, chose, and distributed Ben's clothing. Everyone put on a garment and sighed deeply. I did not anticipate the relief and quiet joy I felt to have these beloved ones wearing Ben's things.

A surprising, somewhat embarrassing opportunity for healing arose in late March. After class one day I exited a door at Wartburg to find a bird dying on the sidewalk. I set down my things and sat next to the bird. I stroked its feathers and sang and talked to it quietly. Its head kept lowering closer to the cement, and its breathing slowed throughout the thirty minutes I was with it. Right before it died, I imagined it bursting into the resurrection with new wings, only to pause and acknowledge Ben as it flew by him.

It sounds strange, but I found the opportunity to be with the dying bird a gift from God. I was still so devastated that I was unable to be with Ben when he died, and being able to be with this little bird as it died was so helpful to me. It was very unexpected.

When the bird was dead, I did not have the heart to just leave it there, so I scooped it up with *The Lutheran* magazine I had just picked up from my mailbox and carried it down the hill to our apartment. I put it in a plastic bag and put it in my freezer. I planned to take it with me to the lake cabin the next day and bury it.

The next morning Jon and Elly were in my apartment drinking coffee, as usual. I tried to be really sneaky in moving the bird from my freezer to the cooler, but they caught me red-handed. "What's that?" Jon asked.

"A bird," I said, embarrassed.

"A what!"

"A bird. I sat with it yesterday as it died, and I am going to take it to the cabin today and bury it." I briefly received the *maybe-you're-cracking-up* look from them, but ultimately they understood. I put the bird in my trunk, drove into the northern woods of Minnesota, and buried it.

In May, Jon and I flew to Boston to see Kez for the first time since the earthquake. The three of us went to her family cabin on a lake for our day together. Kez looked at Jon and me and said: "I used to go to where I thought Ben was buried in the building, just to be there. After Ben's body was removed, I went up there again, and found a chunk of his hair where he was lying. I put it in this envelope to bring it to you." After she handed me the envelope, she and Jon left me alone in the cabin and went for a walk. I looked inside and saw Ben's colorful hair: brown, gray, and red. Tiny pieces of rubble dusted his hair. I felt it and remembered. Kez and Jon came back, and we talked late into the night.

My life and my journey of healing would have been entirely different if both Ben and Jon had died. I cannot even imagine this difficult walk without Jon. Yes, there were many things I had to face on my own, unique to me, but having someone else who experienced the earthquake with me and lived has been an immeasurable gift. Somehow we both survived, and I know it is partly because we each had the other. Many days I thought, *I need to be okay for Jon so he does not give up.* We have cried together more times than I can count, tried to find meaning in it all, and supported one another through an unthinkable loss.

Jon bore his grief more silently than I did, carrying it with him like a sharp rock in his shoe. I felt better just sitting by Jon. Because we both returned to Wartburg to finish our senior year, we were able to see one another almost daily and make sure the other was not headed off the deep end. Every day I thanked God that Jon lived.

Graduation

With the help of each other, our professors, and the Wartburg community, Jon and I finished our senior year and were able to graduate in May 2010. Everyone agreed that the best way to honor and recognize Ben was to read his name and give me an honorary diploma for him.

I stood motionless as Jon's name was read first and he walked across the stage to receive his diploma. I was so proud of him and his accomplishments. I felt the pride Ben might have felt for his beloved cousin who was on his way to becoming a pastor in the church we all loved so much.

Ben's name was read next. Everyone paused as if he were walking across the stage. I looked out and saw my family, Jon's family, and Ben's family all sitting together to support us and one another. I also saw the people responsible for recovering Ben's body: Mytch and Louis Dorvilier and their family, along with Walnes from St. Joseph's. It meant so much to have Haitians there, and it reminded me of the plight their people still had to face every day. If they could survive, I could walk across a stage and accept my diploma.

"Renee Splichal Larson." Hearing my name jolted me back to reality. I tried not to trip as I climbed the stairs and received my diploma and Ben's together. I made my way off the stage, and Jon and I stood next to one another and breathed a sigh of relief. We could easily have been dead, but instead, here we were with the rest of our classmates (except Ben), diplomas in hand.

Later, in a circle holding hands with my closest seminary friends—men and women—I said goodbye to the last place Ben and I called our home. We stood together in the empty living room of our apartment and told stories. We spoke of community dinners and movies, compositions of songs, and a dead bird. We called to mind the laughter in that space followed by all the sorrow and disbelief. We all held hands and prayed together. We prayed fervently for the people of Haiti who had just begun to suffer from cholera, for all those displaced because of the earthquake, for the next people who would live in the apartment, for our futures as pastors in the church, for healing, for hope, for strength. We all wept. Jon ran and fetched Kleenexes for all our runny noses and watery eyes. Everyone left me alone to say my final goodbyes, and we shut the door to the apartment, leaving our prayers in that place.

17

A Sister and a Summer

I HAVE ALWAYS HAD an oldest-sibling complex: self-imposed irrational responsibility, endless worry, telling my siblings what I know is best for them, and so on. Growing up, I had recurring nightmares in which we would go to the zoo and my brother, Eric, would get caught in the alligator pool and my sister, Jessie, would be stuck in the bear cage. The dreams always ended with me trying to save them as the brave older sister, never knowing whether I was successful before I woke up.

In the months following the earthquake, my siblings worried about me. In my grief, I often longed for death. It is not that I did not love life or my family; it was just that I was hurting so much and I wanted so badly to be with Ben.

The night before we buried Ben, Jessie came and sat with me. She always had a "Renee compass" and would know where I was at all times, or gently be as close to me as she could, usually not saying a word.

This time she spoke. "Renee, your life is really important to me. I don't know what I would have done if you had died too. I know it is really hard right now, but I know you will get through this." How odd it felt to have my baby sister, a person I had tried to protect and care for my whole life (even in my dreams!), now taking care of me. "I want you to know that I have decided to postpone this semester of college to come and stay with you in Dubuque," she continued. "I want to help you."

As loving as this offer was, I could not allow her to do it. "Jessie, I am so moved, and I would love to have you with me, but you can't do that. College is too important, and I don't want you to get behind."

"I don't care about college, Renee," she insisted. "I care more about you."

"I know, Jessie. How about this: you can come on the train and visit me during your spring break. Then, we can spend the whole summer together. How does that sound?"

She thought about this carefully and said, "Okay. But if you need me sooner, I will come and stay for as long as necessary."

"Deal," I said.

In March Jessie came to stay with me for a week. I was still exhausted and struggling, but I was getting up each day and attending classes. We went hiking in some of Dubuque's beautiful recreation areas, had a picnic, and simply spent time together. Nights continued to be the toughest, even with Jessie sleeping next to me. I didn't need to pretend around her. Lying face-up in my bed I would say to her, "I need to cry," and then I would let it out. Her tears flowed with mine as she lay silently by me. She rarely said much, but was a quiet and constant presence.

Road Trip

The summer eventually came and I began to feel conflicted about our deal. It was Jessie's summer to complete her nursing internship, and she had been offered a position in the hospital where she was studying on the floor of her top choice. I told her that she did not need to spend the summer with me and that she should complete her internship, but Jessie's mind was made up.

I had to admit, I really needed her. Jessie gave me the courage to face the reality of my life without Ben. I planned to spend the whole summer going from one place to another that had meant something to Ben and me. I felt it was essential for my healing to face my grief head-on and visit the places Ben and I had loved and let my mind, body, and heart feel whatever pains, joys, and emotions each place might evoke. Jessie knew this would not be easy, but she was determined to accompany me on my road toward healing and new life.

We started our journey from our parents' home in Garrison, North Dakota, the day after I interviewed for my first call (more about that later!). We stopped the first night in Billings, Montana, and stayed with Ben's best friend from college, Elisabeth Zant, who was completing her seminary internship year.

The next day we made it all the way to Chelan, Washington, where we ate dinner at a winery before setting up a tent and camping for the night. We woke early to catch the ferry up Lake Chelan to Fields Point Landing, followed by a ten-mile switchback drive in a yellow school bus to arrive at Holden Village, high in the mountains.

One of the first things I saw right by the registration desk was the "Holden Saint" board with a photo of Ben and me from two summers earlier, covered in dirt from work we'd been doing. We were smiling big smiles.

I had never seen that photo, and I loved it. But underneath was the caption: "Ben Larson—died in Haiti." I suddenly felt exposed as the widow. I thought people would recognize me, which bothered me, yet I also wanted people to know what I had lost.

At Holden, Jessie and I spent our days making large burn piles of tree limbs and brush. It was hard work, and it felt good to do some physical labor with my sister. During the late afternoons and evenings we had free time for classes, hikes, or other activities. I took this time to think, to journal, and to grieve.

Coincidentally, there was a poet in the village who was holding writing classes with a special focus on writing poetry through loss. Her name was Rebecca Wee. I had never considered myself a writer, let alone a poet, but she helped me put language to what was going on inside me.

I went away by myself and wrote these words as I sat by the river that ran along the edge of the village. The sun came and went as the clouds passed by.

> Heavy lies the heart
> Beneath a single shadow [. . .]
> Of myself
> Widow, wife of Ben, pastor
> A silhouette of who I was
> Empty, hollow, incomplete, longing
> A shell filled in with darkness, black [. . .]
> Senseless, pointless, innocence
> So many lives, so much destruction
> Concrete, death, wailing, darkness
> Heavy lies the heart beneath a single shadow

In losing Ben, at times I felt like I lost myself as well. I no longer knew who I was. I had so many emotions and thoughts I had never had before. Everything seemed foreign, and I always felt exposed, like my grief was laid out for everyone to see. I felt like a shadow of myself and did not know what the trauma and loss would ultimately do to me as a person.

The next day in the poetry class Rebecca asked whether any of us would be willing to share what we had written. Eventually, I raised my hand. My heart raced as I shared my inner sanctuary with a group of (mostly) strangers. Again, Jessie sat right beside me. I could not make it all the way through without choking up, but I kept reading.

After the class Rebecca thanked me. I told her I had lost my husband in the Haiti earthquake. She, too, had lost her husband very young. He had a two-year battle with cancer and died. Living through his illness and death took a toll on her, and I could tell how much she still deeply loved her husband and that he and his death were a part of her. She said that her family and participating in a marathon helped her cope after her husband died. She told me she waited at least five years to begin dating again, and even then it was hard. She eventually remarried and had two children. She said, "My husband's death was so hard and I miss him all the time. Yet, life is still beautiful in many ways, and I am so thankful for my children. They bring me a lot of joy."

As I spoke with Rebecca, I knew that my sadness over Ben's death and my love for him would never go away. I would have to find some way to live with this reality. Yet, I also felt the first spark of hope that I, too, might still have the possibility of marriage and children in my future. Rebecca's children were with her in the village, and I saw the way she looked at them and ran her fingers through their hair. It was the first time I dared to even consider the possibility.

The next day I received a handwritten letter from Rebecca sharing more of her story with me and some of what she went through as a young widow. She wrote: "I remember that in the days and months after Michael died, one of the huge impulses I felt was to tell everyone about him—who he was, what the world had lost. It was like I'd be introduced to someone and I'd fight the urge to say, 'I'm Rebecca and until he died three months ago I was married to the most phenomenal man.'"

When I met new people, I wanted to say, "I was married to Ben Larson and I wish you could meet him too." It felt so good to hear Rebecca name this longing. It made me feel less alone.

One day, Jessie and I were sitting in the Holden worship center when out of the blue she asked me if I would play the piano for her. She used to do this all the time when we were young, but it must have been nearly ten years since she last asked me to play for her. Ben also used to ask me to play the piano for him. Jessie's request lit a small flame in me. I had hardly played at all since Ben died. Playing the piano for Jessie gave us both great joy, and relieved my stress.

Jessie also gave me the courage to share one of Ben's songs, "Everything I Have," also known as "Earthen Vessel," for open mic night at the end of the week in the village. It felt good to sing and play a song Ben had written—to share him with other people.

At the end of the week Jessie and I hiked a nine-mile round trip to beautiful Hart Lake. As our feet moved softly, one in front of the other, I felt embers of joy and thankfulness burning in my heart for such exquisite mountain beauty and my sister's love. This sense of peace was interrupted only briefly when Jessie put her hands on my back, pushing me forward and saying, "Renee! Walk faster."

I obeyed hastily. "There's a snake, isn't there?" I am terrified of snakes, thanks to a childhood incident with a rattlesnake!

"Yes! Keep walking." As soon as Jessie deemed we were a safe distance away, we both turned around to spot the flexible creature. I screamed and we both laughed and laughed.

My time with Jessie at Holden Village that summer was priceless. As we were getting on the bus to leave, one of the directors approached me and said, "Renee, we have wanted to give you your space while you were here. If there is ever a time you would like to share your experience in some way, talk about Haiti, or anything you'd like, please let us know." I thanked her gratefully, knowing that when I was ready I would accept the offer.[1]

Jessie and I boarded the ferry, *Lady of the Lake II,* and floated back into the world of cell phones and cars. We visited one of my college friends and a couple of Ben's relatives in Seattle. Then we drove south along the west coast and camped near Mount Shasta in northern California. We took our photo next to a "Beware of Bears" sign and sent it to our worry-filled father. We didn't meet any bears, but I met an unexpected challenge. I hadn't realized how it would affect me to try to sleep on the ground near a volcano in earthquake-prone California. I did not sleep the whole night.

After spending a couple of days in Alamo with friends, we made our way across northern Nevada to Salt Lake City, Utah, to spend time with Ben's sister Amy and her family. I loved spending time with my niece, Rachel, who was almost two at the time. Jon also flew in while we were there to visit them. We had the joy of pushing little Rachel in her swing, going to the local swimming pool, playing football (her favorite sport), and staying up late eating ice cream every night. I found these to be the good things in life.

As we drove back to North Dakota, Jessie admitted to me that she had suffered from depression throughout the winter and spring. She had gone to counseling to help her cope with Ben's death. This was hard for me to hear because I never wanted Jessie to be hurt, but it also helped me gain some perspective on what all my family members were going through with Ben's death. I know they were all so thankful for my life and for Jon's, but they were still struggling. Everyone missed Ben and had to deal with his death in their own way. I was so glad Jessie sought professional counseling.

---

1. This invitation would lead to an incredible week at Holden in June 2011 called Haiti Focus Week.

A Reunion

In early July, Jessie and I were home in Garrison, and it happened to be time for my ten-year high school reunion. I had received an invitation the fall before, and Ben had seen it. "We've got to go, Renee!" he had said.

"But I don't know if I want to."

"It will be great. I want to go and meet your classmates. You are from a small town. You need to go." I had agreed at the time, but now I had no desire to go. I could not introduce Ben to my beloved classmates, and I felt that I had changed so much since high school. However, classmates kept calling my house, and eventually two of them came over and said, "Renee, everyone wants to see you. Please come."

I went and it was good for me. Everyone had changed, not just me. Many had loss and grief in their lives. I learned of the suicide of a classmate. Others shared the loss of close friends, family, or pregnancies. People were genuine and caring. Although no one had the opportunity to meet Ben, I felt the support of the people I grew up with.

The Burden of Grief

Near the end of July, Jessie, Jon, Elly, four cousins of Jon and Ben's, and I went on a canoe trip in the boundary waters of northern Minnesota. Ben and I had originally planned to take the trip together, and I decided I would still go, but I invited the others to join me. The most memorable part of the trip was the grueling one-mile portage within the first hour of starting. Our packs were at their heaviest and our canoes were aluminum, unbalanced, and more than 80 pounds each.

That portage was one of the most physically demanding things I have ever done, including four years of collegiate track and field and a marathon in the Rocky Mountains. It was so hard. *Surely, I am carrying the most weight,* I thought when I finally reached the end of the portage. I dropped what I was carrying with relief and went back to see if I could help any of the others.

Within a couple of hundred yards I met Jon and his cousin Jared. Their faces were contorted with effort; beads of sweat ran down their faces. I realized that I was not carrying the heaviest load. I carried what I could bear to carry. The others had the same look on their faces when they passed me. When we all finally reached the end, we collapsed and tried to breathe, nodding our approval of one another's efforts. The high fives would come a bit later after power bars, more rest, and some water.

This experience helped me to see that we all carried what we could carry in our own way, yet we did it together. All of us on that trip deeply loved Ben and missed him terribly. The canoe trip was a journey of grief that we took together. It taught me that all carry the weight of grief differently, and that is okay. Grief feels so heavy to each person, and it can feel as if one individual's burden is the heaviest, but really all of us loved Ben and bore the weight of his loss in our own way.

In August Jessie and I spent some time in Decorah where Ben was buried, taking a little extra time to soak up some vitamin D, floating in a tire inner tube down the Upper Iowa River. We also went canoeing on the river, starting at the spot where Ben asked me to marry him on July 4, 2007. Every step of the way that summer, Jessie was with me as I faced my life without Ben. This was the greatest gift she has ever given me. I love her.

18

The Long Road of Healing

OVER AND OVER AGAIN I heard that "time heals." I would say that God heals—*in* time.

I smelled Ben long after he had died. There were a few white T-shirts he had not washed before we left for Haiti. I embraced his scent each night as I went to sleep, newly thankful that he did not always take the time to do laundry.

At first, I had a lot of trouble eating if I was alone. I would sit with a plate of food and try to eat, but I was too sad and it was too difficult. One evening in the spring of 2010, at Wartburg Seminary, my friend Elly came and spent time with me in my apartment. She sat with me at the table, and I put my fork down and admitted, "I don't want to live without Ben!"

She sat with me quietly and eventually said, "It doesn't worry me that you say that now, Renee. If you say it again a year from now, then I'll be worried." Elly let me be sad, and without diminishing how I was feeling, managed to give me a little hope. Even then, as raw as the pain was, I knew there was truth to what she said. I did not feel the same way a year later. As time went on, I found myself wanting to live more and more, but still carried the loss and the experience with me at all times.

Most people treaded lightly around Jon, Ben's family, and me after the earthquake. Many did not know what to say, and that was all right. What was there to say? Sometimes people did not want to bring up Ben or the earthquake, fearing that it would make us cry. April said a number of times: "I wish people would ask me about Ben. I need to talk about him, and I'm thinking about his death all the time. People are not suddenly putting him on my mind when they ask; it is always there."

It was essential to have the space and opportunity to talk about what happened, especially with the people closest to me. Many helpful friends and family members sat with me, cried with me, worshipped with me, and ate with me. We talked about what had happened, what I was feeling, what I was worried about, and so on. I had a whole community of family, friends, and brothers and sisters in Christ who could bear the sorrow with me, so I did not have to carry the story silently and alone. By sharing what happened, the story could become a part of others as well and be "held" by all.

In my pastoral training, I had seen what happened to people who buried the emotions that inevitably accompany loss. What did not come out in the form of grief or tears came out as anger, resentment, stress, illness, or some other life-sucking thing. I wanted to be the healthiest person I could be, so I just sat in my grief for as long as I needed to. I went to the darkness and made a home there for a long time, and then I invited Jesus to pull up a chair right next to me. There were times when I thought the emptiness I felt would consume me. This was terrifying, but I had people in my life who could accompany me and help pull me out when the loss became too great to bear.

No marriage is perfect. I can honestly say that I only went to bed mad at Ben twice in my life, and both of those times we talked about what happened and forgave each other. Now death had removed our ability to reconcile. For some reason I felt all kinds of regrets, mostly irrational. All the ways I thought I had failed to be a good wife were vividly displayed in the front of my mind. I came across a reading once in my wallowing in regret that was so helpful:

> When the person is dead, what do we do with our regrets? . . . I believe that God forgives me. I do not doubt that. . . . But . . . my regrets remain. What do I do with my God-forgiven regrets? . . .
>
> I shall live with them. . . . But I will not endlessly gaze at them. I shall allow the memories . . . to sharpen the vision and intensify the hope for that Great Day coming when we can all throw ourselves into each other's arms and say, "I'm sorry."
>
> The God of love will surely grant us such a day. Love needs that.[1]

I pictured myself running into Ben's arms and saying, "I'm sorry!" *I am sorry you died and we had to leave your body. I am sorry for not driving with you to your approval interview because I did not want to miss class. I am sorry we did not have children before you died. I am sorry for not playing as much as I could have and for often working instead.* I could go on and on. This helped me not to stay in my regrets and let them have power over me.

Surrounding myself with beauty was helpful, whether it was artwork, flowers, or music. I have always loved images of the tree of life, so I hung some up around my living space to remind me of the leaves of the tree that are for the healing of the nations (Revelation 22:2)—nations like Haiti,

1. Wolterstorff, *Lament*, 64–65.

devastated by an earthquake. I also had great joy in gardening. Putting my hands in the dirt, planting seeds, watching them grow, and caring for the plants was very therapeutic for me, not to mention beneficial in putting food on my table that I could share with others.

Like my sister, my mom came to stay with me at Wartburg for a week. (They spaced their visits out so that I would not be alone so much.) My mom spent the week going to classes, helping me clean and go through things, going to campfires and worship with my classmates, and basically doing anything she felt I needed.

My mom was with me when I was getting ready for the Wartburg senior banquet. I stepped out of the shower and wept. I did not want to go without Ben. She quietly came into my room, sat cross-legged on the floor with me, and laid my head in her lap. I could feel her silent tears as she stroked my hair and said, "You don't have to go, pumpkin." I cried with my head in my mother's lap just as I had done growing up. I took my mom to the banquet instead of Ben, and we had a great time.

Ben's family did not have to call me daughter, sister, or "Aunt Nae" after Ben died, but they did. They let me know again and again how much they loved me, how much Ben loved me, and how much they wanted me in their family. This had incredible power. I am a daughter, a sister, and an aunt in the Larson family, and I could not be more blessed.

The people in my home community of Garrison, North Dakota, did their best to care for me as a daughter of their town. When a few individuals in Garrison found out that I had lost my glasses in the earthquake, they immediately went to the optometrist's office. Within a week I had a new pair of the exact same glasses delivered to me at no cost.

I eventually sought out a spiritual director. I needed someone who would go to the depths of God with me, to struggle with me, and she did.

Even four years after the earthquake I still needed healing. I had tended so acutely to my grief over the loss of Ben that I overlooked my own trauma of being in the earthquake and trapped under concrete for a while. I told myself I was fine, but my body sent other signals. While writing this book, I began to have extreme fatigue, what one might describe as "brain fog," intense lower back pain, heart palpitations, and numbing on my face. Although it was years after the earthquake, I had to admit the trauma was affecting me in a new way and that I needed help.

I tried physical therapy, chiropractic care, and acupuncture, all of which helped. Along the way I heard about something called EMDR (eye movement desensitization reprocessing) therapy. EMDR is a way to reprocess trauma. In my sessions, my therapist helped me remember and stay in the most terrifying moments of the earthquake and notice how my body responded. My eyes would follow a light back and forth as I recalled the terror. There are also auditory and sensory methods to EMDR, and the therapist used all of them with me.

I could not have imagined the magnitude of my physical response as I purposefully relived the most traumatic moments of the earthquake. My whole body shook intensely. Both sides of my face, my chest, and my upper back tingled, as though my nerves were plugged into an electrical socket. Over the course of a few months, my physical response lessened as I recalled the event. After my final session, my therapist said, "Even though the effects of PTSD have dramatically decreased, your physical response to the trauma of the earthquake may never fully go away, and that's normal." I'm okay with that; at least, I have to be.

I would not be where I am today without the assistance of people in helping professions. It has been an incredibly humbling experience letting others into my deepest pain and fears. The connection of mind, body, and spirit is truly a mystery. I could not simply tell my body, "You are fine!" I needed the help of others to heal properly, and I am so grateful to those who walked with me.

Healing through Inspiration

After Ben died, someone once said to me, "I think Ben is going to touch even more lives in his death than he did in his life." This was very hard for me to hear and I did not know if I agreed or not, but I could not deny the effect Ben's death was having on so many people. All who knew Ben knew he loved, trusted, and followed Christ, and those who did not know Ben quickly discovered this as they heard about his life and his dying witness.

When people learned of Ben's death and heard about the Haiti earthquake, many searched for God and any meaning in all of the senseless death and a city left in ruins. Ben was good friends with so many people who considered themselves to be agnostic (searching) or atheist. He loved and respected people who practiced Islam and other religions. He understood the arms of God to be wide and embracing. He emphasized this in his song, "Made":

> My Maker's arms are wide enough for you
> She breathed you too, she breathed you too

Ben, Jon, and I had met one person who considered himself an agnostic at best just days before the earthquake. He survived and remained in Haiti for months. I found out from his sister, who had been living in

Haiti for years at Wings of Hope, that he kept listening to Ben's songs off the Internet, all day every day, especially one song called "Hush." In that song, Ben acknowledged the atrocities of the world, but he spoke of resting in God's arms for now:

> Hush child, do not be afraid, do not fear the dark
> Hush my little child, do not be afraid
> I'm with you till the end . . .
>
> The world can be bitter sometimes
> And I know it may be all of the time
> But it is how it is that's how it is
> And you're on this world making it better than it was before . . .
>
> And when you feel tired, my child
> Put your trust in me
> I will rise you up on wings like the eagle's
> You'll find strength in me and be renewed
>
> But for now
> Hush, hush, hush, hush my child
> Hush, hush, hush, hush my love
> Hush child, I'll bring you rest

Because of people's compassion and outreach, more than $12.5 million was raised through the ELCA to help with the relief efforts in Haiti for at least three years after the earthquake. This included tens of thousands of dollars from individuals, organizations, churches, and schools that poured into the ELCA Disaster Response's Haiti Earthquake Relief fund in memory of Ben.

Also in Ben's memory, Wartburg Seminary set up an endowed J-term scholarship of $25,000 to assist future students in traveling to developing countries. Minneapolis Bishop Ann Svennungsen inspired the rostered women leaders in the ELCA to create another endowed "Fund for Leaders" scholarship, which pays for tuition for ELCA seminary students. I was happy to learn that the first recipient of the scholarship was a man from Zimbabwe who decided to attend Wartburg Theological Seminary.

Every year on Ben's birthday, First Lutheran Church (where Ben's parents served as pastors) in Duluth, Minnesota, made Lutheran World Relief kits to send all over the world to disaster areas. They called them "Bundles for Ben's Birthday." The first year (2010), 1,500 kits were made on a Sunday morning, setting a new record with LWR.

A cantata called *Peace Ascends* was written by Dr. Stephen Johnson of Southwestern Baptist Theological Seminary, who was inspired by Ben's singing in his dying. It was performed for the first time in the spring of 2011, and April, Judd, and I were flown in for the performance. It was also performed at the Lincoln Center later that year. The blurb on the CD of that recording says: "*Peace Ascends* portrays the peace of God amid life's tragedies. It was inspired by the story of missionary Benjamin Larson, who died in Haiti's massive 2010 earthquake. Buried under rubble, he breathed his last while singing, 'God's peace to us we pray.'"

Another composition came from Joshua Shank, who had known Ben from Luther College. His piece was called "He Was Singing" and was performed by The Singers, a professional forty-four-voice chamber choir from Minneapolis. Joshua told the *Duluth News Tribune*: "The one thought I couldn't shake was: He gave his last breath up for a song. And that resonates with me as a musician more than I have the capacity to put into words."[2] I had the opportunity to hear the piece performed live by the choir in the spring of 2012.

Music . . . Ben's music, hymnody, choral pieces, the music of creation, became the pulse of my healing. Music, especially hymnody, touched the depths of my soul when nothing else could. Even when my heart was heavy, music declared to me that God is still good. Dietrich Bonhoeffer wrote this about music and Martin Luther: "Luther knew [music] has dried an infinite number of tears, made the sad happy, stilled desires, raised up the defeated, [and] strengthened the challenged."[3] It was too difficult at first to listen to music Ben wrote, but over time I was able to let his music strengthen my faith and give me joy once again.

Letting Go

After seminary graduation I started to read every grief book I could get my fingers on, hoping that one would contain the magic potion to bring Ben back or make everything better. No book had either of those, but some were quite helpful. At least I knew I was not alone in what I was going through.

One book I read was called *Found Through Loss* by Nancy Reeves. She writes this about healing:

2. Passi, "Story of Duluth Pastors' Son," para. 10.

3. Bonhoeffer, *I Want to Live These Days with You*, 349.

> I define healing as a shift of energy whereby energy for life-enhancement is added to that used for survival and grieving needs. Healing also involves the ability to think about the loss without feeling overwhelming emotion, a change from "existing" to "living," and the experience of grief shifting from the center of awareness to a less demanding position.[4]

Although tears fell from my eyes at some point every day for at least a year and a half after Ben died, I cried less each day as time went on. Over time I felt more energy for decision-making and my vocation to ministry. I definitely noticed a shift from existing to living again.

I used to wonder if Ben got the easier part of the deal by dying rather than having to survive the trauma and the loss. What was really challenging was when people said how important and special Jon's life and my life must be since we survived the earthquake. I know they did not mean this, but it felt like they were saying, "God has a great purpose for your life since you lived, but not for Ben because he died." I think God had great purposes for all who died in the Haiti earthquake. My life is no more special than someone else's who died. Why some buildings fell the way they did and why some people died and others did not remains a frustrating mystery to me.

Even after trudging through the first year after Ben's death, I was clinging to the memory of Ben and our marriage and our life together like it was breath itself, and it was not good for me. I needed to release Ben to God, not as if I was "moving on," but in a way that was a blessing.

During our marriage I would always write the days of the new month on our large dry-erase calendar and add all the important dates and appointments. After the earthquake, I left the month of December 2009 on that board for more than a year. I would look at it with misery and long for the life I once had.

On April 4, 2011, I woke up, ate oatmeal, drank coffee, and gathered my courage to erase the board. I knew it was not just about erasing a stupid whiteboard; it was a symbol of letting go and releasing Ben. Before I erased the board, I wrote pages and pages in my journal and also wrote down every day that was on the whiteboard so I could remember. Here is some of what I wrote in a letter to Ben:

> I am tired of being sad, but I do not know what or how to be. It is like my sadness and grief are so familiar. If I let them go, then it feels like I am letting you go. I keep thinking of C.S. Lewis's words I read last spring about when he "let his wife go" he was able to grow more fully in relationship with her. Will that be true

---

4. Reeves, *Found Through Loss*, 8.

for us, my love? I am afraid. I am afraid of living without you. I am afraid of letting go of the grief that has been my constant companion; I am afraid of what others will think and how they will judge me. "Didn't she love him enough? Is she 'over him' already? It's only been fifteen months." Well, let me tell you, it may as well be fifteen years!

I need your help today Ben, for I am going to begin the process of letting go from my end. I am pretty sure you have already and death has forced us to "let go" in physical ways. I think I need to let go too, in hopes that I will be brought out of the pit and be able to continue my God-given work and call, be more present to others who are living, have more energy, and by the grace of God, grow more fully into my relationship with you. If you are experiencing true joy like I believe you are, then I would like to experience that in any ways I can with you.

I know I have been brought to this place today through grievous hard work and struggle. I am going through a very painful birthing process and I know I cannot stay in the womb . . . We have not been given a Spirit of fear in our baptism, have we, Ben? No, we have not. Through Christ we are more than conquerors, are we not, my Ben? You know this fully now, Sweetie Pie; it's just taking me a little longer to come round. Help me release you to God.

I thought of the Haitian woman who looked at me the day after the earthquake and said boldly, "Kouraj." So, I wrote "COURAGE" on the whiteboard and erased everything else. I was not expecting it, but when I finished, I felt astonishing relief. I breathed in deep. I was not forgetting Ben or our life together; I was releasing him to his Creator as I rested in the hands of God for my future and our resurrected future together.

19

Widow

WHEN I BECAME A widow I began to notice how many widows and widowers were around me. So many people, young and old, had felt the deep pain of losing the one with whom they had been one flesh.

I remember one time in seminary when Ben and I quickly grabbed dinner at Kentucky Fried Chicken in Dubuque. Two booths away from us I noticed an elderly man eating alone. He seemed sad and lonely. Right or wrong, I assumed his spouse had died. My heart ached for him. I told Ben that I could not bear it if he died. But within the year, Ben was dead and I was the one seated at an empty table.

Some of the significant days, especially anniversary dates and birthdays, I would dread for weeks, only to have them come and go like any other day. And then there would be a "normal" Tuesday when I would wake up and the tears would already be flowing. I would be numb and drained of all energy. I never knew when these hard days would come.

Before Ben died, I did not think about how hard it might be for the surviving spouse to get the bills in order and remember other simple things. I was driving on the interstate in North Dakota late one night when I saw flashing lights behind me. The officer approached my window and said, "Your tabs are expired. You needed to renew them more than a year ago. Why haven't you taken care of that?"

"Well, it's a long story," I said, not wanting to get into it or to have him to feel sorry for me.

"I have time."

"My husband died and it wasn't at the top of my priority list to renew the tabs on my car . . ." I paid a small fine and took care of the tabs the following week.

Scripture notices widows. Before the earthquake I would pass over the word "widow" in the Bible as a mere adjective. Now I pause and imagine the depth of loss, the complexity and uncertainty of the future, and the greater details of that one's life, which we rarely get to hear in the story.

Acts 9 tells the story of Dorcas and the many widows she cared for. When Dorcas died, the community called for Peter. They wept as they showed him the tunics and other clothing Dorcas had made. They wanted Peter to see the work of her hands and know how much she had meant to all of them. When the widows wept, they did not mourn only for Dorcas, but for the spouses they had lost, perhaps children who had died, and for the finality of death in this world. Grief compounds upon grief. However, the story ends with new life when Peter resuscitates Dorcas. Mourning turns to dancing.

After Ben died I had a number of conversations with other widows. One woman lost her husband to suicide. She told me she spent time in the "grief room" of her being. She said, "There is a room in me where I go to grieve. There are times I enter it and stay for a short time. There are times I just sit in it for hours. Other times I move to different corners of the room and explore what I find there, never putting pressure on myself to explore the whole room at once. When I need to, I leave the room and continue with the necessary aspects of my life, whether caring for my children, going to class, or working. If I can't get out of the room, I ask someone who loves me to help escort me out. When I'm ready again, I go and visit my 'grief room' that will be in me for the rest of my life." This is how I envisioned much of my grief work.

Another widowed woman told me she gave away all of her husband's things within days of his death because it was simply too painful for her to have his stuff around. It quickly became clear to me that everyone dealt with the loss of their spouse differently and that was okay.

One widower told me he eventually had to move out of town and find a new job. Otherwise, everywhere he went, and with everyone he met, he felt like he was "bleeding all over the place."

In some places in Haiti widows wear black for two years after their spouse dies. The color of their garments tells the whole community: "I lost someone. My life is different. I am in mourning." One of my Haitian friends told me, "Wear something of Ben's to give you strength. He passed on his strength to you and his life when he died. He helped you survive in Haiti, and he will continue to help you."

I also had a conversation with a woman who lost her husband in a horrible car crash fifteen years before. She was in the car with him along with her infant grandson and two family friends. It was midday and they were driving on a two-lane road. Someone heading their way in the opposite direction crossed the centerline and hit them head-on. This woman's grandson died as well as her husband. She was hurt, but her injuries were not fatal. We sat at my kitchen table, and tears streamed down her face as she told me this story even fifteen years later. I could feel the sorrow that remained in her and also her deep love for her husband and grandson. "There were times," she said, "early on after my husband died when I felt his presence in the room, almost like he was sitting next to me." Through her tears she spoke of her gratitude for life.

The word *gratitude* stands out to me because of a phone conversation with another widow. I knew her from Wartburg Seminary, but she had graduated and was serving a congregation in Texas. She had become a widow at age twenty-five, ten years before; her husband had died of cancer. She spoke of the way he would smell after mowing the lawn with fresh-cut grass on his skin. She described his smile and what their home together meant to her. They did not have children, so after his death, she poured herself into improvements on their house. A few months later she finished the construction, sold the house, and moved out. When I spoke with her, she was engaged to be married. I asked her how her life was now, a decade later. She said one word: "Gratitude." She was so thankful for her life with her first husband, to have known and loved him like none other. She was also thankful for her life now and the man she was going to marry. "Gratitude," she said, "to God and for life."

I have had other widows look me straight in the eye and say, "Renee, you will be okay." They would say it over and over to me. Not, "Everything will be okay," but rather, "You, Renee, will be okay." They could say that. They had been through it. They trusted that God would help me be okay.

After Rebecca Wee[1] lost her husband, Michael, a fellow widow named Gertrude paid her a visit. Rebecca told me about the depth of pain she felt after Michael's death and Gertrude's helpful words:

> After Michael died, I wasn't prepared for how painful it was
> to navigate people's efforts to be comforting. Everyone meant
> well, but the platitudes and wrongness of most of what was said
> scraped me raw; I felt worse and lonelier. There simply wasn't
> help for that level of hurt, for a very long time.
>
> The one encounter I carry though, still, because it felt right
> and true at the time, and has proved to be exactly that, was
> with eighty-six-year-old Gertrude Lundholm. When Gertrude's

---

1. Poet I met at Holden Village (see chapter 17) and professor of English at Augustana College, Rock Island, Illinois.

husband Beanie died she was bereft, and after I returned to Augustana in 1999, she invited me over for coffee and got right to it. Bright blue eyes flashing, she said, "Well, I bet everyone's telling you it's going to get better, and you want to slap them across the face. But you also want to believe they're right because it doesn't seem possible that anything will ever feel better, does it? It *doesn't* really get better—it will never be all right that you have to live the rest of your life without the man you loved. You should have had a long, beautiful life together. You were just getting started.

"But it will get *different* Rebecca, and you'll see that that will be enough. It will. You will have a good and full and meaningful life because you know what love is. You're going to miss him all of your days, but it's not always going to hurt like it does now."

It was the truest thing anyone said to me in those terrible years. No platitudes from Gertrude. And she was right.

Through these conversations with other widows and my own experience of living after the earthquake, I realized that God does not promise us a better life after such loss, or the same life, but rather *new* life. And this new life is still good and worth living.

The Grave

As a widow, I have lingered in Phelps Cemetery in Decorah, Iowa, where Ben is buried at the feet of his maternal grandparents, Joe and Aleta. There are many beautiful, mature trees where Ben is buried, including a maple tree whose canopy shelters the grave. Over time, I have been at his grave at sunrise and at sunset, in the heat of a July day, and in the bitter cold of January 12. I have seen fireflies dance in the night sky, filling the air with a small glow. Deer always enjoy the delicious flowers people bring to beautify the place of sorrow. I have watched squirrels chase each other through the trees and listened to the wind rustle the leaves, creating a shimmering, peaceful sound. Birds seem to enjoy the cemetery, just as I enjoy their songs. There is so much life and beauty in that place that houses resting, lifeless bodies.

Because many people wanted to spend time at Ben's grave, we decided to put a community bench at his feet where they could sit. Late in the summer of 2010, we went to choose a simple, unfinished stone bench from Decorah Memorial Company. April and Judd asked me, "Renee, what are you thinking? You can have any type of stone you want."

I pointed as I said, "Well, I'd be perfectly happy with this one, that one over there, or that one in the back."

The store owner chuckled a bit and said, "Well, you're in luck, because they are all the same stone! They are Mahogany granite from North Dakota."

April and Judd laughed. "Ben would think it was so funny that his wife from North Dakota unknowingly choose all three stones from North Dakota!" I was relieved because it made my decision so much easier.

We chose to have Romans 14:7–9 carved on the bench. That was the Scripture that came to me in the lot with the Haitians the night of the earthquake:

> We do not live to ourselves, and we do not die to ourselves. If we live, we live to the Lord, and if we die, we die to the Lord; so then, whether we live or whether we die, we are the Lord's. For to this end Christ died and lived again, so that he might be Lord of both the dead and the living.

I have loved sitting on that bench under the maple tree, even when I am thinking about the earth that will be opened to embrace me someday too. God's Word gave me a sense of peace the night of the earthquake, and it continues to give rest to my soul beside Ben's grave.

I have spent hours upon hours at Ben's grave, and I am so thankful I can visit the place he is buried. At first I could barely walk there without my knees buckling. Sometimes I would lie on the ground trying to talk to Ben, trying to talk to God, straining to hear anything that God might give to me. Ben felt very dead and very far away. When I let myself think about his body right there under the earth below me, it took all my strength to not lose my sanity. At the same time, I needed to be there.

When Ben was first buried, the ground over him looked like a wound in the middle of pristine grass. It symbolized how we all felt. When grass started to grow over the grave, April would hoe it up. Over time we began to feel comfort at the grave site, and eventually, we allowed the grass to grow in. There was still pain, but it became more of a dull ache than a piercing sword.

Sometimes I would just walk through the cemetery and read headstones. I always felt sad for the people whose dates on their tombstones indicated how long the other lived after their spouse died. I noticed how many children were buried there. I started to feel less sorry for myself when I walked the rows. All people suffer loss. I thought the most poignant grave in Phelps Cemetery was that of Phelps himself. His stone was massive and right by the gate. I noticed that he survived two spouses, four infant children, and a son who lived to his early forties. I could hardly imagine the loss Phelps bore throughout his lifetime.

After the first anniversary of the earthquake passed, we started working on getting a headstone for Ben's grave. I struggled because I knew Ben would not want anything that stood out too much,[2] but I finally chose one that had a fairly large cross at the top. There was no other cross anywhere near the grave, and it was appropriate for Ben, who had died singing about the Lamb of God.

How could we describe Ben's life and death on a single stone? We knew we needed to include Ben's dying song and witness, so right under his name, Benjamin Judd Ulring Splichal Larson, February 27, 1984–January 12, 2010, we wrote:

> Buried in the rubble of the Haiti earthquake, Ben sang his last words:
>
> "O Lamb of God, you bear the sin of all the world away;
> eternal peace with God you made, God's peace to us, we pray."
>
> Child of God, Beloved Husband, Son, Brother

Ben's sister Katie drew the likeness of the cross that Jon clung to on the roof of St. Joseph's and we had it etched into the stone. Ben's life and death would be forever linked to Haiti. We had a plaque made to tell as much of the story as we could:

> As an infant Benjamin Judd Ulring Splichal Larson was wrapped in the arms of God in the waters of baptism, and from those waters his life was an outpouring of love and joy, laughter and play, music and song, in response to God first loving Ben.
>
> Ben's love of Jesus Christ, walking in accompaniment, passionately loving others, listening and learning from those who are poor across the globe, drove his serving.
>
> We give thanks to God for the incredible joy of knowing Ben. His laughter, playfulness and passionate heart for those who are hurting were manifest in his daily life. He delighted in the privilege of serving and knowing Jesus Christ, laying out his life in joy.
>
> Most of the people who died in this deadly Haiti earthquake were the poorest of the poor in this hemisphere. Ben went to Haiti to teach theology and Scripture in the new Lutheran Church of Haiti, but more deeply to learn from these people loved by God. In his young death his life joins the bodies of the poor. In the Haitian rubble Ben's life joins these dear beloved people of God: all those parents crying for their children; young

2. Ben used to say to me: "When I die, just put me in a wooden box and lower me into the ground." This desire was inspired by the burial of Olaf in the movie *Sweet Land*.

widows calling out for their husbands; new orphans searching for their parents.

In memory of Ben from his wife Renee; parents, Judd and April; sisters, Katie and Amy

We also wanted to include one of Ben's songs on the stone. Choosing one out of 130 was no easy matter, but we eventually decided on "Rain Song," also known as "Pitter Patter," which he wrote as a young teenager. It spoke to the beauty of the place, it revealed Ben's spirit of joy in creation and God, and it called all who read it to gratitude:

> Here comes that rainy day feelin'
> With a sweet pitter patter again
> A peaceful breeze now joins the rain
> So a shimmering of leaves has begun
>
> So come now, rejoice with me
> For the beauty around us
> Come now rejoice on bended knee
> As we praise the Lord for this day
>
> Like a song it starts with a melody
> As the droplets fall in harmony
> And the puddles form the percussion
> As the wind howls through the grass

After at least ten eyes looked over the proof and the stone was cut and set, Ben's parents noticed a year later that there was one mistake. Instead of the leaves "shimmering," the word "simmering" appeared on the stone. Perhaps leaves can "simmer"? We all decided Ben would think it was funny, and now we laugh about it.

Anniversaries

Ben dying any month of the year would have been difficult, but his dying in January has been really tough because he is buried in Iowa, where temperatures routinely drop to ten or twenty degrees below zero (Fahrenheit!) and the snow is deep. Every year on the anniversary of his death many have stood shivering around his grave.

The first year, Judd and April paid someone to plow the road so we could get roughly fifty people to the site for a worship service. People came, and people froze. That night Jon, two other seminary classmates, and I went back up to the grave and lit the many candles Ben's parents had put there.

We huddled together with blankets and barely said a word. That first anniversary was so very hard, and the bitter cold cut into our bones like a knife.

The second year we were in Haiti over January 12, but we still spent as much time as we could at Ben's grave after we returned. I built a snowman and a snow lady near the bench and wrapped up in a wool blanket April gave me that used to be her mother's.

The third year we got smart. It was so important for Ben's family to spend time at his grave around the anniversary that we decided to purchase an ice fishing house so we could be near Ben's body for more than ten minutes without freezing. Judd placed the icehouse right over the headstone. We crawled in and sat in it for a good hour telling stories and continuing to grieve our loss.

The fourth year Luther College Ministries in Decorah put on an event called "Lespwa fè nou viv," which is Creole for "Hope makes us live." Musicians gathered to play music and raise money for various nonprofit organizations in Haiti. They included Hans Peterson (of Dakota Road) and Peter Mayer (from the Peter Mayer Band and Jimmy Buffett Band). Bill and Walnes from St. Joseph's Home for Boys were also able to come. The night before the concert, all of us were gathered in Judd and April's home (now in Decorah), and two hours of spontaneous music sprang up and out of us as if we could not keep it in. The morning of the concert, about thirty of us stood around Ben's grave freezing once again—especially the Haitians! We sang, prayed for Haiti's continued recovery, read Scripture, and told stories. We sang and sang and gave thanks to God for Ben and for the power of music.

Over the years in summer or fall when Jon, our friend Elly, and I visit Ben's grave, we stop first at a coffee shop—either the Magpie or Java John's—and purchase four coffees, one for each of us and one for Ben. We take them up to the grave, lay out a blanket, and play cards. Occasionally one of us will pour out a libation of Ben's favorite drink and say, "Here you go, Ben." This practice has been strangely comforting.

It has been difficult over the years for me to observe Jon at Ben's grave. Mostly he stands still and silent, hardly saying a word, as he stares at the ground and Ben's headstone. The heaviness about him has been hard to bear, and I ache for his loss. Often he leaves and takes a walk through the cemetery. He always gives me my time alone at Ben's grave, and I give him his.

It has been special for me, especially in the winter, to see evidence of how many people visit Ben's grave. Path after path has been carved into the snow, almost like a pilgrimage site. At times I have found little trinkets and things people have left at his grave. It makes me happy to think how Ben continues to touch so many people's lives. God provided the beautiful place for people to visit and enter into the greater story of Ben and Haiti, and there is a bench there where people can read the Word, sit down, and rest.

Once within the first year of Ben's death, April was by herself at the grave. Like any mother who had lost a child, she stood there lost in grief. Then something quite surprising and unexpected happened. She heard a voice as clear as day: "Why do you look for the living among the dead? He is not here, but has been raised." She looked around and saw no one. She did not feel as if the voice was criticizing her for grieving at her son's grave, and she knew her son's body still lay beneath the earth. The mysterious words became a proclamation of good news to her and to all of us. It gave me great hope that Ben was already living a resurrected life with Christ.

PART V

Reflection

Haiti
Corrine Denis

faithful faces
veiled in dust
searching for Adonai
for the One who neither slumbers nor sleeps
oh my sisters, the Good Shepherd
is overturning rocks to find you
oh my brothers, the Light
desperately rushes to your dark and doubt.
The Lord is collecting the salt
from your tears
mixing them with ours
in a velvet pouch
to sprinkle along the Caribbean shore
forever joined
with all the saints.

20

The People of Haiti

In conversations in the U.S. concerning Haiti, a few themes often come up: poverty, corruption, government, danger, Vodou, charity, mission work, pity, and HIV/AIDS. In her book *Dèyè Mòn: Behind the Mountains,* written years before the earthquake, my friend Renee Dietrich describes "Haiti: The Other Story."

> Images flash across the screen.
> 30 second sound bites don't accurately describe the situation.
>
> All the outside world sees is;
> Violence;
> Bloodshed;
> Angry mobs shouting anti-American sentiments;
> Self-destruction in the name of national sovereignty.
>
> Those who don't bother to look any further into the story will
> never know or see any more than that.
> They will only see what they want to see.
> What is easy to see.
> What countless other stories before these have taught them to see.
> Foolish savages ruining their own lives;
> Looking for handouts;
> Lazy, backward, dirty, ignorant.[1]

Haiti appears on the U.S. news only during uprisings, government coups, or major hurricanes. After the earthquake on January 12, 2010, people turned on their TVs to see collapsed buildings, broken and bloodied bodies, and men, women, and children crying out while wandering the streets in a concrete-dust haze. Perhaps some of those watching were like my brother Eric, vomiting in the toilet after seeing the devastation and not

1. Dietrich, *Dèyè Mòn,* 74–76.

knowing if his older sister was buried somewhere in the rubble. Perhaps some were like my brother's wife, Janessa, fiercely scanning the television screen, hoping against hope to see three fair-skinned seminarians alive and well among the crowds. Most, I suppose, could not believe their eyes as they watched helplessly from afar.

Haiti has a certain negative reputation in the U.S. Every time I have traveled to Haiti, our government's advisory recommended against it. I understand the need for caution, and it's true that Haiti has not always been the safest place to be. Still, it surprises me how much we misunderstand and misrepresent a country that is just an hour and a half flight from Florida. Haiti is so close, yet so poorly understood. Many Americans don't understand what life is like for the Haitian people, what Vodou culture and religion are, what they mean when they speak of Guinea,[2] or the generations it will take to "recover" from the earthquake.

Dietrich continues in "Haiti: The Other Story":

> What they won't see is the love and courage a mother shows for
> her children;
> Rising before dawn to walk barefoot across the rocks to gather
> water;
> Cooking for hours over hot charcoal;
> Spending the day under a burning sun to eke out an existence
> for her family;
> Carrying a child on her hip and a bundle on her head as she
> returns to the stream to beat her clothes on a rock;
>
> Then returning to her preparation of a simple evening meal of
> rice and beans;
> Allowing herself to eat only after her children have had their fill;
> Stooped over candlelight, hand-stitching magnificent creations
> out of scraps while her children sleep;
> Finally laying down on a straw mat to rest her eyes and her mind
> for a few hours before rising to begin again.
>
> What they won't see is the father;
> Shedding his own dignity to become a human donkey;
> Pushing and pulling his cargo up and down the hills
> for a few gourdes to feed his family;
> Bare feet and bare back showing the strain;
> Sweat, burden and pain aging him beyond his years.

2. Haitians I know speak of Guinea as the place where they will return when they die, much like many might speak of heaven. They long to return to West Africa, from whence they came, where they were always supposed to be.

What they won't see are the children;
Crowded into a classroom, sharing one book, one piece of
paper, one pencil, if they are lucky;
Soaking in all of the knowledge they can to help them improve
their lives before they are forced onto the streets to help the
family survive;

Taking time to play;
Like children everywhere;
Not with Air Jordans and big league athletic equipment;
But with bare feet and rocks;
A piece of plastic and some string;
A rusted out bicycle tire rim and a stick;
Taking immense pleasure in the simplicity of still being able to
be a child.

These are the other stories.
The stories of simple dignity and profound love.
But, these are the ones often left untold because they aren't as
sexy or exciting.
They don't ring with gun shots and angry shouts at the camera.
They aren't colored with blood and burning buildings.
They don't rock with political upheaval.
But, they are how the country continues to survive.
Angels on earth, simply striving for a quiet, dignified existence.
Life goes on, even when the government doesn't.[3]

In a country that continually hosts crowds of visiting white people in
matching T-shirts on mission trips, it was in Haiti that I was ministered to,
cared for, and witnessed to.

Somehow it is assumed that if a white person is in Haiti they are there
to do some kind of "mission" work, whether that means starting a church,
playing with children at an orphanage, building something, or setting up
a medical mission. Of course, these are good things to do, and I have met
many Americans who went to Haiti hoping to change lives, only to come
back and say, "I am the one who was changed." Haiti has that kind of power.
But for many, the perception is that Haiti just needs help, which makes it
more challenging to describe what I "do" in Haiti.

Jon and I were once dropped off at the airport in Port-au-Prince in
a "normal" five-person vehicle (not a tap tap, van, or bus) by a Haitian

---

3. Dietrich, *Dèyè Mòn*, 78–88.

husband and wife. These two are like family to us, and we went to visit them in February 2011. A group of people from the U.S. in lime-green mission T-shirts stood nearby as Jon and I said our goodbyes to our dear friends. We went through security and made the short flight back to the U.S. When we arrived in Miami, a member from this group joined us in line at an airport fast-food restaurant. He struck up a conversation with Jon and me.

"So, what kind of mission brought you to Haiti?"

Jon and I replied, "We were just visiting people we love."

The young man looked puzzled, but said, "Yes, I noticed you hugging two people and it looked like you knew them really well."

"We do! We love them."

He kept trying to understand: "Right, but what were you *doing* there? Did you go to an orphanage or something or where were you doing your mission work?"

Jon and I were worn out from our trip to Haiti for the first time since the earthquake. We simply said again, "No. We were just visiting people we care about." An awkward silence followed as we all waited for our food. When we parted, we knew we were on different wavelengths. We politely said, "Nice talking with you."

It is not that Jon and I don't have a sense of mission. We do. We believe God has called us to be in relationship with our brothers and sisters in Christ in Haiti. We see this as accompaniment; we are in mutual relationship with one another.

Jon and I do not have any more to offer the Haitian people than they offer us. We change and transform one another primarily through being in relationship. This is hard work because it takes a lot of time and effort to truly get to know one another on both sides of the cultural divide. We are prepared to be changed—our mind-set, our values—walking in accompaniment. In fact, this is guaranteed to happen when horizons of culture, language, race, theology, and social class meet.

Haitian Spirit and Hospitality

What I have learned from the Haitian people, especially through the earthquake, are strength and courage, as well as what it means to have faith in the face of death and despair. Jon and I felt paralyzed after the earthquake. We were so shattered by Ben's death and the trauma of having two floors of concrete fall on us. It was in this crushed state that the Haitians accompanied us, even though they had just experienced exactly what we had. They lost family and friends, as well as their homes and life as they knew it.

Their songs and prayers carried us; the sheet that was graciously given to us warmed our shaking bodies; they watched over us and let us know that they would do anything for us.

I received looks of compassion from Haitians who lost family members. They were so sad for me and sorry they could not save me from my loss. They were devastated that my husband died while visiting their country. As Sylvia Raulo from LWF Haiti told me later, they were shocked that because of our love and commitment to Haiti we became victims of this terrible, monstrous event.

So many Haitians lost everything, yet they still gave their energy and time to care for our family, Jon, and me after the earthquake. A team of Haitians expressed incredible hospitality and accompaniment by risking their lives to dig Ben's body out of the rubble. We are forever grateful, and we can never repay them. The only thing we can do is accept *their* "mission work" as sheer gift.

The Haitians' courage and perseverance were an inspiration to me as I grieved Ben's death. Every day I thought about what they must be going through with their losses, injuries, and ongoing fear of more earthquakes or aftershocks. Kez, our nurse friend in Haiti, once told me that the fear on the street was: "When the next earthquake happens, how long will it be before someone digs my body out?" In the Midwest I was safe and did not have to worry about the earth beneath me moving again—and I still struggled.

Even those whose homes were still standing could not sleep in them for fear of another earthquake. That is why the tent cities remained so large for so long. It is also why I travel to Haiti only for as long as I can survive on little or no sleep. It is impossible now for me to sleep under a concrete roof in Haiti.

There is a saying in Haiti about the earthquake: "Everyone lost someone; someone lost everyone." In Port-au-Prince and the surrounding area this is true. Some people lost their *entire* families, including their homes and whatever future they had planned.

I heard about an elderly man in Port-au-Prince who had only a hammer, but slowly chipped away every day at the side of a building that had fallen into the street. He was demonstrating the incredible spirit of the Haitian people to "degaje," to do what you can with what you have.

I thought: *If the Haitian people can get up every day, I can get up every day.* So I did, and so did they. They gave me incredible strength.

At one point after the earthquake I heard from one of my Haitian friends that many of the people in Port-au-Prince were engaging in a communal fast to ask God for help. They proclaimed, "God is with us." My own faith has been strengthened through the Haitian witness to Christ.

My experience of the Haitian people is that they are full: full of resilience, faith, joy, love, music, and dancing. When Jon and I returned to Haiti in February 2011, we found out that the Haitians didn't just sing the night after the earthquake; they sang every night, all night, for weeks.

We also had the opportunity to meet Pierre, the local Haitian man who took the lead on digging Ben's body out of the rubble. When Jon and I saw him, our eyes filled with tears. We reached for the hands that had worked so hard for three days to unearth a total stranger. We knew that he had risked his life in the hospitality he showed our family. I learned he had a wife and a small child. He had been living in a tent for the past year because his house collapsed in the earthquake. We gave him a photo of Ben, and he stared at it long and hard without saying a word. He slipped the photo in his wallet. Through a translator we were able to communicate some of our gratitude to Pierre.

It is impossible to make sense of a disaster like this. The Haitians interpreted the earthquake in various ways, just as anyone might who has suffered a terrible disaster. Some thought that the earthquake must be some kind of punishment. Other Haitians only knew that the earth moved and their loved ones died; they threw up their hands to the Creator to ask for mercy. Some Haitians wrestled and wrestled theologically, as I did, shaking their heads in disbelief that the loving God who came to earth incarnate in Christ would ever allow such a thing. Some Haitians became angry; others became numb.

One Haitian man said to me: "I really struggled with my faith after the earthquake. I could not understand why it happened. What helped me was seeing so many people on their knees praising God through it all. Even with God's allowance of the earthquake, the important thing is to still have faith." I am continually amazed at these people of deep faith, courage, and strength.

A story in Kent Annan's book, *After Shock*, describes the response of some children to the continuing aftershocks:

> The day after the nighttime aftershocks in the little tin-roof house, we visited another friend in town. Their house was damaged but nobody had died. And though they were sleeping outside, during the day they used the concrete house. (Reasoning: you'd be fast enough to get out in time when awake, but not while asleep.) We sat on the porch talking . . . and then some shaking started. Following their lead, I stepped quickly off the porch into the front yard as we kept talking.
>
> Meanwhile, as soon as the earth started shaking, neighbor kids who were playing out in the next yard began jumping up

and down cheering it. Fists pumping in the air. Whooping it up like their favorite team just scored a World Cup goal.

It was a dissonant scene in the midst of it all. It was defiant joy: a kind of "Mock the devil that he may flee from you." Or "You've stolen everything we have, including all our tears, but you can't get our laughter." Or just kids being kids. . . .

Those kids don't cower or pretend the shaking isn't happening. They know it's dangerous, but they're alive, and after each aftershock they let God and the tectonic plates know exactly how alive they still are.[4]

Woven Into the Fabric of Haiti

Jon's life and my life are forever woven into the fabric of Haiti. (I have even been called a "daughter of Haiti" by a Haitian man.) We started to discover this more and more as time went on. First, many people started asking us where they should send donations and about the best ways to help. In the U.S., Jon and I learned that we were viewed as authorities on how to send aid to Haiti, although we felt quite inadequate. We could tell people about the organizations and people we knew in Haiti who were doing good work and how funds would best reach them. Other than that, we had no special information to offer. We felt so helpless in the face of such devastation and loss ourselves.

We found that Haitians who were in the U.S. at the time of the earthquake saw us as a bridge for them back to their beloved country. Mysteriously, we became a link for those who had become disconnected.

For example, in May 2010, Jon and I flew to New Jersey to thank the twenty people who took us under their wing at the U.S. embassy in Haiti in the days following the earthquake. We happened to be at the Presbyterian Church of Lawrenceville on the Sunday they were celebrating their relationship with Haiti. The congregation supports a ministry called "Harmony Ministries" in Port-au-Prince, which Haitian pastor Luc Deratus helps to operate. He had come to speak. The congregation asked Jon and me to say a few words as well.

I do not remember a word we said, but I do remember a man who was standing in the hallway, on the periphery of the group. When we finished speaking, he came into the midst of the assembly, deeply moved and with tears in his eyes. He said, "I left Haiti twenty years ago and I thought I would never look back. I have made a life for myself here in the U.S. and

4. Annan, *After Shock*, 37–38.

have become very successful as an educator. When I found out about the earthquake, I was distressed and didn't know what to do. I haven't really done anything to help my country and my people. Now I hear you speak, and something has awakened in me. I know I need to help. For the first time since I left Haiti, I know I need to go back and do something. Thank you for being here and for caring about Haiti."

Jon and I were surprised, but similar things kept happening in different circles. We discussed this with Rev. Dr. Winston Persaud, a long-time professor at Wartburg Seminary who is originally from Guyana. He said, "You two are a bridge between the U.S. and Haiti, but especially for those who were not there during the earthquake. You are a symbol of hope for people and a connection to Haiti."

A Haitian man who lived in Duluth, Minnesota, had first connected with Ben's parents when they served as pastors at First Lutheran Church. He told Judd and April that his brother had been murdered a year and a half earlier in Haiti and he had not been able to cry. But when he heard our story and how Ben was killed in the earthquake, he said his heart cracked open and he finally began to cry. He finally mourned the death of his brother as well as the chaos in his beloved country. He said to them, "I feel responsible for your son's death because he died in my country."

It seems totally irrational, but there are many Haitians who blame themselves for Ben's death. How could this be? I tried to understand. It seemed to come down to the fact that we were guests in their country. Sometimes I, too, blamed myself for Ben's death. When Jon or Haitians blamed themselves, it seemed so obvious to me that they were not responsible. This helped me to stop blaming myself. I blame no one for Ben's death. That being said, I remain crabby with God about the whole thing.

In the fall of 2010, I attended an ELCA "Glocal" (global and local) Mission Event in Grand Forks, North Dakota. I discovered that a number of Haitian women were there, cooking a meal for the event in order to share their culture and raise awareness about the earthquake. My knees buckled. I did not expect to meet Haitians in North Dakota. I felt my body moving toward the kitchen. I was compelled to be near them. I walked into the kitchen and they all turned. I blurted out, "My husband died in the earthquake!" They all looked at me with such compassion and sadness. Then they proceeded to simply name the people in their families who also died. None of them had been in Haiti during the earthquake, but I was, and there we were together in Grand Forks, mourning the loss of our loved ones.

"Lespwa fè nou viv," the Haitians say: Hope makes us live. The Haitians give me hope all the time. If I could give hope in return to any Haitian, or any person, I would be filled with gratitude. I suppose that's the main reason I am writing this book.

To be honest, it is not clear to me what to "do" now for Haiti and its people. With its layers of history, outside involvement, inside corruption, a culture of dependency, poverty, numerous non-governmental organizations and charities, and multiple sources of authority in Haiti (i.e., the Haitian president, the United Nations, USAID, and so on), it is so hard to know what will actually break down systems of injustice, restore the society to health, and empower people to make a life for themselves. What I do know is that the leadership must come from within Haiti. We must listen: listen to the people of Haiti, listen to the Spirit, and listen to one another.

I have seen incredible examples of communities being created and sustained in Haiti through the constant presence of people who were there to empower Haitians. My Haitian friend Louis Dorvilier used his incredible gift for community organizing while working for the Lutheran World Federation in Haiti. He helped the community of Thiotte establish a coffee project and a reforestation project. There is also a community cheese-making business near Thiotte, as well as micro-loans to help people get on their feet and start businesses.

There are great things going on in Haiti, and relationships are being developed and deepened all the time. One of the most phenomenal accomplishments since the earthquake was the creation of a "Global Village," another project Louis led through the LWF. In August 2010, Louis traveled to Haiti to spend time with the Eglise Lutherienne d'Haiti. While he was there he had a dream in which he, his wife Mytch, Jon, Ben, and I were all playing soccer with a number of children. It was excruciatingly hot and windy. Louis became tired and decided to sit out of the game to catch his breath. As he was sitting on the sideline, he dreamed that Ben ran up to him and said, "Come on, Louis! It's time to keep playing."

"I know, Ben. I'm just resting," Louis replied.

Ben encouraged, "Don't worry, I will be with you. Come on!"

Louis called me from Haiti and told me about the dream. He said to me, "We must do something for the young people of Haiti. They are on the street with nowhere to go and nothing to do, especially when schools are not functioning after the earthquake. I have an idea."

Louis's vision was a village in which 200 families who had been living in tent cities after the earthquake would each have a solid home—designed to withstand hurricanes and earthquakes—and access to a community center. This community center would have after-school programs and opportunities for young people to discover their gifts. It would be a place to hold meetings and where doctors could provide medical care for the community.

It could even house worship. There would not be a school in the village, however. The children would be required to attend school a walking distance away in order to avoid creating a "gated" community. Everyone who lived in the village would still be connected to the larger community, actively engaging in and around the "global village."

Trying such a thing in Haiti seemed like an insurmountable challenge. The first miracle came when Louis convinced four mayors to agree on the jurisdiction of the area that would become the global village. The next miracle was when he persuaded the government to donate the land, even though land was becoming increasingly expensive in Haiti. The third miracle was when he talked the United Nations into constructing a road into and out of the village. The fourth miracle was LWF staff interviewing family after family among the hundreds of thousands in order to select 200 qualified families to have new homes in the community village. The fifth miracle is that it all actually happened—within about two years.

I always learn from the people of Haiti and their tenacious spirit. They embody hope and perseverance. They have changed me and will continue to change me for the rest of my days. They help me to see things differently and to trust God. They only ask me for a few things in return: to pray for them, to pray that God would change their situation, to remember Haiti, and to continue to be an advocate. These are things I can do.

Renee Dietrich wrote another poem in *Dèyè Mòn* titled "The Knowing." It sums up well how I hope the grace of God transforms us as our horizon meets with the horizon of Haiti and its people.

> Haiti isn't simply a feature on a map.
> It is not only a place with steady geographic boundaries.
> To profess knowledge of Haiti solely through history books and
> news clippings is a lie.
> A false sense of security that leads to misunderstandings and
> frustrations.
> Haiti is much more than a place.
> More than a time.
> Haiti is a way of being.
> A way of seeing the world and your place in it.
> A feeling.
> An attitude.
> A sense of profound joy in the face of adversity.
> Hope in a sea of hopelessness.
> To really know Haiti,
> To really understand all of her idiosyncrasies and nuances and
> subtleties of character,

One must leave all past knowledge at the door,
And enter with an open mind and an open heart.
Being ready to experience, appreciate and imprint the life breath
of the people on your soul.
Taking with you much more than memories,
Snapshots of people and places.
But going forth with a passion for life,
And justice,
And peace.[5]

5. Dietrich, *Dèyè Mòn*, 46.

21

Why So Many Died

In a conversation with Judd and April, the late Rev. Dr. Richard Jensen said, "The earthquake does not care whether anyone lives or dies, but God does."

Many people have tried to come up with explanations for the Haiti earthquake and attempted to justify why there were so many casualties on January 12, 2010, and in the months that followed. Sometimes I think people are trying to convince themselves that somehow they are exempt from such a fate. The most ridiculous explanation I encountered raised its ugly head a couple of months after the earthquake. I heard a knock at the door of my seminary apartment. I opened it to find two young men who said, "Hello, we are selling magazines." I told them I was not interested in buying any. They persisted, "Well, is your husband home?"

"No, he's not."

"Where is he?"

"He's not here."

Unbelievably, they kept pressing, and I should have simply closed the door. They asked again for my husband and I finally said, "He is not here because he died in the Haiti earthquake two months ago."

You would think this might have drawn some sympathy from them. Instead, one of them actually said, "Oh, I'm so sorry, but praise Jesus that he's with God because I know you were doing good mission work down there. And you know, it's a good thing that God caused that earthquake to happen because there's only so much oxygen to go around on the planet. Hundreds of thousands of people need to die every once in a while so the rest of us can survive."

This is the most extreme example I have encountered of such ignorance and arrogance. It puts other terrible reasons I have heard to shame. Reasons such as: "Haiti and its people are evil because they practice Vodou. That's why the earthquake happened! It was God's punishment."

In Luke 13, some people asked Jesus about a number of Galileans who had died a tragic death. Jesus said to them: "Do you think that because these Galileans suffered in this way they were worse sinners than all other Galileans? No, I tell you . . . Or those eighteen who were killed when the tower of Siloam fell on them—do you think that they were worse offenders than all the others living in Jerusalem? No, I tell you . . ."[1]

The complexities of Haiti and why so many people died would fill several books. In *Haiti: After the Earthquake*, Paul Farmer writes: "[T]he earthquake can be understood as an 'acute-on-chronic' event. It was devastating because a history of adverse social conditions and extreme ecological fragility primed Port-au-Prince for massive loss of life and destruction when the ground began shaking on January 12."[2] The actual number of casualties is unknown, but it is estimated that between 150,000 to 220,000 people died, and 1.5 million were displaced.[3] Much of the death toll and devastation has to do with Haiti's history and foreign involvement. I am no historical expert, but I am aware of the basics.

Occupants of Haiti

Back when Christopher Columbus first arrived on the island, there were native people there who helped him. He named the island Hispaniola, meaning "the Spanish island." The Spanish "introduced Christianity, forced labour in mines, murder, rape, bloodhounds, strange diseases, and artificial famine (by the destruction of cultivation to starve the rebellious). These and other requirements of the higher civilisation reduced the native population from an estimated half-a-million, perhaps a million, to 60,000 in 15 years."[4] In the end, *no native people survived.*

The island's non-native people did not choose to be there; their ancestors were enslaved. They were taken from their beloved homes in Africa and brought across the ocean in shackles on overcrowded boats to work in forced labor for the financial gain of individuals and European nations such as France, Spain, and England. These three nations fought over the fertile lands of Hispaniola. "French, British and Spaniards raided and counter-raided and burnt to the ground, but in 1695 the Treaty of Ryswick between

---

1. Luke 13:2–5a.
2. Farmer, et al., *Haiti After the Earthquake*, 3.
3. Muggah and Kolbe, "Haiti"; O'Connor, "Two Years Later."
4. James, *The Black Jacobins*, 4.

France and Spain gave the French a legal right to the western part of the island."[5]

The French's brutality toward the African people on the island was horrifying. Countless people died from conditions and treatment not meant for any creature, let alone human beings.[6] The slaves united, forming a common language (Creole), and miraculously overthrew their captors.

From Haiti's independence in 1804 as the first ever free black nation (less than thirty years after the U.S. gained its independence), it remained under an unjust, high-interest, crippling debt from France for more than 120 years.[7] "In 1825,[8] France finally agreed to recognize Haiti's independence, but she demanded 150 million francs[9] for the privilege (the money was earmarked to indemnify French planters who had lost their fortune in Saint Domingue)."[10] Basically, the French wanted to be paid for the plantations they had lost in the revolution, including the enslaved people whom they considered property.

Because of the outside influences of affluent nations and for-profit companies, as well as the internal corruption that has plagued Haiti's history, the nation has been unable to get ahead or become truly independent from foreign powers. When I visited the mountainous rural areas outside of Thiotte, the people there spoke about the devastation of deforestation.[11] Some Haitians used the trees for charcoal, but we were also told that certain American companies harvested the trees. They paid Haitians for the wood, which led to forests being cut down because people needed money. The loss of the forests meant that hurricanes and mudslides became more deadly.

Haiti has remained dependent on foreign aid. In the 1980s and 1990s, U.S. rice imports were so numerous and cheap that they put many rice farmers out of business. As a result, the native varieties of rice are scarce, the rice industry in Haiti has collapsed, and Haitians rely on the U.S. for a staple food that is not as nutritious as locally grown rice.

Not many people know that the U.S. occupied Haiti from 1915 to 1934. Some say it was to restore order as a result of a failed government, some say

---

5. Ibid., 5.

6. For detailed stories, read *The Black Jacobins* by C.L.R. James.

7. Haiti finally paid off its debt to France in 1947, but only by receiving more loans from other nations—and going further into debt.

8. The U.S. did not recognize Haiti's independence until 1862. See Farmer, *The Uses of Haiti*, 66.

9. Roughly half a billion U.S. dollars.

10. Girard, *Haiti*, 71.

11. Fortunately, when I visited the area in February 2011, a reforestation project through the Lutheran World Federation was becoming quite successful.

it was to secure U.S. corporate interests, others say it was so a European nation would not gain control of Haiti, and still others say it was to maintain political and economic stability. Whatever the reason, in my visits to Haiti, my impression has been that the majority of Haitians were unhappy about it. Who would want to be occupied in their own "free" country? Not only that, the occupation led to the government and its politics being influenced toward American interests. "For example, the Haitian army that today claims to have the country 'in its hands' and seeks to be reestablished was created not by Haitians but by an act of the U.S. Congress. . . . This state of affairs—military-backed governments, dictatorships, chronic instability, repression, the heavy hand of Washington over all—continued throughout the 20th century."[12]

One of the results of the occupation were American-influenced Haitian presidents (although I have heard many call them dictators), none more notorious than François Duvalier (later known as "Papa Doc"), who was in power from 1957 to his death in 1971. His son, Jean-Claude Duvalier ("Baby Doc"), was in power from 1971 until his flight from Haiti during the uprising in 1986. These leaders ruled ruthlessly and kept foreign aid to Haiti largely for themselves, resulting in little infrastructure, more debt than ever, and abject poverty for seventy-five percent of Haiti's population.

Why would the U.S. government back such injustices?

> A tyrant who would look out for U.S. interests was quite good enough to deserve Washington's support. . . . A new phase in the history of the Haitian economy had been initiated in the last years of François Duvalier's tenure, when offshore assembly for U.S. corporations and markets was touted by both nations as "aid" to Haiti. . . . The Duvaliers' Haiti offered enormous benefits for offshore assembly—generous tax holidays, a franchise granting tariff exemption, tame unions, a minimum wage that was but a tiny fraction of that in the United States. . . . Shortly before the fall of Jean-Claude Duvalier, Haiti was the world's ninth largest assembler of goods for the U.S. consumption—the world's largest producer of baseballs—and ranked among the top three in the assembly of such diverse products as stuffed toys, dolls and apparel.[13]

Cheap labor, subsidized imports that put rural farmers out of business, and a military-backed dictatorship created a recipe for disaster, especially in Port-au-Prince. Because Port-au-Prince was the center of the Duvaliers'

12. Farmer, *The Uses of Haiti*, 379–80.
13. Ibid., 94, 98–99.

power, most aid and goods flowed into and out of the capital city. In fact, Haitians told me that the Duvaliers closed down all other ports in the country to ensure this. People who lived in the countryside or on other coasts of the island now had to go to Port-au-Prince for food, work, and other necessities. Once in the city, they stayed. Port-au-Prince and its surrounding areas grew exponentially with no infrastructure to support the tremendous influx of people. Amy Wilentz, author of *The Rainy Season: Haiti Since Duvalier*, writes: "When I first went to Port-au-Prince in 1986, it was a sleepy little city of about 800,000 people ... But when I visited last year [2009] ... This city of almost 2 million now stretched out over the nearby farmland and farther."[14]

Little shacks sprung up everywhere made out of any material people could find to build their new homes. Because Haiti is visited by hurricanes, those who were able to do so built their homes out of concrete. However, there were no regulations and corruption was rampant, so corners were cut and unsound housing structures rose up practically on top of one another. There were too many people, living in too little space, living in poverty. When the 7.0 earthquake occurred in the heart of the most populous area in the country (around three million people), thousands died within forty-five seconds.

Poverty

I have witnessed with my own eyes that the first disaster of Haiti is poverty. It is not an exaggeration to say that people die every day of hunger-related causes in Haiti. People lack basic necessities such as shoes and clean water. Education is a luxury. Child slavery is alive and well. Preventable and treatable diseases kill people all the time. Following Haiti's history of slavery, occupation, and corruption, the systemic problem of poverty is not difficult to understand.

Poverty is one of the main reasons why so many people died on January 12, 2010. In this sense, Ben was a victim of poverty. Ben had always told me that he was not afraid to die, and I know how privileged he would feel to die alongside the Haitian people, having his life forever linked with theirs. This is solidarity in its purest form. We all suffer when there is poverty, whether directly or indirectly.

The horrible infrastructure of the crowded city made it impossible for a medical or emergency response to help those who could have lived. Because it took days for any medical personnel to arrive in Haiti, many people died from infections and injuries that should not have been fatal.

14. Elliott, et al., *Haiti: Tragedy and Hope*, 58–59.

Many doctors and nurses were killed in the earthquake, and some medical facilities collapsed. Even if injured people reached the hospitals, there was little or no help for them there. It was chaos.

Here is tragedy upon tragedy: those who survived the earthquake had to face the cholera epidemic months later. Cholera is a rampant terror; it is easily contracted, and without treatment, a person can be dead within twenty-four hours. Haitian graffiti artist Jerry Moïse Rosembert said: "Cholera, I guess it's worse than the earthquake, because it kills people day after day." Thousands died of cholera during the months following the earthquake. A terrible irony is that a likely source of the cholera outbreak was traced back to United Nations peacekeepers from Nepal, who had been sent to help.

Another sad reality is that after the earthquake, many people fled the area, but at the same time, another flood of people arrived in Port-au-Prince from the countryside. Many people in the country were starving, so they went to Port-au-Prince to the tent cities, where they knew there would be supplies of food. These are people who barely felt a rumble beneath their feet!

It will take much time, effort, money, and other resources for the area of Port-au-Prince to "recover." But, recover to what state? There is no quick fix, and it will take nothing less than generations of accompaniment, money, work, and prayer to rebuild Port-au-Prince and its surrounding cities, not to mention the regulation of for-profit foreign vested interests.

When Jon and I went back to Haiti for the first time after the earthquake in February 2011, it looked as though the earthquake might have happened the day before rather than more than a year earlier. If the bereaved Haitians felt anything like I did (which I am sure they did and worse!), then they had little energy to clean up, make decisions, rebuild, and so on. There was survival—and survival only. Those who were able or had money recovered the bodies of their loved ones. But so many were unable to give their deceased family members a proper burial, a situation with unique cultural implications in Haiti. Yet, there was no other choice but to dig mass graves, move bodies in dump trucks, and cover them with dirt. Many people did not even know where their loved ones were buried. It is hard to comprehend such loss and trauma.

When Jon and I visited St. Joseph's on our first trip back, we were told that the neighbor's home still had an uncle and a niece buried in between two floors (keep in mind this was thirteen months later!). Some family members had started digging, but they ran out of money and were forced to wait until they could afford to dig again. The uncle's head was exposed, and someone had covered it with a baseball hat.

I saw the hat and the black hair underneath. I felt horrible that there had been a team of people digging Ben out weeks after the earthquake when right next door were a man and a little girl who would continue to be buried well into the next year. The injustice of it all is unnerving. There was no closure for so many people.

Jon and I also learned that we, along with all the other survivors in St. Joseph's Home for Boys, owed our lives to a tree. As what remained of the home was torn down, bucket by bucket, it was discovered that a single standing oak tree was holding up the pancaked, leaning concrete building. Everyone understood that if the tree had given way during or after the earthquake, the whole house would have collapsed. Likely everyone in it would have died, including Jon and me. This means the crew that dug Ben's body out were taking an even greater risk than we realized.

Unfortunately, the tree had to be cut down in order to make the foundation for the new building secure. The St. Joseph Family held a special service thanking God for the tree, and they hired a local wood-carver to carve its trunk into a beautiful statue of St. Michael the Archangel, the protector. As the carver chipped away at the wood, Jon and I gathered up fragments of this "tree of life" to keep for ourselves and give to our family members.

Sharing

When Jon and I went back to Haiti, we discovered that some people had not talked about their experience of the earthquake at all.[15]

It seemed natural to me to ask the people I knew in Haiti about the earthquake and how they were doing with the threat of continued aftershocks, but they told me that they try not to think about it. Then someone said, "This is the first time we have talked about the earthquake." They started to tell us that people would often feel "phantom" aftershocks and panic. I understood this because I felt them, too, even in North Dakota. They also said there had been real aftershocks (continuing as much as a year later) and some kids had jumped out of school windows, thinking there was going to be another big earthquake. A number of children had broken their legs when they hit the ground.

Even two years later, some people still had not shared with one another what had happened to them in the earthquake. I traveled back to Haiti with Jon and a number of our family members for the two-year anniversary. Our final day there we were invited to participate in a sharing time at the

15. I have heard others say that when they went to Haiti they had the opposite experience—people wanted to talk about the earthquake all the time.

Lutheran World Federation office in Pétionville. We were there for hours as every staff member went around the circle and shared about the earthquake for the first time: where they were, what they were doing, what they had experienced, and whom they had lost. Our experiences were so similar.

One woman shared that she was working at a telephone corporation in downtown Port-au-Prince. She had an awful dream the night before, but did not quite know what was wrong. She went to work the morning of January 12 with a feeling of impending doom, so much so that she called all her family members from work to tell them that something bad was going to happen. Eventually she was sent home from work to rest, and when she stepped out of the building, the earthquake hit and the building collapsed behind her. She passed out and woke up some time later to death and chaos.

I will never forget the way one woman robotically shared the loss of her sister. I started to imagine if my sister, Jessie, had been with me and died. I cried for the woman and for each person who shared. Jon and I also shared, along with Ben's parents, my mother, Ben's sister Katie, and Ben's aunt, Janet. Everyone listened intently and felt our loss as well.

There was healing in the sharing. Jon and I had the opportunity to be removed from the threat of imminent death; the Haitians did not. They lived in constant fear of another earthquake. In their struggle to survive, they did not have time to share their emotions and process what had happened. With their loved ones still buried in rubble or in unknown mass graves, there was not much room for closure, processing, or healing.

Mass Grave

Jon and I knew we needed to visit one of the many mass graves for the sake of our grieving. In February 2011, Mytch and Louis Dorvilier took us to the one outside of Cité Soleil, near a tent city that had sprung up called "Clintonville." There were rumors that President Clinton was going to give everyone a house who owned land in that area, which had no water source and was exposed to the ocean in the event of a hurricane. Gangs (mostly started by Haitians who had moved to the U.S., become involved in the gang culture, and then were deported back to Haiti) gained control and "sold" pieces of land to people who were hoping to get a house from President Clinton. In reality, the government owns most of the land. Now thousands were living in the area who had "rightfully" paid for their piece of property—with no house yet from Clinton.

We passed Clintonville as we made our way to the mass grave in St. Christophe, just south of Titanyen. It was windy, hot, and dusty. We saw only four people: two white people who seemed to be filming something, and two young children who were orphaned by the earthquake. The two children walked to the mass grave every day, believing that was where their parents were buried. Jon spent some time with them.

When I first stepped out of Louis's vehicle, I could feel my heart pounding. The whole grave was marked with hundreds of small, wooden black crosses. *I could be in this grave*, I thought. *Ben could be in it . . . or Jon.* I slowly walked to the edge of the black crosses and fell to my knees at that holy and wretched place. I turned my face up to the sky and wailed, just as I had one year earlier on the shores of Lake Superior. I wept for all my brothers and sisters whom I saw dead in the streets the day we walked by them after the earthquake. I wept for Haiti's continued plight. I wept for all the unknowns and injustice. There was so much senseless and preventable death.

I looked up and saw the beautiful ocean in one direction, and then my eyes turned to the hill that overlooked the mass grave. A pathway led up the hill to a large white cross. This "pathway" was a long piece of purple cloth that lay on the ground, creating a sort of via dolorosa. The cloth had all kinds of writing (most of which I could not read) on it with memory tokens strewn on top and on all sides. Strips of ripped black cloth were tied around the white cross and blew in the wind. I sat at the foot of the cross trying to take in the reality of everything that had happened to me, to Ben, to Jon, and to the people of Haiti. I sat with my head in my hands and listened to the *flap, flap, flap* of the black cloth whipping in the wind.

A Future with Hope

Yes, it is true that Ben died as a result of poverty as well as tectonic forces, but I also think about his death in another way. I think about why Ben, Jon, and I went to Haiti: because we were invited, because we wanted to be better pastors, to follow God's call, to support a fledgling church, to accompany the Haitian people and grow as a result, and for the sake of relationship. I have to admit that we would make the decision again (not, of course, knowing there would be an earthquake).

I have spent time reflecting on what is worth dying for. Are relationships worth dying for? Yes. Is accompaniment with people living in poverty worth dying for? Yes. Is the message of the gospel and going where God calls me worth my death? Every time I answer, with trepidation: Yes.

On my good days, it gives me some peace to conclude that Ben also died because we were following where we felt the Spirit was leading us, to those people who would shape us and teach us and love us. Probably much to my family's dismay, I believe this discipleship is worth my life, and I will more than likely continue to go where God leads me, even at great risk. I do not like it, but call is call, and sometimes Christ bids us, "Come and die."

When Jon and I returned to Haiti in January 2012, the progress of cleanup and rebuilding was clear, and it made me happy to see. People were just shell-shocked for a while. For example, the second time Jon and I returned to Haiti we visited the same mass grave again, but this time there were hundreds and hundreds of people there. There was a memorial built as part of the grave, there was an orchestra playing music, and the president, Michel Martelly, gave a speech to mark the second anniversary. How different it was to hear orchestral music in that place rather than the flapping fabric of our desolate, desert, holy experience at the grave the year before.

I do not know what the future holds for Haiti, but I cling to God's promise for the Haitians and for us all in Jeremiah 29:11: "For surely I know the plans I have for you, says the LORD, plans for your welfare and not for harm, to give you a future with hope." Lord, have mercy. Christ, have mercy. Lord, have mercy.

22

Theology of the Cross

CENTRAL TO LUTHERANS' CHRISTIAN faith is the "theology of the cross," which is also a theology of resurrection. This theology is a lens through which we see the world, including events like the earthquake.

The theology of the cross means that when we experience things like suffering, pain, violence, and death, we understand that Christ is there in all of them, present and real. It means naming death as death—not minimizing it—yet also from the cross seeing through Christ's empty tomb into eternal life.

The theology of the cross takes suffering seriously as people struggle with unanswered questions and endure atrocities. Nicholas Wolterstorff writes of this struggle to understand suffering, the cross, and the way of God in the world through Jesus Christ:

> How is faith to endure, O God, when you allow all this scraping and tearing on us? You have allowed rivers of blood to flow, mountains of suffering to pile up, sobs to become humanity's song—all without lifting a finger that we could see. You have allowed bonds of love beyond number to be painfully snapped. If you have not abandoned us, explain yourself.
>
> We strain to hear. But instead of hearing an answer we catch sight of God himself scraped and torn. Through our tears we see the tears of God.
>
> A new and more disturbing question now arises: Why do you permit yourself to suffer, O God? If the death of the devout costs you dear (Psalm 116:15), why do you permit it?[1]

I have found that many people like the *idea* of the theology of the cross, but no one actually wants to live it, including me. It means picking up your cross to follow Christ to his death. People like Dietrich Bonheoffer,

---

1. Wolterstorff, *Lament*, 80.

Mother Teresa, Dorothy Day, and Martin Luther King, Jr., lived a theology of the cross.

Many of us find ourselves beneath the cross because of loss, tragedy, disease, or some other trauma. When I spoke with Dr. Schattauer in one of our pastoral care sessions, he said to me: "Only through the reality of the cross will you be able to have life, new life. One cannot go around it; one must go through it." The theologies of the cross and resurrection were the only ones that spoke to me in my grief.

Martin Luther rejected outright a "theology of glory," which says that if you are a good person and one of God's elect, God will bless you and no harm will befall you. He said, "A theology of glory [*theologia gloriae*] calls evil good and good evil. A theology of the cross [*theologia crucis*] calls the thing what is actually is."[2]

What does it mean to call a thing what it actually is? After the earthquake, Bishop Elizabeth Eaton said, "The correct theological term for this is . . . this sucks." Eaton said it well. A theology of glory attempts to call the earthquake and the suffering of its victims good (a punishment for those who practice Vodou, or a way to free up extra oxygen), whereas a theology of the cross confirms that it is anything but good. The suffering Christ is with those who suffer.

Some examples of a theology of glory in our world today, especially in popular U.S. religion, include: *Believe this and you will be rich; give money to this ministry and God will bless you; God wants you to have five cars and a mansion for a home.* Many people like and believe in this message. But where is the cross in this "gospel" of worldly power and prestige? Where is Christ in it?

At times I too want to live a theology of glory. I covet a God who will bless me with all the things I want and need. I want a God I can control. I don't want a God who suffers and dies, and asks me to do the same. I want a God who fixes things and comes to the rescue, a God who takes my suffering away instead of walking with me through it. But when I am rational, I know this kind of God is shallow and cannot go to the depths of grief and pain that we all experience. I am thankful for the suffering, dying, and rising God.

It is awful to be in the depths of despair, to be nailed to the cross with no way to come down. In my agonized grief following the earthquake and Ben's death, I would have clawed my way out of the miry clay if I could have; I would have saved myself and come down from the cross, but I could not. Living the theology of the cross was darkness and the ache of nothingness.

2. Hall, *The Cross in our Context*, 16.

It was silence. It was Christ crying out on the cross, "My God, my God, why have you forsaken me?"[3]

The theology of the cross taught me that God suffered with me. I found solace in knowing that the Creator of the universe could know my emptiness, because Christ knew emptiness. In that knowing, there was a strange companionship of Christ with me and me with Christ.

I experienced my first Ash Wednesday service about a month after the earthquake. As I received the ashes on my forehead in the sign of the cross, I discovered that for the first time I was okay with my own mortality. I was not thrilled with mortality in general, but I could accept the sign of the cross I first received in my baptism, a sign that represented both death and life.

The reality is that *no one* is exempt from suffering and death. Suffering has been universal among humans everywhere for all time, just as it was in Port-au-Prince on January 12, 2010. There is a quote attributed to St. Augustine: "God had one [child] on earth without sin, but never one without suffering." Why should Ben, Jon, or I have some sort of protective bubble around us when we travel to places like Haiti, or even when we take a walk around the block at home?

I live in a culture that wants to convince me that I do not have to suffer if I see the right doctors, or if I have the best insurance, or if I have enough money to fix whatever is wrong. Various cosmetic products and surgeries promise that I can even deny the aging process of my body and delay thinking about death altogether. The Haiti earthquake (not to mention other tragedies around the world) strips away all my comforts and assumptions. What I am left with is the cross of Christ, and I cling to it with all my strength, like Jon embracing the iron cross on the rooftop of St. Joseph's during the aftershocks.

The Suffering God

A theology of the cross is really a theology of suffering. How do I think about God and my life in relation to suffering? I would much rather contemplate joy or grace, but suffering was on my mind for a long time as I tried make sense of life and death, injury and healing. For one thing, nothing really seemed fair. When I was deep in the pit of my grief, I lamented and wondered with the Psalmist:

> Do you work wonders for the dead?
> Do the shades rise up to praise you?

---

3. Mark 15:34.

Is your steadfast love declared in the grave,
     or your faithfulness in Abaddon [the land of destruction]?
Are your wonders known in the darkness,
     or your saving help in the land of forgetfulness?[4]

There were times when all I could see was the cross . . . death. The empty tomb seemed unreal and far away. I thought of all the suffering I had seen, not only in Haiti after the earthquake, but also the injustice in poverty-stricken areas of Denver and the U.S./Mexico border during my years of volunteer work. I wrestled with God like Jacob in the night, and have wondered time and time again about Christ and his cross. As a Christian, I understand and even expect that I will continue to experience suffering because I follow Jesus. Yet, it is so difficult for me to reconcile the love of God for the world—which I feel and believe with all of my being—with the incredible misery I have seen and known.

What really helps me in my struggle is the concept of the "suffering God," which says that God suffers with and alongside those who suffer. The entire New Testament witnesses to this through the life, death, and resurrection of Jesus. Jesus did not avoid suffering, but faced it head-on for the sake of those he loved.

The most profound witness I know of to the suffering God is in the book *Night* by Elie Wiesel, which describes his experience in a World War II concentration camp. In this passage, the SS hang three prisoners, including a child:

> The SS seemed more preoccupied, more disturbed than usual. To hang a young boy in front of thousands of spectators was no light matter. The head of the camp read the verdict. All eyes were on the child. He was lividly pale, almost calm, biting his lips. The gallows threw its shadow over him. . . .
>
> The three victims mounted together onto the chairs.
>
> The three necks were placed at the same moment within the nooses.
>
> "Long live liberty!" cried the two adults.
>
> But the child was silent.
>
> "Where is God? Where is He?" someone behind me asked.
>
> At a sign from the head of the camp, the three chairs tipped over.
>
> Total silence throughout the camp. On the horizon, the sun was setting.
>
> "Bare your heads!" yelled the head of the camp. His voice was raucous. We were weeping.

4. Psalm 88:10–12.

"Cover your heads!"

Then the march past began. The two adults were no longer alive. Their tongues hung swollen, blue-tinged. But the third rope was still moving; being so light, the child was still alive. . . .

For more than half an hour he stayed there, struggling between life and death, dying in slow agony under our eyes. And we had to look him full in the face. He was still alive when I passed in front of him. His tongue was still red, his eyes were not yet glazed.

Behind me, I heard the same man asking:

"Where is God now?"

And I heard a voice within me answer him:

"Where is He? Here He is—He is hanging here on this gallows. . . ."[5]

The God of the cross is a God who suffers as Jesus, the Son of God, dies. Because of Christ, death is taken up into the very being of God. The theology of the cross taught me that God is with God's beloved ones in their suffering. I know this in Ben's dying song, as he sang to the Lamb of God who bears the sin of all the world away, the one who died for him. Even through other events that night and the days that followed, I could feel God's presence and love accompanying us. I knew my grief was also the grief of God. Do I believe that God could have saved people from the terrible earthquake, just as Christ could have come down from the cross? Yes. I wish all the time that there could have been another way, just as Jesus' disciples may have wished that Christ would have bypassed the cross.

Instead of preventing the earthquake, God empowered Ben to sing as he died. God gave strength to the woman in the middle of the field who sang all night. God guided Jon and me after the earthquake through the streets of Port-au-Prince and provided Ronald, the man who accompanied us to the U.S. embassy. God embraced us at the embassy through the staff and the people from New Jersey. God showed us mercy through those who dug Ben's body out and returned him to us. God gave us the promise of eternal life that will come to fruition only on the other side of death.

I do not understand the cross, but because it reveals God's action in the world through Christ, the cross gives me unceasing hope. And because of the cross I can know the mystery and the hope of the resurrection.

I have come to believe that Christ was in Haiti when the mountains shook with all their tumult, Christ with those who died, and Christ with those who lived. In Matthew 24:40–41, Jesus says: "Then two will be in the

---

5. Wiesel, *Night*, 60–61.

field; one will be taken and one will be left. Two women will be grinding meal together; one will be taken and one will be left."

Because of my earthquake experience, I interpret this text in a new way. Within seconds, Ben was taken and Jon and I were left. Some Haitians were taken and others left, people who were sitting at the same table together. It was a terrifying reality. So which one was Jesus with . . . the one taken or the one left? Was it better to be taken or better to be left? I do not know the answer to the latter question, but to the first one I answer: both. I have no doubt that Jesus was with Ben and the rest of those who died, and I know Christ was also with me, Jon, and the rest of those who lived. If Christ is Lord of both the dead and the living because of his death on the cross and resurrection to eternal life, then he was with those who were "taken" and with those who were "left."

The earthquake gave me a glimpse of what the "Day of the Lord" might be like when Christ returns. Matthew 24:29 says, "Immediately after the suffering of those days the sun will be darkened, and the moon will not give its light; the stars will fall from heaven, and the powers of heaven will be shaken." Even though this sounds like a fearful thing, I am not afraid of it. In fact, I welcome it with joy and anticipation because I know the one who comes has already died for me and all people and he will bring with him the fullness of the kingdom of God. Then, the vision of Revelation 22 will come to be, when the leaves from the tree of life will be for the healing of the nations.

I know that when Christ comes again, peace will finally reign and all things will be made new. Because of the cross and resurrection, I believe that God works in all things for good, creating life where there seems to be only death and nothingness.

I know that following Jesus will take me into the belly of suffering at times because Christ calls me to engage fully in the world. Dietrich Bonhoeffer wrote: "It is not the religious act that makes the Christian, but participation in the suffering of God in the life of the world."[6] As much as I do not want or like to suffer, I have come to understand God's profound presence with me in my darkest days. As much as I do not want or like to witness the suffering of others, I have come to recognize God's presence in the people and places that suffer.

Christians believe the source of all life came to earth as a human being, Jesus of Nazareth, and died rejected, abandoned, and humiliated. What a mystery it is that God would become human! God came into the world as a vulnerable newborn baby, subject to illness, disease, violence, and death

6. Bonhoeffer, *I Want to Live These Days With You*, 63.

just like every other human. The world was waiting for a mighty warrior who would crush God's enemies and fix all that was wrong in the world. Instead God sent the Son to teach, to love, to eat, to drink, to call, to heal, to embrace, to set right, to weep, to suffer, to die, and to rise.

On one level, God becoming human did not make any sense, and on another level it made all the sense in the world. God gave to us God's very self in order that we might grow to love and trust God. There is no greater gift and no greater love. The paradox of the cross is that it brought life. Through suffering and death comes redemption and new life.

I can say and believe all this with confidence now after years of healing after the earthquake. Yet the theology of the cross still causes me great discomfort, because if I am honest with myself, I still do not want to live it. Even though I know God is in the pit with those who suffer, I still do not want to be there! Yet I clearly recognize that death and resurrection are happening all the time all around me in a myriad of ways. When death penetrates my life once again, and I know it will, God will sustain me as God has faithfully done before.

23

Thoughts on Resurrection

TOGETHER WITH THE WHOLE Christian church I confess and believe in the resurrection of the *body* . . . whatever that means. I cling to the promise of Romans 6:5: "For if we have been united with [Jesus Christ] in a death like his, we will certainly be united with him in a resurrection like his." I understand that the new creation began when Jesus Christ was raised, the first fruits from the dead, and that somehow we are living in this new creation where heaven and earth overlap, where the living and the dead are one in Christ, and where God's promised future has already broken into this world, and continues to break in where we least expect it.

When Christ rose from the dead, resurrected and made new, some did not recognize him. Others recognized him only through what he said or in the breaking of bread. Those closest to him needed to know he was real, so Jesus ate food and let them touch his pierced hands and side.

Although the details of Christ's resurrection remain a mystery, that does not change the witness that Jesus' physical body was raised and eventually ascended into heaven. When the women whom the Spirit chose to be the first witnesses and preachers of the good news arrived at the tomb, the angels did not say to them, "Here is his body. But don't worry, he's in a better place now." Rather, they said, "Why do you look for the living among the dead? He is not here, but has risen."[1]

The most powerful writing I have ever come across regarding bodily resurrection was a poem by Carol L. Gloor inspired by Luke 24:36–42:

> He could not give up the flesh.
> In the moments before we leave forever
> we want to say what he did:
> *I have hands, feet, bones; touch me,*
> *and is there anything for breakfast?*

---

1. Luke 24:5.

We are tethered to tubes,
nails hammered hard,
spear in our side, soon
to pass through, but still
this is my body,

with the scar on my hand from the bike accident,
the lungs shredded with chemo,
the broken left foot never quite healed,
but still all I have ever known:
this is my body.

If I rise, let it be not
as a ghost, no metaphor
for new life; please something
like this body, some flesh,
something I can understand.[2]

In one of the resurrection stories, Jesus' disciples mistake him for a ghost. Then he says to them: "Look at my hands and my feet; see that it is I myself. Touch me and see; for a ghost does not have flesh and bones as you see that I have."[3] The disciples needed some flesh, some bones, some scars to recognize the one they knew, loved, and followed before his death on the cross.

The theology of the resurrection of the body is fundamental for me. One day I will see Ben's broken and battered body restored and alive. I believe this is Christ's promise of resurrection to Ben, to me, and to all people's tired, disabled, worn, or damaged bodies.

When Ben died, I raged at God and demanded to know, "Where is Ben?" The only available answer was that Ben was "with God." *That is nice, but what does it mean?* Part of me felt that Ben was so dead and so gone; yet, another part of me knew he was more alive than ever, more alive than I was. This is confusing. I believe in the resurrection and restoration of the body, and yet I know where Ben's body is . . . it is decomposing in Phelps Cemetery in Decorah, Iowa. Therefore, I am left with a mystery and somewhat of a problem.

I have struggled and wrestled with the concept of resurrection and its "timing." After Ben died, I received much affirmation (through Scripture and the witness of other people) that he was very much alive and well and in the presence of God, but I could not reconcile this with the way I thought

2. Gloor, "Luke 24:36–42," 30.
3. Luke 24:38–39.

about the resurrection of the body. I also understood Jesus to be very present when Ben died, especially as he sang. After I received the vision and
letter from Philip Moeller, I imagined the real possibility of Ben joining in
the choir of angels and saints the moment he breathed his last. But in what
form or consciousness?

Once in the months following the earthquake, Ben's family was gathered in his sister Katie's kitchen and talking about "where" we thought Ben
was and what he was up to. April said, "Even if Ben was fully living in the
resurrection, I think he would be sad because Renee is not there with him."

Katie confidently replied, "No, Mom. Ben is not sad because Renee is
already there with him. We all are!" Strangely enough, I had been thinking
about this. The concept of time is mysterious: there are multiple dimensions
of time, it bends, and it is not as linear as we assume. However, I found this
train of thought disappointing. In fact, it made me miserable because I actually felt as if Ben was even further away. I was still facing the rest of my life
"in time." It seemed that there was a party going on called eternal life and I
was not invited yet.

One thing I knew for sure was that those who had died were no longer
subject to time like those of us still living. How could I possibly wrap my
mind around what it is like for someone to be outside of time, as God is? The
confusing, unanswerable nature of this question has not stopped me from
thinking about it.

Because of Romans 6, I know I have already died and risen with Christ
in my baptism, but there is always the question of heaven and the final resurrection. There are a few different examples in Scripture pertaining to the
"when" of resurrection from the dead. For example, when two criminals
were being crucified with Jesus and one said to him, "Jesus, remember me
when you come into your kingdom," Jesus replied, "Truly I tell you, today
you will be with me in Paradise."[4] Jesus said "today," not "don't worry . . .
you'll wait in the ground for a while and then you'll be with me in Paradise."
This has always been comforting, yet mysterious. How can this work? Does
it have to do with consciousness or something different? How do we think
about paradise or heaven in relationship to our confession of the resurrection of the body? I do not fully know.

A couple of examples that support some kind of waiting come from
Paul in 1 Corinthians 15:51–52 and 1 Thessalonians 4:13–14, 16:

> Listen, I will tell you a mystery! We will not all die, but we will all
> be changed, in a moment, in the twinkling of an eye, at the last

---

4. Luke 23:42–43.

trumpet. For the trumpet will sound, and the dead will be raised imperishable, and we will be changed.

But we do not want you to be uninformed, brothers and sisters, about those who have died, so that you may not grieve as others do who have no hope. For since we believe that Jesus died and rose again, even so, through Jesus, God will bring with him those who have died. . . . For the Lord himself, with a cry of command, with the archangel's call and with the sound of God's trumpet, will descend from heaven, and the dead in Christ will rise first.

These Scripture passages seem to indicate that there is a time of waiting and then everyone will be raised together. Yet, it also sounds like the dead are with Christ while they wait. Although this is hard to understand, it is also very hopeful.

I found passages like Luke 20:37–38 helpful. Jesus said to some sneaky Sadducees: "And the fact that the dead are raised Moses himself showed, in the story about the bush, where he speaks of the Lord as the God of Abraham, the God of Isaac, and the God of Jacob. Now he is God not of the dead, but of the living; for to him all of them are alive." This Scripture begs the question: As long as the dead are in and with Christ, then does it really matter whether or not we "wait," or even where we wait?[5] When I entrust Ben to God, the details cease to matter as much.

However, the Sadducees didn't stop there. Not believing in the resurrection and trying to trick Jesus, the Sadducees asked Jesus whose wife a woman would be in the resurrection if she had married seven brothers, each after the other had died, and no children were born to any of them. Jesus responded: "You are wrong, because you know neither the scriptures nor the power of God. For in the resurrection they neither marry nor are given in marriage, but are like angels in heaven."[6]

This bothered me a lot. I was no longer Ben's wife in this world, and evidently I would not be his wife in the next. Death had completely severed our marriage, and it would never be restored. I wanted to have that unique relationship with Ben in the resurrection. Jesus' words made me feel that I would be no more special to Ben in the resurrection than the next person, and that hurt.

It took me a long time to become comfortable with the idea that I was no longer Ben's wife, either now, in heaven, or in the resurrection. What

5. If our deceased loved ones are "with Christ," then it is not wrong to say they are "in heaven," for that is where the crucified and resurrected Jesus ascended.

6. Matthew 22:29–30.

finally helped me was thinking about our primary relationship to one another as brother and sister in Christ. Because of Christ—and only because of Christ—Ben and I are still intimately connected. Yes, we are no longer married, but we still have our love for one another and our relationship in Christ that remains real in the mystery of the communion of saints. I was working all this out in one of my pastoral care sessions with Dr. Priebe when he said, "Your relationship to Ben in the resurrection will be no less than marriage." I desperately needed to hear these words.

The relationship that was our marriage was not ultimate, either in this life or the next. The primary and ultimate relationship here on this earth and beyond the grave has always been our relationship to one another as brother and sister in Christ. This is the only relationship that endures beyond death, and it is the relationship that blesses us most. Once I let this sink in, I finally had peace.

Life After Life After Death

N.T. Wright's concept of "life after life after death" is helpful. When Ben and I were on internship in Lincoln, Nebraska, we studied Wright's book *Surprised by Hope* every Saturday morning in the spring with a group of college students from the Lutheran Center. We also went through the book with the adult Bible study class at Ben's internship church. As we prepared for each study session, Ben would be in our living room reading the book and burst out, "Ha! Yes! My whole life I have been thinking this and finally someone has put language to what I have always known to be true."

Much of what Wright wrote challenged people's existing beliefs about death and resurrection, but it should not have, because the church has been confessing the resurrection of Christ and the resurrection of the dead since the women first went to the tomb and found it empty. Yet this concept often comes as a shock to modern Christians because they grew up believing that when someone dies their soul separates from their body and goes to heaven, where it will stay for all eternity. Ben and I showed them that this belief is not scriptural and is not what the church confesses. It makes heaven the ultimate goal, instead of God's resurrection of the dead (body) and restoration (or re-creation) of all things, including heaven and earth.

Making "going to heaven" the ultimate goal of life also carries the danger of not caring about creation and the kingdom of God that is present in this world. When our college students and adult Bible study participants stopped and thought about what they were confessing in "the resurrection of the body," it rocked their worlds. It raised many new questions and challenged their perception of God's redemptive plan for all things. Everyone began to think about death and resurrection in a totally new way. Never had I seen such transformation and excitement for the resurrection and what God is doing in this world through all of us.

Wright presents this view based on his deep study of Scripture. He shows that our ultimate hope is not "heaven"; it is the new creation, which has already begun with Christ being raised, and will culminate in the resurrection of the dead to eternal life. He describes heaven, or paradise, or whatever people want to call it, as a temporary "tent" of waiting for those who have died. Heaven is life after death. (It is not the same as purgatory, a doctrine which Wright believes has no evidence in Scripture.) Heaven is where God resides and the seat of God's power. It is where Christ ascended, and he will descend from heaven when it is time for judgment and what Wright calls "life after life after death"—the resurrection of the dead. Wright points to Revelation 21:1–5:

> Then I saw a new heaven and a new earth; for the first heaven and the first earth had passed away, and the sea was no more. And I saw the holy city, the new Jerusalem, coming down out of heaven from God, prepared as a bride adorned for her husband. And I heard a loud voice from the throne saying, "See, the home of God is among mortals. He will dwell with them as their God; they will be his peoples, and God himself will be with them; he will wipe every tear from their eyes. Death will be no more; mourning and crying and pain will be no more, for the first things have passed away." And the one who was seated on the throne said, "See, I am making all things new."

This is one of my favorite Scripture passages. It speaks of God descending once again, much like Christ in the incarnation, in order to dwell with God's creation. It describes the overlap and joining of heaven and earth, as if heaven is right around the corner in our everyday lives. I believe there are times when heaven breaks into this world, probably more often than we can ever know. These are times I hope and look for; the ways God is already making all things new. What does resurrection look and feel like in this life? I can't always put my finger on it, but I know it's real.

A Visit from a Messenger from God

The second time I went back to Haiti after the earthquake was in January 2012 over the second anniversary. Ben's parents, one of Ben's sisters, one aunt, and my mother joined Jon and me for the trip. On one of the days we all went to the heart of Port-au-Prince near the capitol building, which still looked like the earthquake happened the day before. Every time we drove by a collapsed building the pit in my stomach expanded and I felt a wave of nausea. We parked near one of the tent cities across from the capitol building. Standing there looking at the capitol, I recognized the all-too-familiar feeling of dread and vulnerability—in addition to the chaos that can be a Haitian street! People, animals, tap taps, and other vehicles filled the roads. People were trying to sell us things, or patting their tummies to indicate hunger while the other hand strained forward in hopes of being filled with a few gourdes (Haitian currency).

Our purpose downtown was to visit the ruins of the Episcopal and Roman Catholic cathedrals that had collapsed in the earthquake, killing many who were inside. My spirit was very heavy as I wondered about God's presence in the whole mess. We dodged cars and people and did our best to walk on what was left of the sidewalk. I could feel my mother's anxiety, too. After spending her whole life in North Dakota, the hectic scene was not something she was used to. I grabbed her hand to try and help her feel more comfortable.

As we were stepping around people, a young Haitian man began to walk beside me. I assumed he was simply traveling in our direction, but then he turned his body slightly toward me and slowly said, "I . . . love you." Surprised, I thought, *Great. Here I am wondering if this building is going to fall on us if there is another earthquake, trying to care for my mother, and visiting places where lots of people died, and this guy is hitting on me!* I gave him the best smile I could muster and said, "Thank you." I tried to speed up a bit.

He kept up. He said more confidently in perfect English, "My heart burns with love for you." *Whoa. This is not normal.* I slowed my pace.

He kept walking with me until we entered the courtyard of the ruined Episcopal church, where we stopped. He turned toward me and said compassionately, "You know that we will be together again with all of those who have died, right?" Shocked, I looked at him and wanted to say, *My husband died here*, but all I could manage to squeak out was, "Yes . . . thank you."

He threw his arms open, wide to the sky, with a huge smile on his face and said joyfully, "Isn't it wonderful that we will all be together again in eternal life!" He took my hand and kissed it, then took my mother's hand and kissed hers, turned, and walked away.

I watched him until I could see him no longer. I wanted to run after him, to ask him to tell me more, to hug him and weep. My feet would not move, nor would my lips. God had visited me in the form of a young Haitian man on the street, with a tattered red T-shirt and black shorts, worn shoes, a rusty gold hoop earring in his torn left earlobe, and a scar on his right cheek.

I stood in shock, trying to absorb that a perfect stranger (or angel!) would come up to me in a foreign land and speak the good news of the resurrection to me in my own language.

I could hardly have been more vulnerable and terrified at that moment, or more in need of hearing the promises of God. There in the collapsed ruin of the house of worship, which had become a tomb for so many in the earthquake, the last thing I expected was a proclamation of life from a stranger. God sent that messenger, and it is one of the greatest gifts of grace and love God has ever given me.

The message did not change the fact that Ben died in the earthquake, nor all of the others who died right where I was standing, but renewed my confidence in the promise of the resurrection of the dead and that one day, in the words of Julian of Norwich, "All will be well."

I stood in shocked silence for quite some time while all the others listened to the story of the Episcopal church. Some of the walls were still standing, and a large tent was placed in the middle of the ruins where people could worship. The church had held incredible art pieces, many of which were damaged or ruined in the earthquake. As everyone was looking in the art shop, I approached Louis Dorvilier (who was guiding our group) and told him what had happened. I said, "And I didn't even say anything to him! I am a pastor and all I could do was nod and say, 'Yes' and 'Thank you.'"

"You said exactly what you should have said," Louis comforted me. "Yes and thank you. God sent you a messenger and he said what he needed to say and left."

Our group came out of the gift shop and we stepped out of the courtyard and onto the street again. I looked around for the man in the red T-shirt, but he was nowhere to be seen. We continued on to the Cathedral of Our Lady of the Assumption where the Archbishop of Port-au-Prince, Joseph Serge Miot, and the vicar general, Charles Benoit, were killed. I felt my heart sink again. We approached the huge pillars that once held up the massive ceiling of the cathedral. People were scattered here and there near the ruins. There was a man holding a little girl, trying to convince some of us to give him money. Someone said to us, "It's not even his daughter. He's just using her so you will give him money." These are the meager options people have in Haiti. This man's dignity was reduced to almost any means simply to eat and survive day to day.

As I entered the ruins of the cathedral, I stared at the altar, which was still standing. I drew near it and pictured the mass being celebrated by thousands over the years. Christ's table, the table where all were fed, stood empty and alone. As a pastor, I thought, *What if these were my people? What would I say to them? Where are you, God? Where are you in all of this?!* I have never heard an audible voice from God, but in this moment I "heard" again the voice of the messenger: "I love you. My heart burns with love for you." I wept near the altar for all who had died and trusted in God for protection, yet my heart warmed with the love God has for me, for all who survived, and for all who died.

That night I was in charge of devotions for our group, and at the end of our singing and prayer, I shared with everyone my encounter with the man and what he said to me. Everyone said that they had seen us talking. Judd said, "I thought it was someone you knew. You both looked like you knew each other."

"Surely, God visited you," everyone agreed, and gave thanks to God for such a gift. We spoke together about the words of the young man, and we knew and felt them to be true because of Scripture's witness to the resurrection of Jesus and our promised future.

Months later my mom and I were out on a walk together and were discussing the incident. She said, "Renee, was the man whispering? Why couldn't I understand him? You know way more Creole than you give yourself credit for."

"What do you mean? No, he wasn't whispering, and I really don't understand Creole. He spoke clearly in English as I am speaking to you right now."

"No, Renee," my mom insisted, "he was speaking in Creole. I heard Creole."

"What?" I asked, confused. "Mom, he was speaking perfect English."

"I have been trying so hard to think about what he said, but all I heard was Creole. I know he kissed my hand, and we were all so close together. How is it that I was right by you and couldn't understand what he was saying to you?"

"I don't know, Mom. I don't understand it either. All I know is what he proclaimed to me." We walked in silence for a while, both perplexed.

Glimpses of the Resurrection

I have felt the power of resurrection in my own life since the earthquake. The clearest sign is that I once felt dead and now I feel alive. This is only possible through the mercy and grace of God, who is "making all things new." The Holy Spirit helps me understand that the new creation is present in this world and that I am privileged to be a part of it, even after such loss and devastation. I want to live. I want to live for a long time and give this world all I have.

Resurrection tastes like oatmeal and coffee. Seriously. There were many mornings when I would not have risen from bed if it were not for my favorite food and drink.

Worship and music are agents of resurrection for me. They serve as an icon, a window into and an experience of heaven. At Ben's funeral, the Luther College Nordic Choir sang a version of "How Can I Keep From Singing." As we buried Ben, how could we keep from singing?

> No storm can shake my inmost calm since to that rock I'm clinging.
> Since Christ is Lord of heaven and earth, how can I keep from singing?

In a conversation after the earthquake with Rev. Dr. Craig Nessan, he said to me, "Sometimes resurrection is just getting up every morning. Laughter is also a sign of resurrection in the midst of such sadness."

When many of us were planning Ben's funeral, we were all crying as we tried to put something meaningful together. In the middle of it my mom's phone rang. It was on the loudest possible setting, and her ring tone started blaring "I like big butts and I cannot lie . . ." We all erupted in laughter as tears of sadness remained on our cheeks. My mother was mortified and tried hard to shut the ringer off. I looked suspiciously at my sister, who had a sly grin on her face. I said, "Did you set Mom's ring tone to that song?" She nodded her head in pleasure, as if it could not have worked out any better in her wildest dreams.

Laughter itself is not the resurrection of the dead. Obviously, we are not quite there yet. But in these signs or gifts from God—laughter, food, coffee, worship, and music—God holds us and communicates to us that death does not have the final say.

Resurrection for me is also labor in the Lord. In 1 Corinthians 15:58, Paul writes: "Therefore, my beloved, be steadfast, immovable, always excelling in the work of the Lord, because you know that in the Lord your labor is not in vain." God, had I labored! I have labored with grief in order to live. A friend once told me, "Renee, your labor in the Lord right now is grieving." It was important for me to know that all the hard work of grief and fighting for life would not be in vain, that there was purpose and meaning in it. By living I participate in the work of the kingdom, the work of heaven and the new creation, and it is not in vain. I receive glimpses of the resurrection. And somewhere within the great cloud of witnesses, Ben is cheering me on.

Even in this life, our bodies are being renewed all the time. We "lose fifty to a hundred and fifty strands of hair a day . . . [and] ten billion flakes of skin a day, every twenty-eight days" our bodies regenerate "completely new skin, and every nine years" our bodies are entirely "renewed!"[7] Yet who we are stays remarkably *the same*. Something inside of us remembers who we are even with such drastic changes. Surely this is a glimpse of the resurrection of the body.

It is no small thing that Ben died where the Resurrection Dance Theater of Haiti performed, a place where dances of storytelling and new life now continue in the newly built home. Ben loved the Resurrection Dance Theater. He had a permanent smile as he watched the dancers and drummers share the history and culture of Haiti. His death in that space reminds me that because of Christ, the cross is not without the resurrection and the resurrection is not without the cross.

Do we know with certainty what happens in and after death? No. But because of Christ's resurrection, I am okay with not knowing. I believe the promise that our dead are "in" Christ, and I believe that Christ lives. I am not called to know; I am called to trust and look forward to the day when the resurrection of the dead will come to pass in all its fullness. The resurrection is not a puzzle to be unlocked or figured out, but a promise that moves me and gives me hope.

The resurrection of Jesus does not make the horror of the cross less evil or less awful. So, too, the resurrection of the dead does not make the Haiti earthquake less evil or less horrific. Yet, in the mystery of faith, there is hope in and through death. God, "who gives life to the dead and calls into existence the things that do not exist,"[8] is making all things new.

---

7. Bell, *What We Talk About*, 50.
8. Romans 4:17c.

PART VI

Call and Marriage

Incarnation
Corrine Denis

dwelling in wilderness
fearing in the dark and the doubt
numb, unable to move
Eternal Presence steps into the chasm
standing and beckoning from the periphery is not good enough.
No, Love Incarnate comes close,
sits down next to you,
so close your bodies are almost one,
waits with unwavering patience.
and when it is time—no sooner—
clasps your hand,
intertwining fingers
completely hemming you in
and leads you out.

24

Ordination and Call

THE ELCA "DRAFT" HAPPENED in February 2010, one week after Jon and I returned to seminary after burying Ben. This is the assignment process the ELCA uses to place new pastors, first in regions (via the "draft"), then in specific churches. Congregations within the assigned region interview the prospective pastors. When a congregation votes to "call" a seminarian as their pastor, he or she is ordained and begins their "first call."

The regional draft is a Spirit-filled, exciting event when each senior seminarian receives a regional assignment and then a phone call from the bishop of their new synod. All of my classmates were looking forward to that call; Jon, Ben, and I had been waiting for that day since beginning seminary.

Because of the earthquake, Ben would never receive a phone call from a bishop welcoming him to a synod. And because of the earthquake, Jon and I did not go through the standard process of assignment and call like every other seminarian our senior year.

Instead, Jon and I were put on "administrative assignment." Basically this meant we were placed under the care of our home bishop and synods of candidacy: I with the Western North Dakota Synod, and Jon with the Southeast Minnesota Synod. Throughout the spring of 2010, my bishop, Mark Narum, met with me a number of times and gave me pastoral care. Now and then he would mention the possibility of a congregation and an interview. In late April 2010, he asked me if I would consider a half-time call with Heart River Lutheran Church, a congregation that provided worship services for the youth on the campus of the North Dakota Youth Correctional Center in Mandan, North Dakota.

I received the paperwork for Heart River Lutheran Church in early May and fell in love with the congregation immediately. They were a mission start congregation in the early 1980s, and had been worshipping on the campus of the North Dakota Youth Correctional Center (the only juvenile detention facility in the state) every Sunday for the last thirty years with the youth who were court-ordered to spend time in corrections. The membership of Heart River consisted of a diverse group of people from the Bismarck and Mandan area. They were "salt of the earth" and "hands in the dirt" people: social workers, ranchers, organic wheat farmers, professors, teachers, conservationists, geologists, advocates, and plenty of gardeners. They brought their children to worship, gave them communion as soon as they reached for it with longing hands (and could adequately digest it!), and were unconcerned about their children worshipping with "incarcerated" teenagers.

This ministry was made possible because of an original invitation from the correctional facility director in 1982. In the middle of the campus was a free-standing, beautiful chapel called "Hope Chapel." It was built in 1964 for the spiritual care of the youth who were housed on campus. The director wondered what it would be like to have a "traditional" worshipping community who would be willing to worship with the youth on campus every Sunday, and invited the people who eventually became Heart River Lutheran Church to be that community. They enthusiastically said, "Yes!"

Heart River members began to worship every Sunday with the young people in Hope Chapel, where they were able to embody God's grace and love to teens who were really struggling. The congregation encouraged the youth to be leaders within worship, creating a mutual ministry environment. The youth served as readers, ushers, communion servers, and occasionally the musicians for worship. Their attendance and participation were strictly voluntary.

These young people, who had barely stepped foot in a church on the "outside," were now leading worship in Hope Chapel and were integrated into the life of the community of faith that was Heart River Lutheran Church. Some of the youth heard the Word for the first time, were invited to share in Christ's presence at the communion table, and experienced a church setting without judgment.

As I reviewed Heart River's paperwork, I saw that they did not own the chapel on campus and had no alternative place of worship. This community lived by grace and invitation, guests in their own house of worship. On average, forty-five young people from the correctional facility attended worship each Sunday, making up half of the faith community. I had never heard of a church quite like this one, a group of Christ-followers whom I could only hope to pastor.

I had my initial phone conversation with the call chair in early May, and before I hung up the phone, I knew I would accept the call if it was offered it to me. I interviewed formally with the call committee on Sunday, June 6, 2010. My sister, Jessie, accompanied me to worship at the chapel. I dressed in my best suit, the one I wore at Ben's funeral.

I had never visited the correctional facility, so I did not know what to expect. As worship began, a number of teens—both boys and girls—filed into the chapel in their uniform clothing. *This could be my congregation*, I thought as the first hymn began.

Following worship and a tour of the correctional facility, my call interview started. One of the questions from the committee was, "Where do you see yourself ten years from now?"

I replied honestly: "I used to be a person who planned out much of my life. I had a good idea of what I wanted to be doing two, five, and ten years from now. The earthquake changed all that. I am grateful for today, and if I am alive in ten years, I hope I am where God calls me to be."

Our conversation continued, and it was evident that Heart River Lutheran Church had a clear mission with endless opportunity for outreach. The call committee wanted their new pastor to explore ways the congregation could better support the young people who were released from corrections. They explained: "Too many of the youth come back to campus because they are not making it on the outside."

It was this request that truly grabbed my attention. Even though worship was the heart of what Heart River did as a congregation, the people wanted to dig in and do the hard work of engaging the wider community to wrap support around the youth who were in the juvenile justice system in North Dakota. They did not know what this would look like or what was possible, and they wanted their new pastor to lead them in this effort.

After two hours of conversation, the committee asked if I had any questions for them. I said, "Yes, I do," and pulled out two pages of questions! I had plenty of trepidation because they, too, would be pulled into my reality of grief and loss, no matter how hard I might try to protect them. I was very honest about what had happened in my life and my need to continue to be able to grieve, travel to Haiti, possibly write in the future, and so on. I wanted to be sure God was initiating this call—from both sides.

Within three days of the interview, the call committee chair called me and said, "We want you to know our recommendation to call you has already been approved by the church council and we will move it to a vote for the congregation in three weeks. We hope you will consider coming to be our pastor if the congregation officially calls you."

I was excited, yet apprehensive. Jessie and I were already making our way through Montana on our summer road trip, and I knew I needed to engage in some serious conversation with the Spirit of God. I felt called to Heart River, but I was still so very tired and deep in grief. The people of Heart River were ministering and being ministered to by young people who had endured such suffering in their young lives. True, the youth had hurt others and themselves to be in such a place, but most of them had been victims, too—victims of physical or sexual abuse, neglect, and other forms of atrocities on their minds, bodies, and souls.

The gospel in Hope Chapel and its people was so tangible and real I could reach out and touch it and let it pulse through my veins. Death was real there, and so was resurrection. I sensed it the minute I walked into the sanctuary and saw those who gathered in that place. I needed real. I needed purpose. I needed new life. These are things all of us need, and I wanted to be in a place where the gospel really mattered and spoke to all who gathered to be fed, renewed, challenged, and invited to engage more deeply in a life of faith and community. *Could God bring me back to life through this incredible congregation of people and the mission they shared together? Could I lead them well?*

Apparently in the congregational meeting before the vote, one member said, "She's going to make us do stuff, isn't she?" Then they unanimously called me. They had been fostering a three-decade relationship with the correctional facility, carefully respecting all separation of church and state boundaries, and now they were ready to take the next step and try something new to care for the youth who were released from the North Dakota Youth Correctional Center.

My official letter of call came in the mail in early July. It took me two weeks to bring myself to open it. I read it for the first time with Judd and April at their family-owned walnut tree farm in northeast Iowa. The grasses and weeds were taller than my head. It was sweltering and humid. I was scared, but I knew God was calling me to pastor the people of Heart River Lutheran Church. They cared so deeply about the teenagers who had been caught up in systemic suffering. They were my people and I knew it. I felt fire grow in my belly: fire for justice, for the gospel, and for tough work with people who lived on the fringes of society. The fire reminded me that I was not dead and I had a life to live and gifts to share.

I accepted the call to shepherd the people of Heart River Lutheran Church, Mandan, North Dakota, and set my ordination date for August 2, 2010.

Ordination

In July I received a letter from my good friend Katie, whom I had met as a fellow volunteer at Girls Inc. in Denver. Besides her incredible leadership and organizational skills, dreams are one of Katie's spiritual gifts. When Katie's letter said she had a dream to share with me, I paid attention.

There was a large group of people at a church. You and I were there, but I couldn't see anyone else's face. You were surrounded by tons of people who were hugging you. They were gathered in a circle around you. You had your eyes closed, and somehow you were taller than they were and they could all reach you (around you). It was another peaceful moment. I remember hearing Rebekah's name, but then I heard the name "Ruth" over and over. People kept saying it. When I woke up I had this strong inclination to read the book of Ruth in the Bible. I ignored it at first, but it became so strong. I have never read this book. I didn't even know where to find it. Then I read that it is the story of two women who lose their husbands. The intro in my Bible says it is a story about love that thrived in suffering . . . I hope you feel peace, piece by piece—and I pray for the day you will feel the peace in my dreams.

Katie's dream gave me new confidence that God was calling me be ordained to the office of Word and Sacrament even though Ben was dead. I still had a ministry, and God would use me even in my brokenness.

I was captivated by Katie's mention of the book of Ruth, which I have always treasured. Ben and I even had a reading from the first chapter of Ruth at our wedding. When Ben died, I felt like Ruth. I could not leave Ben's family, and I felt drawn to his mother, April, who had lost the son she bore into the world.

April's support was essential as I prepared to be ordained. I will never forget the compassion and faith in her voice when she looked me in the eyes and said, "Renee, whatever you are lacking, God will give to you on the day of your ordination." There was power in her words, and they gave me the courage I needed to step forth with confidence to say my vows to God and to the church.

August 2 came, and I spent time that morning in the sanctuary of the church I grew up in, St. Paul Lutheran Church in Garrison, North Dakota, where I would be ordained. Ben and I were married in the very spot. I was facing another first without Ben, but I knew I would be surrounded by family and friends, just as in Katie's dream.

That evening I was ordained. My parents, as well as Judd and April, read Scripture and placed my stole on me. Bishop Narum presided and Rev. Dr. Priebe from Wartburg Seminary preached. A number of my seminary classmates were there, along with people from St. Paul's and around the Western North Dakota Synod. I felt supported and at peace with this new step in my life, as hard as it was.

I rejoiced when I read the card April wrote to me that night and felt the strength of all the women of faith who had gone before me. She wrote:

Dearest Renee, beloved Pastor Splichal Larson,

Proclaimer to the proclaimers,
Priest to the priests,
Christ bearer to the Christ bearers.
You *are* and *have been* and *will be* a blessing to so many!
Your mothers raise their hands and bless you . . .
Apostle, Mary Magdalene
Evangelist #1 from Samaria
The great confessor, Martha
Prophets of the great reversal, Mary and Hannah
Women of courage and vision, Esther, Ruth, Deborah
Prophet, musician, liberator, Miriam
Women of justice:
    Syrophoenician woman,
    Shiphrah and Puah,
    Daughters of Zelophehad
Models of Christ:
    The widow who gave up everything,
    And the unnamed priest, pastor to Jesus
Mothers in the faith, Sarah and Hagar
Missionary Priscilla
  To you dearest Renee, priest, pastor, daughter, your mothers in the faith bless you and give thanks to God for your call as priest, leader, mother in faith, shepherd to God's people.

Love,
Mom (and your sister in Christ)

I knew the shoulders of the women of faith I stood on and the hard work that made it possible for me to live out my calling as priest and pastor. They all endured loss and hardship, much more than I had, and they still proclaimed and served the God of love, justice, and mercy. If they did it, so could I.

After the ordination service my family invited everyone over to our home in Garrison. We set out table after table of food and opened the garage doors, where two lovely ladies supplied us with music: my great aunt played accordion, and her ninety-five-year-old friend played bass.

Pastor and Mission Developer

I was installed at Heart River Lutheran Church on September 12, 2010. My call was affirmed when I walked into the chapel and there was an ensemble playing recorders to my favorite hymn, "Lord, Whose Love in Humble Service." Tears of joy filled my eyes. I knew I was in for an adventure, and I could feel life and healing burrowing its way into my chest. The lay minister, Peder, said to me after worship that day, "Right when you were being installed my son heard a chickadee singing outside and he said to me, 'Dad, I think Pastor Renee is supposed to be here with us.'" I agreed.

I dug into ministry. It felt refreshing to have purpose and be in mission with the people of God. I was still tired, but I sensed a renewed strength as I discovered needs and opportunities. I started getting to know my people, including visiting the youth on campus. I began helping young people with their fourth and fifth steps in the twelve-step addiction treatment program. I heard story after story from the mouths of teenagers of sexual abuse, tragic loss, neglect, betrayal, parents in prison, drug and alcohol use and addiction, and hopelessness. After hearing what were essentially confessions, I would wash my hands as a symbol of letting it all go and giving it to God.

When I would ask the young people in our one-on-one time if they had sober people in their lives they could count on, many said, "No. I don't know anyone who isn't using." I thought to myself, *How on earth are you going to make it?*

I started learning about what reentry was like for the youth. When they were court-ordered to corrections, many of the youth voluntarily began attending worship twice a week. They also had access to spiritual care from chaplains on campus, as well as a sense of what it might be like to be part of a congregation with Heart River. The wider community of Bismarck and Mandan had a number of agencies working to help the young people find work, housing, jobs, and so on upon release, but unless the youth went into a structured transitional living situation, no one was tending to their spiritual well-being or connecting them with a faith community on the outside.

I was visiting with a youth who was soon to be released, who served communion regularly at Heart River Lutheran on Sunday mornings. I asked him if he intended to seek out a worshipping community once he got out. He, a Native American with tattoos and piercings, said to me, "Like I'm just going to walk into some white church, Pastor Renee!" He asked, "Why can't I come back to Heart River?"

This youth and others like him grew to know and love this congregation where they felt so welcome, not judged. They belonged within the worship community on Sunday mornings: participating, leading, or simply hearing the Word and sharing in the Lord's Supper. Heart River would re-joice to have any youth come back and become an official member of the church, but it was not allowed for security reasons. Therefore, our only way to give the young people greater support when they left was to educate and empower the whole community, especially other congregations, to continue to be the hands and feet of Christ for these young people.

Our goal was to create a bridge of people to assist in the transition from life on campus into the community, focusing on their entire well-being and integrating them into a faith community of their choosing. We would do this through mentor relationships and working with other community organizations, the correctional facility, the Division of Juvenile Services, and other organizations that were already working with the young people to help them in the transition process.

To invite other congregations and people into God's mission for us as a faith community, we put out a request for quilts. Within a couple of months we had more than one hundred handmade quilts to give to the youth who left corrections. Whenever someone was released, we gave them a quilt and said, "There are people all over North Dakota who care about you and want healing and wholeness for you in your life. This quilt is a reminder to you of God's love for you and that we continue to pray for you. Wrap up in it and feel the presence of this community and God in your life." The youth loved the quilts; they were something they could have with them always, even in the midst of homelessness or couch surfing.

In addition to giving quilts, we also gave each youth a card printed with the promise from Jeremiah: "For surely I know the plans I have for you, says the LORD, plans for your well-being and not for harm, to give you a future with hope."[1] A future with hope was something many of them did not believe in for themselves. Many thought they would be dead before their twenty-fifth birthdays because of the tumultuous lives they lived. While they were with us, we did all we could to build them up and help them realize their self-worth. We truly believe that God has a future with hope in mind for all of them.

Throughout my first year we identified the steps it would take to create a more in-depth reentry ministry. The discoveries seemed endless: sustain-ability, release of information documents that needed to be signed, all case managers' participation and support, the correctional facility's approval every step of the way in development, appropriate church and state separation, a governance structure, hiring another person, understanding the work of

---

1. Jeremiah 29:11. In this ministry context, we replace the word "welfare" (with its political connotations) with "well-being."

various organizations who worked with out-of-home placement youth, development of sound mentor training, recruitment of people to be mentors, piquing the young people's interest in such an opportunity, follow-up and evaluation processes . . . the list went on and on.

Throughout the challenging development of what came to be called "Heart River Bridges of Hope," I kept wondering, *What are you getting yourself into, Renee?* But every time I would meet with the young people and realize their needs on the outside and their hopelessness for being surrounded by healthy community and continuing their faith formation after they were released, I committed to doing everything in my power to find a way. What greater purpose could I have than to walk with the young people and seek out possibilities for them to continue to hear the Word and be nourished in community? I loved them and wanted a better life for them, as did the people of Heart River.

To my surprise the Youth Correctional Center was open to what we were trying to accomplish, mostly because they had witnessed a revolving door—seeing the youth come back for addiction treatment time and time again. They could not tend to the young people's spiritual needs after they were released or create a volunteer network of people after youth transitioned out of the Division of Juvenile Services, so we jumped at their openness for us as a congregation to try something. The Spirit of God had been making a way for this opportunity long before I arrived on the scene. The soil was rich for seed planting and growth.

Most people were supportive, but some said, "Do you know how many people have tried to work with this population? Many . . . and many have failed. Do you know how hard this kind of work is?" I did not, but the congregation knew God was calling them to this work and I was called to be their pastor.

In November 2011 we formally named the ministry "Heart River Bridges of Hope." After six weeks of a focus group meeting in my living room, we finally emerged with a purpose and vision statement, helping us give focus to what would prove to be an endless well of need:

> Heart River Bridges of Hope is an outreach and reentry ministry on behalf of the ELCA and the whole Church. As an expression of God's grace and love, this ministry will provide youth opportunities for community worship, mentorship, wellness, and mutually enriching relationships. Trusting and believing that God heals and creates new life, our intent is to accompany and empower youth toward a future with hope.

We suffered many disappointments, but had numerous small miracles and joys along the way. I am continually amazed at the difficulty of life on the outside for the young people and the evil power of addiction. One hundred percent of the youth we worked with had addiction issues, and most went back to using after a time of being out. They went from an incredibly structured environment where they had few decisions to make each day to having hundreds of decisions a day and little or no structure in their lives. Some were even welcomed home with a six-pack of beer. How could we develop relationships that were strong enough to weather the storms of their turbulent and chaotic lives?

We continue to ask this question to this day as we are animated by God's Spirit to be manifestations of God's love and grace in the world, particularly for the youth we serve and love. We continue to believe in the power of loving relationships to change lives. We also know that this serves as a seed-planting ministry for now. We will possibly not see the results of our efforts for five or ten years. We know that the young people are resilient and survivors. We also know that they need to desire change and make that decision for themselves. Until then, we will offer ourselves and opportunities for faith formation, pro-social activities, worship, community, and mentoring as they grow into who God is calling them to be.

Sometimes I find myself thinking that mission development is just as hard as surviving the earthquake. I do not know if this is entirely true, but it certainly feels like it in the many complications and struggles we face each day. But until God calls me elsewhere or closes the door to this opportunity for ministry, I, along with Heart River Lutheran Church, will keep at it.

Take Off Your Shoes

Stories like Sarah's[2] help me keep at this labor in the Lord. When Sarah arrived at the Youth Correctional Center, she said to me in a Bible study, "I hate God." As I began to develop a relationship with Sarah and know her better, I came to understand that she was abused and neglected as a child, her father was in prison, and her mother dealt drugs on the street. I thought, *Of course you hate God.*

What surprised me about Sarah, however, was that even though she said she hated God, she was in worship every Sunday. She eventually started to serve communion, serve as an usher, read Scripture lessons, and even sang special music. One day on the way out of worship, Sarah asked me,

---

2. This name has been changed to protect the identity of the young woman.

"Pastor Renee, do you think it would be all right if I could be baptized?" I was shocked and elated.

Sarah and I began baptismal classes. She was brilliant and had such knowledge of Scripture and understood grace. She even chose a member from Heart River to serve as her baptismal sponsor. Since her foster family was Seventh-day Adventist, full immersion baptism was imperative for her. Our tiny font in the chapel would not do. We had a special liturgy for her in worship on Sunday morning, celebrating her upcoming baptism among the community of faith, and then afterward we made our way to the swimming pool on campus with a few people from the congregation and her foster family. There, in the correctional center swimming pool, Sarah was fully immersed in the chlorinated baptismal waters three times in the name of the Father, Son, and Holy Spirit, and marked with the cross of Christ forever. She rose up out of the water to her new life as a child of God.

It was a day I will never forget, and so was the day we wrapped her quilt around her and bid her Godspeed. I was afraid for her, and she was too. She was excited, but she also harbored many fears and uncertainties. We were able to pair her with a mentor who also happened to be her baptismal sponsor.

Sarah moved out of state, and there is rarely a day in which she and her mentor do not speak. Her mentor sends her weekly bulletins from Heart River, and Sarah has sought out a faith community and continues her baptismal journey.

I am continually moved with joy and love when my people call me "Pastor" as I embrace my identity as shepherd of a little flock in Mandan, North Dakota. I am also so thankful to be engaging in something I find to be challenging and fulfilling. It gives me life and purpose. It makes the gospel more real to me than ever before. I am a living, walking example of death come back to life, and I believe it for the young people, too. More than ever, I know in my bones that God wants life for the youth, real and good life. I desire to be a vessel through which it can come about, along with the rest of the people God calls along the way. God is opening up the graves of hopelessness, systemic systems of poverty and broken families, and addiction, and breathing new life into those who have been in the pit for so long in their young lives. God is breathing new and renewed life into the dry bones of all the people, including me.

One Sunday a young girl volunteered to serve communion for the first time. She was nervous because she thought she would forget what to say. She asked if she could write the words on her hand. Among her tattoos she found a space for more ink to write: "The blood of Christ, shed for you." Yes, indeed.

25

Marriage and New Life

FREDERICK BUECHNER WROTE: "JOY is a mystery because it can happen anywhere, anytime, even under the most unpromising circumstances, even in the midst of suffering, with tears in its eyes."[1] Joy happened for me all the time in the midst of suffering. Mostly it came in quiet beauty: the early spring green of flowers appearing after long winters, sunsets on the prairie, singing hymns with the people of God, having dinner with family and friends, and many other simple joys of living. After Ben died and Jon and I survived the earthquake, I experienced the slow growth of new life year by year.

Many times I wanted my "old life" back. I wanted Ben to be alive and to have my energy renewed. As time went on, all I could do was live and let God give me new life. I knew my life would never be the same, but I believed it could still be good and filled with joy. Smiles came more readily. Laughter became more frequent and without guilt. I enjoyed spending time with my nieces and nephews, and I wanted to watch them grow up. I planted perennials in my garden and looked forward to seeing them each year.

The earthquake forced a kind of "kenosis" in my being, an emptying out of what I knew and how I understood myself. In many ways I felt empty and hollow, and yet it was in the emptiness that I could feel God filling me back up, filling me with love, presence, breath, existence, joy, and call. My name, "Renee," means "rebirth." Never did I think it would come to mean what it does for me today. I do feel as though I have been reborn. I, along with so many others, have risen from the rubble and still have life to live.

When Ben died I became a widow. All of our dreams and the life we knew died on January 12, 2010. I truly believed that no one would ever love me the way Ben loved me, and I also thought that I could never again open up my heart to love another within the intimacy of marriage. Even if I ever felt ready to date again or consider the prospect of marriage, I never again wanted to feel the pain of losing a spouse.

1. Buechner, *Hungering Dark,* 94.

I was so angry at God for creating marriage. It made no sense to me that God would foster such love and intimacy between life partners only to have one die before the other. It was like losing half of my own self. There seemed to be no mercy in it. The marriage liturgy itself speaks of death, reminding those who wed that they will someday be parted by it. Even though the spouse dies, the love for them does not. At the age of twenty-seven, I did not know whether I would or could ever open my heart to another.

After graduation Jon and I went different directions. It was hard and strange to separate, because we had survived the earthquake together and lost Ben together. We were together at seminary with all of our close friends in the months following the earthquake, receiving care from them and from each other. Seeing Jon every day throughout the semester reminded me that I was not alone. He understood how I was feeling, and I didn't need to say a word. When we parted, I felt another loss—the loss of someone whom I did not know how to categorize in my life. Friend? Cousin-in-law? Seminary classmate? Fellow survivor?

I moved to Bismarck, North Dakota, for my first call to Heart River Lutheran Church in Mandan. Jon interviewed with a number of churches in Minnesota and Wisconsin. In the meantime, he took a short-term position at First Lutheran Church in Duluth where Ben's parents were pastors. April and Judd needed the help, and Jon wanted to be doing ministry while he interviewed. Late in the fall of 2010, he called me and said, "Renee, your bishop called me and asked if I'd be willing to interview at a congregation in western North Dakota, but he didn't tell me which one. Do you know of any openings?"

I said I didn't, at least not what he was describing. A couple of weeks later, though, I found out that the associate pastor of Faith Lutheran Church in Bismarck was leaving. My jaw dropped. I lived one mile from that congregation and on the same street. Sure enough, in late December Jon interviewed at Faith Lutheran Church in Bismarck. The call committee went forward with their nomination immediately, and within the month the congregation voted to call Jon as their pastor.

Call is such a mysterious and amazing process. If I were a bishop, I would definitely want Jon as a pastor in my synod! He is so communal, an advocate for justice, a faithful pastor, and a terrific colleague. I knew Bishop Narum could see these things in Jon, but only the Spirit of God determines call.

I have to admit, I was conflicted. I was excited because I missed Jon and it was challenging to support one another from a distance, but at the same time I was confused and scared. *What did this all mean?* Mostly, I was happy for Jon and for Faith Lutheran Church. More than anything, I wanted Jon to have a call and for a congregation to be blessed by his leadership.

Jon started at Faith Lutheran Church in Bismarck in March 2011, right after we returned from our first trip to Haiti after the earthquake. Now that Jon was so near, we had the opportunity to explore our relationship now—who we might be to and for one another. In the summer of 2011, we had an honest conversation and found out we cared deeply for one another—perhaps even *loved* each other.

This was frightening and troubling, especially since I was still so sad about Ben's death and still deeply loved him. We also did not know what our family and friends would think if we started dating.

The first people we talked to about the possibility were Ben's parents. Judd and April said, "The first thing we prayed for when we knew Ben was dead was that you two would fall in love." This surprised both of us. How could these two grieving parents pray for such a thing? I knew they thought of me as their daughter and that they wanted me to be happy and to find love again. They had known Jon his whole life as both their nephew and godson, and they knew his integrity and character. They wanted happiness for Jon, too, and they could see that he and I shared life experiences that no one else could ever come close to understanding. Looking back on it, it makes sense, but it was mind-boggling for us both at the time.

After we received April and Judd's blessing to start dating, we told Ben's sisters and their husbands. They celebrated as well and told us they were waiting for this to happen and hoping for it. This was the same response we received from all of our family members, cousins, and friends. No one wanted to push us into a romantic relationship, but they all wanted us to discover love in our own time.

Our next step before our first date was to have a conversation with our bishop. When two pastors date, it can be fairly complicated, and our story was particularly unique and public. We asked him if we should tell our congregations before we went on a date, and he had great wisdom for us when he said, "Goodness, no. Go on your first date and see first whether it's even going to work!" Duh.

The Heart Expands

Jon and I went on our first date on September 9, 2011. I was nervous the whole day. *Would opening my heart to Jon feel like betrayal to Ben? Would I lose what little I still felt of Ben? Would I forget what our marriage was like? What would other people think?*

All my anxieties were laid to rest when Jon showed up at my door. He was holding a large bouquet of flowers and a letter for me to read. In it, he wrote about how much he had been thinking about Ben all day long before our first date, how much he loved and missed Ben, and how he was ready to care for me in new ways. Reading Jon's letter and seeing him there before me willing to step out in risk and love, my heart cracked open.

I was so scared that I was not capable of loving both Ben and Jon at the same time. Ben's love for me had felt so far away and gone for so long, but in that moment of reading Jon's letter, I felt it flooding back to me. I never expected this. It was as though I was free to have my love for Ben grow and now to let my love for Jon grow as well. It was certainly an epiphany in my life, and I am so grateful to God for designing our hearts in such a way that they have the capacity to expand with an infinite amount of love.

I had been clinging to my life and marriage with Ben, and I could never have them back. Once I let that go, I found I could love Ben even more for who he was becoming in God and what we were becoming together in our continued relationship in Christ. But I also had a life to live, and there was an incredible man who knew me and wanted to love me. One does not exchange one love for another love. The heart expands.

I remember when I first realized I loved Jon, even before we went on our first date. He was washing my dishes as usual and we were talking about something unimportant. I asked him about singing in choir at Augustana College and whether he had a favorite choral piece. He thought about this for a long while as he continued washing dishes. Just when I thought he had forgotten I even asked him a question, he answered: "'Salvation is Created' by Pavel Grigorievich Chesnokov."

Surprising even myself, I asked, "Could you sing some of it for me?" He did not respond, but kept looking down and scrubbing the plates. I went back to whatever I was doing, and then all of a sudden I heard his beautiful tenor voice singing in Russian. His eyes never looked up at me, and he continued to wash the dishes as the beauty of the piece rang out in his voice. I saw him as if for the first time. I am so thankful he never looked up, because I was awestruck and staring. I could hardly move because I suddenly understood that I loved him; not in the way that I have always loved him as Ben's beloved cousin and my friend, but with a new love that was deep and different and surprising.

Opening my heart to Jon was frightening, and I know it was scary for him as well, but we stepped into it trusting that God had given us an opportunity to discern if marriage was in our future. On November 14, 2011, Jon pulled out Ben's guitar and sang "Can't Help Falling in Love," but with a twist. He inserted some lyrics from "Certainty," the first song Ben wrote for me: "But in this world not all is uncertain / There's the love of God and my love for you." With that, he asked me to marry him and I said yes. I was touched by Jon's thoughtfulness in honoring Ben and his love, even as he proposed our new marriage to one another. Our memories of Ben would always be so important to both of us. Jon put a beautiful ring with a pear-shaped diamond on my finger, and we set a wedding date for April 14, 2012, in the season of Easter.

A few months before Jon and I were married, he wrote this to me in a card:

> Renee,
>
> Remembering and abiding in hope are closely, tightly knit together. We remember Ben and we hope for a time when we will meet him again and we hope for a time when pain and suffering and emptiness are no more.
>
> My ultimate hope in this world is for your healing. I care so deeply for you and I constantly question God as to why life is this way. I wrestle with God like Jacob did, and I too will always limp. We all will, for the rest of our days.
>
> I will walk with you; I will limp with you; all the days of my life. And, I will hope with you, trusting in God's mercy to carry us when we fall and the pain is too hard.
>
> You are loved, Renee. May the incarnate God dwell deeply within you.
>
> God's peace,
> Jonathan

We decided to invite everyone and anyone who wanted to come to our wedding. Still to this day I have no idea how many people actually came to celebrate and witness our vows to one another, but we had a sanctuary that seats 900 close to full. All of our brothers and sisters stood up with us, including Ben's sisters and their husbands. We left the best man spot open to remember Ben and his importance in both of our lives. Bishop Narum presided, and we asked Rev. Amy Current, a staff member at Wartburg Seminary who knew what we had been through and what we had lost, to preach. We wanted Amy to name it all as it was, as we knew she would: to name Ben, to name the crucified and risen Christ, and to name the hope and new life God gives us on this earth. We needed the gospel proclaimed to all of us who still loved and missed Ben so deeply.

We chose the Scripture for our wedding very carefully. Song of Solomon 8:6–7: "For love is strong as death, passion fierce as the grave." Psalm

126: "Those who go out weeping, bearing the seed for sowing, shall come home with shouts of joy, carrying their sheaves." 1 Corinthians 15:19–26: "The last enemy to be destroyed is death." And the gospel, from Matthew 28:1–10: "And suddenly there was a great earthquake . . . 'I know that you are looking for Jesus who was crucified . . . He has been raised from the dead.'"

The gospel reading at our wedding was the same one we read at Ben's grave on the first anniversary of the earthquake. Our lives were steeped in the reality of death and resurrection. Rev. Amy Current proclaimed the Word we all needed to hear:

> The crucified and risen Lord meets us here—meets you, Jon, and you, Renee, in this place in the midst of your fear and great joy—meets us all, this whole assembly, gathered to witness the solemn promises that you share today as you become husband and wife.
>
> Yet there are many who are not here in body today . . . two in particular among the saints: Miriam (Mim) Joy—Jon, your mom—and Benjamin, the beloved of Renee and cousin-brother of Jon. The grief is indeed palpable, for while the power of death is destroyed, the sting remains.
>
> The crucified and risen Christ met Renee and Jon in their darkest hours—as the earth literally crumbled around them—as their beloved Ben sang his last breath—and as they clung to one another—in utter fear, terror, and trembling—as their Haitian sisters and brothers trembled and the news spread to the rest of the world—as your family waited in fear.
>
> It is the crucified and risen Christ who reminded you, "Do not be afraid, for by my death I have destroyed the power of death"—and who allows you still to feel the sting of death and suffering, as the risen Christ bears the marks of death. We all carry with us real pain, suffering, and grief.
>
> It is the crucified and risen Christ who met you as the months moved forward and walked with you both and began to give you this new gift of love . . . Renee and Jon's love. Not new in the sense that the past is wiped away—but new in the fact that the promise of eternal life is real for all those who have died . . . God is still speaking and declares, "Do not be afraid—go and tell"—and this is new.
>
> New creation where Jon is not a replacement for Renee's beloved Ben—and Renee does not replace the love and loyalty between Jon and Ben—but instead the crucified and risen Lord makes all things new—

And has brought a new tender and fierce love shared by these two—who are now called to carry their fear and joy together—as one—one witness to hope, joy, and renewal. What joy it is to celebrate new creation!

And it is the crucified and risen Christ who meets us now—who meets us all now—greets you, welcomes you, allows you to cling to him—worship him—and then beckons you forth, saying, "Do not be afraid. Go and tell."

Many hymns were sung and communion was shared. We sang "Jubilate Deo" of the Taizé community, a song we had sung so many times following the earthquake, except this time we sang it with tears of joy. After the worship service, which lasted an hour and a half, and a two-hour receiving line, we ate at the potluck and danced the night away to a polka band. It was a day to celebrate new life, resurrected life, which still bore the scars of death and sorrow. Jon and I held both death and resurrection in our beings on that day. We boldly proclaimed and felt that life and love prevail.

A Baby

On May 12, 2014, I found out I was pregnant. Words cannot describe the joy and fear in me upon discovering that Jon and I were going to have a baby. When Ben died, I truly believed children would never be possible for me. How thankful I am that I was wrong!

At my first doctor's appointment, Jon and I were able to hear my heartbeat along with our child's rapid beat of life. I thought I might burst from happiness and expectation. The doctor told us the due date: January 16, 2015. *January!* I thought. *Of course . . . January.* "We cannot help when babies come, Renee," Jon said.

Sharing the news with our families, including Ben's family, brought us so much joy, but telling them the due date was tough at first. When we told Ben's parents, though, the first thing out of their mouths was, "We are so happy! January is perfect for a baby. New life in the midst of sorrow!" January is always hard for all of us, but on the fifth anniversary of the earthquake we would all be anticipating the birth of a baby boy.

When I told the people of Heart River Lutheran Church that Jon and I were expecting our first baby, they erupted in cheers and hugs. It did not take long for four of the women from my congregation to stop me in a hallway and ask if they could lay hands on me and pray. "Of course!" I said. They gathered around me and all put their hands on my abdomen. They prayed for my health and well-being, they prayed for the development of the child that was now growing inside my womb, and they gave thanks to God that they could witness my pregnancy and be a part of the life of our child. All my fears subsided in that moment and I was left with pure gratitude.

I marveled at the life in me that moved and grew. I felt it in my body and in my soul. Instead of immense sadness as January approached, I felt anticipation and expectant joy with the advent of our son. I started serious contractions on January 11, and I prayed fervently not to give birth on January 12. My labor subsided, and my water broke at 7:15 a.m. on January 15. Twenty-nine hours later, at 12:12 p.m. on January 16, Gabriel David Splichal Larson was born into the world God loves so much. He was eight pounds, five ounces, and twenty-one and a half inches of sheer gift! I stared at his beautiful face, completely exhausted and amazed by the God who knit him together in my womb. Gabriel David . . . fearfully and wonderfully made!

Gabriel means "God is my strength," and David means "beloved." We named our child after the angel Gabriel, who visits Mary and shares with her the news that God has big plans for the redemption of all of creation. Gabriel, the bringer of the good news of Jesus Christ for the sake of the world. Gabriel, our son, bearer of God's presence and promise of new life.

The day we were to take Gabriel home from the hospital, I decided to take a bath. I let the waters run over my weary and thankful body. Unexpectedly, I started to cry. I let the tears silently flow. I had not cried at all that week during the fifth anniversary of the earthquake because my focus was on birthing Gabriel. Now I grieved, and I gave thanks in the water. Not knowing I was crying, Jon knocked on the door to speak with me. He noticed my tears and asked me what was wrong. I simply said, "I'm so happy."

I realized I truly was happy. I could scarcely believe that I had given birth and that we had a healthy, beautiful baby boy, who would soon have a smile that takes up his whole face. I bathed in the waters of resurrection and gratitude.

Love and Life

I have come to discover that love knows no bounds. I am so grateful to God for Ben and our marriage, and also so thankful for Jon, for our relationship now as husband and wife, and for our child.

A year and a half into our marriage, I asked Jon if there was a moment when he knew he loved me. He sat quietly for a long time, as he usually does when I ask him a thought-provoking question. Finally, he looked at me and said, "I can't remember a specific time. I just knew I wanted to take care of you."

One time early on after Ben died, I asked Jon what he thought Ben would want for me. He paused thoughtfully before answering. "I think Ben would want you to reclaim some of the things in your life that give you joy, things like music, dancing, and making bread. I know you are not the same person, but that is okay. Let God shape you into who you are becoming through all we've been through. Know that Ben loves you and is so proud of you. You are a wonderful pastor, Renee, and are so gifted. I think the Bible is not necessarily full of faithful people, but desperate people. God is doing great work through you. And I, too, long for the day when our every day is not Good Friday."

I am so blessed to have been loved by Ben, and to now be deeply loved by Jon. I find it hard to put into words my love for Jon and what I know his love is for me, and now our passionate love for our child. We are bonded by a force that is beyond both of us. My love for him is deep, steady, and strong. He is my person. He makes me laugh every day, and we are building a wonderful life together. He is the one person on this earth who can relate to my innermost trauma. He has walked with me faithfully through it all.

We wear our grief differently, but it is helpful simply to be near one another. I can easily tell when Jon is missing Ben. His body slouches, his eyes become watery, and there is a depth of sadness I can see in him that can only be born out of such loss. Yet, there is an incredible joy in him that has never been lost. His passion for service, his love for Christ, his witty and quick humor make him someone I want to be around. Besides, he has an incredible gift for washing dishes (I call him the "dishes fairy").

Although Jon and I are very happy, we both live with the wish that Ben was alive. A few months after we were married, we traveled to Portland, Oregon, to Jon's internship placement site. A woman in his congregation who was happy to see us said: "I'm just so happy you two are now married. Everything has worked out in the end." We know she meant well when she said this, but our hearts sank. It is difficult for us to feel resolution with what we have lost, what we lived through, what we have seen, and what seems still to be undone. Ben being dead still feels wrong, along with the countless Haitians who lost their lives in the earthquake. Our marriage is wonderful, good, and sacred, but we do not feel as if everything has "worked out." It is a painful reality that we live with every day, and yet we embrace the new life God is giving us through our marriage and life together.

Some time after the earthquake, Jon wrote this to me in a note:

> You (and me too) do not always understand how/why you have
> the faith you do in the midst of your own brokenness, but that
> is the definitive power of God coming through. The gray-ness of

faith becomes clearer when we realize we can't understand it, it just is, and there is power in the is-ness. And then, as you say, it is about the transformation of our lives by the very God who instills in us faith. Through that instilled faith, somehow God's good work happens.

Those of us who survived the earthquake are living in the "is-ness," along with all others who have loved and lost. Perhaps all of us are living in the "is-ness" of faith and God and life. I treasure the man, Jonathan David, and our life together. The laughter of our son is a wellspring of life. Yes, I am terrified of Jon's death, and now Gabriel's, and I do not know how I would live through it if it happened, but I try not to think about that too much and enjoy my life with them. I thank God every night for the day God has given us together and ask that God might bless us with a long life with one another. Together, we are truly one witness to hope, joy, and resurrection in Jesus Christ.

There is so much life still to be lived. There is beauty all around. There are family and friends and those I have yet to meet. There is an amazing child to watch grow. There is the call to discipleship and ministry and the work of the Kingdom of God in this world. There is music and gardening. There is love and the promise of resurrection.

I am happy and I want to live.

Ben Still Sings

PLEASE VISIT WWW.BENSTILLSINGS.COM TO download some of Ben's songs. You will also find photos, Ben's liturgy ("Behold, I Make All Things New"), and other information about his story.

Afterword and Acknowledgments

WENDELL BERRY ONCE WROTE: "New grief, when it came, you could feel filling the air. It took up all the room there was. The place itself, the whole place, became a reminder of the absence of the hurt or the dead or the missing one. I don't believe that grief passes away. It has its time and place forever. More time is added to it; it becomes a story within a story. But grief and griever alike endure."[1] I will miss Ben and grieve the Haiti earthquake for the rest of my life, yet I know I will endure.

This book has been a labor of love. Many have asked me if writing it has been healing. I suppose it has in that getting the story down on paper has been a personal calling of mine. Now I know it will not be lost. Certainly while writing this book I experienced some re-traumatization, which I would not call "healing." It has been incredibly difficult to form language, not only to articulate the event of the earthquake, but also to be so vulnerable in sharing the dark nights of my soul. I have also learned there is much more to writing a book than just writing a book.

If I have missed an important detail, misunderstood something, or misrepresented anyone in these pages, I am deeply sorry. My goal has never been to paint an idealized picture of Haiti, the Haitians, Ben's life, or my own. We all have faults. I have simply strived to tell the story as I know it.

In one of my post-earthquake conversations with a Haitian friend, she said:

1. Berry, *Jayber Crow,* 148.

> We must honor the memory of those who have died. Some good
> must come out of the earthquake. We need to allow ourselves to
> believe that the country will be better than it was before. That is
> what I am hoping. I don't know how we can change our mental-
> ity. We as Haitians cannot just rely on others to do it for us.
> We Haitians and people who actually love Haiti and the Haitian
> people . . . we all can do it together and help each other to make
> it happen.

I am thankful to God for the strength and the will to start and complete this book.

I must lift up my gifted editor, Jennifer Agee. Without her I imagine I would still be finding the courage to begin the editing process. She has given me the confidence to release this work into the hands of the public.

Words cannot express my appreciation of and respect for my first reader, Rev. Dr. Norma Cook Everist. Her care, attention, and time given to the faithful reading of the raw first material is a gift that cannot be repaid. I am also grateful to Heart River Lutheran Church for the four-week writing sabbatical and for inspiration along the way. They have been a tremendous community of faith.

I would not be who I am today without the support of my family and friends. When I placed a draft of this book into some of their hands, they wept. They have reminded me often how important this witness is and have patiently walked with me in all aspects of my life.

A special thank-you to those who read drafts or chapters and gave me feedback: Ben and Jon's immediate families, my own family, Evon Flesberg, Kent Annan, Shelly Satran, Luther Kistler, Patricia Hansen, Mary Delasin, Renee Dietrich, Mytch Dorvilier, Louis Dorvilier, Craig Nessan, Susan Briehl, Elizabeth McHan, Corrine Denis, Katie Amaya, Lindsay Melaas, Peder Stenslie, Shera Nesheim, Lauri Desir, Michael Gibson, Carolyn Carlson, and Paul Hoffman.

Thank you to Corrine Denis, Kalen Barkholtz, and Renee Dietrich for the use of their beautiful poetry. Special thanks also to Renee Dietrich for providing photos, descriptions, and technical assistance. Thank you to Wipf and Stock Publishers for publishing my witness and to ELCA Global Mission for deepening my understanding of accompaniment.

Thank you to those who returned Ben's body to us: the ELCA, particularly Rev. Rafael Malpica-Padilla and Louis and Mytch Dorvilier; the Haitians who dug, especially Pierre; the St. Joseph Family; Paul and the U.S. embassy in Haiti; and the U.S. military. We are so grateful for the gift of being able to bury Ben.

I give thanks to and for Jonathan David, who loves me more deeply than I ever thought possible. His wisdom, faith, and humor lift me up and make me smile each day. I could not have completed this book without his unconditional support and encouragement.

I give thanks to Gabriel, who makes me marvel and wonder at life and growth. One day he will have the chance to read these pages. I never expected to be in mourning and feel so dead on the eve of January 12, 2010, and six years later on January 12, 2016, to be dancing with my son after returning from visiting Ben's grave. I held him in my arms, closed my eyes, and rested my forehead on his, my body swaying to the music. I breathed him in. I breathed life in. I used to think God's promise to turn mourning into dancing was eschatological, but I have already experienced it in this life and I am so grateful.

Last but not least, I wish to recognize Ben and his profound impact on my life. Ben taught me about playful joy and shared his deep appreciation for music. Being in relationship with him has undoubtedly changed me for the better and has taught me how to love more deeply. Not even death can take this away. I pray this book has honored him and spoken truth to who he was, even knowing that no one can ever be confined or defined by words on a page.

Ben and the Communion of Saints
Kalen Barkholtz

When I was a little girl I loved saying Communion of saints,
Communion of saints
Communion of saints
Communion of saints.

I still love to say it.
Communion of saints.

Communion of saints sounded like
Christmas lights to me.

Christmas lights tangled in a knot
the way they come out of the box from the Christmas before.
And the first thing you do of course is plug them in before untangling
and when you are a child, and when you are an adult
there is a startling beauty when all the lights blink on in an instant.

This is what I see, still,
when I say Communion of saints,
a tangled, lit universe, a studded cloud of bright and sparks.
Every tiny bulb makes its own unique light:
distinctive pink, sharp green, bleeding blue.
And there is the glorious light of the whole bundle,
an iridescent glimmering like the angels bunched together in the sky,
singing down on the shepherds
who looked up and listened
to a twinkling, shining mass of Gloria and peace on earth.

And this is how I picture Ben.
He is a bright yellow gold
among the communion of saints, singing with us,
Peace on earth, peace on earth,
Glory to God in the highest and peace on earth.

The Longest Night

By Keziah Furth

Ben, Jon, and I met Keziah Furth while we were staying at St. Joseph's Home for Boys. We quickly became good friends and spent as much time together as we could in the days leading up to the earthquake. Kez is a nurse by profession and was the only medical caregiver in the open lot where so many of us gathered right after the earthquake. She describes in detail what it was like for so many that horrible night. Our stories interweave, yet are so different.

A few months after the earthquake I gathered up the courage to read her blog, where she documented her experiences in the weeks and months following January 12, and to look at her photos. I could hardly believe what was I was reading and seeing—and I had been there! I finally realized how very fortunate Jon and I were to have escaped all physical injury. I was also very thankful that Ben did not survive only to die after immense suffering like so many others.

On the third anniversary of the earthquake, Kez sent me eleven unpublished chapters describing her experience before, during, and after the earthquake. The following is her account of "The Longest Night." —RSL

MEMORY LIKES TO PLAY games, letting certain things fade to a blurry haze while keeping others poignant and perfectly detailed. When I think back to the night of the earthquake, most of it seems to have disappeared in a melting pot of adrenaline and tragedy. The timeline of events is more like a toddler's scribble than a straight line across a page. I have completely forgotten some things and only recall them when I reread my journal or my blog. And yet, in the midst of the fog over that night, there are certain sights and sounds that I can remember as if they happened yesterday.

I remember when I was doing my second round through the crowd in the field, handing out pain meds and encouraging words. A man called to me from the farthest corner, "Miss, do you know how to sew people up?"

A woman was lying with her head in his lap, a jagged cut on her forehead, just at the hairline, oozing blood across her face. I put on gloves, the non-sterile kind because frankly, I was in a field in semi-darkness; nothing was going to be sterile. I didn't have enough lidocaine in my E-pack to numb the whole area. "Ma'am, I'm sorry, but you're going to feel this a little. Can you hold still for me?" Wincing internally, I started to sew her up. She held perfectly still and didn't make a sound to show the pain that I know she was feeling. When I was done, I gave her a shot to prevent infection and moved away to the next victims.

Sometime after that, I returned to Bill to check on his status. He was still stable, but in agonizing pain. All around him, the St. Joseph's boys had gathered and were trying to get comfortable among the pieces of broken wall and the trash. I set my bags down and began to walk toward my Shoebox.[1] "Where are you going, Kez?!" everyone exclaimed. "I need to get pads and sheets and more supplies from my house," I answered. "Don't go inside!" they cried in panic. "Don't go inside. If another quake hits, you'll die!"

I went anyway, the first of many forays into my chaotic house that night. The entire city was without power since the quake hit, but my inverter batteries were charged, so I was able to turn them on and have lights for a few minutes. I tried to get online to tell my family that I was okay, but I was unsurprised to find that the Internet was down too. I climbed through the hallway, over dozens of boxes of birthing kits that had tumbled down, into the back bedroom where all the extra supplies are stored. Could it be coincidence that a few weeks earlier I had reorganized all the cases and duffle bags in that room? I knew exactly where to find more lidocaine, more bandages, more sutures, more sheets. I dragged my mattress and a few pads out and coaxed one of the St. Joseph's boys to help me carry it all to the field.

Night had fallen and it was dark and cold. I distributed water and sheets to as many of my child neighbors as I could. Someone had brought TiPatrick, the little boy I'd seen on the hillside when I was running home, to join the rest of us. I was taking care of him when Bill's phone rang nearby. One of the boys answered, "No, you can't talk to Bill, he's barely conscious. Here, why don't you talk to the nurse who's taking care of him?"

Haiti has two major cell phone providers; neither had been working since the quake hit. Bill, despite much peer pressure, had stayed faithful to Haitel, a small phone company that was considered practically defunct.

---

1. Kez's house.

Haitel was working. I took the phone and spoke to the person on the other end, a reporter for ABC who had met Bill during one of his speaking engagements in the U.S. She was looking for a report on the quake and the current conditions. I bristled and told the woman brusquely that I was taking care of dying people and I didn't have time to talk. Fortunately, she was persistent and I agreed to let her call back an hour later for a proper interview.

When she called back, I stepped away to a quiet part of the street for about ten minutes and described everything I was seeing and doing. When it was over, I remember distinctly saying to her, "I just helped you out, now I need you to help me. Please email my parents and tell them that I'm alive." She agreed, but I was skeptical; in the rush of breaking news, would she really remember to email?

I wish I knew that reporter's name, because I would dearly love to thank her. I found out days later that she not only emailed my parents; she somehow found their phone number and called to tell them personally that I'd survived. It was five hours after the quake had hit and after countless unsuccessful attempts to contact me, my parents were convinced that something awful had happened to me. When my mother answered the phone, the reporter asked if she was Keziah's mom, and apparently, my mother was sure that the lady was calling to tell her I'd died. Seconds later, she heard the beautiful truth, "I just got off the phone with your daughter and she's fine," and burst into tears. My parents don't like to talk about those first hours or even first days, but I have gotten small glimpses of how terrible it was for them. I don't doubt that I had it the easiest of all of us; in the heart of the tragedy, I was too preoccupied by the needs around me to worry. For my parents, all they could do was wait and pray.

Back on the field, my neighbor Alix had rigged a solitary lightbulb to a large tree and was running a small generator to power it. Victims continued to stagger in and congregate around that tree so that I could inspect them and provide care. I quickly realized that the lightbulb wasn't enough, and I looked around for someone to hold a flashlight for me. The only person I recognized right then was Jean-Andre, a young man with tattoos across his arms and back who usually sat at the top of my street smoking and playing cards. His nickname was G, and three days earlier he'd helped me find a new place to buy water. I didn't know him well and under normal circumstances, I probably wouldn't have chosen him, but there he was and when I called his name, he came without a second's hesitation.

As we settled into our improvised triage site, word spread: Kez is here and she has medical supplies. The men from my neighborhood took the cue and began to search the collapsed buildings nearby, looking for victims. They carried them in on pieces of wood, broken doors, or just on their backs. G and I greeted each group with a cursory look-over: "OK, those three just need pain meds. Sit 'em over there. This lady can survive with a couple Band-Aids. And those guys are going to need to be stitched. Put them right beside the tree."

In the dark, crouching or kneeling on the ground, I tried to patch up the ugliest wounds I have ever seen. The walls and roofs that fell had left deep gashes, entire chunks missing from some limbs, and crush injuries that seeped blood. To make matters worse, most of these wounds were full of tiny pieces of concrete, the telltale sign of blocks collapsing and crumbling upon impact. I used syringes full of sterile water to try to flush the white chunks out of people's arms and legs; when flushing failed, I attacked with tweezers. Sometimes I spent thirty minutes just cleaning a wound before I could begin to close it.

G stayed beside me the entire time, winding a little crank flashlight and focusing it on my patients. He learned quickly how I work and was able to hand me materials as I needed them. My E-pack was lacking one essential tool: needle drivers. I was forced to hold each tiny needle in my gloved fingers as I closed the wounds. My hands slipped as they got covered in blood and I kept losing sight of the needle in the poor lighting. Did I change gloves between patients? I hope I did, but I honestly don't remember.

The earthquake had happened shortly before five o'clock and tremors had continued to hit once or twice every hour. Each time the ground started to shake again, I paused in my work and prayed silently, "God, make it stop. Please God, make it stop." All around me, my neighbors exploded into cries of terror and shouts for help and prayers for deliverance. With the first few tremors, there was a mad rush as everyone tried to get to the very center of the field, as far from the adjacent structures as possible. By late evening, the panicked running had ceased, but the terrified crying had not. The tremors lasted five or ten seconds and when they ended, G and I went straight back to stitching, as if nothing had happened.

Meanwhile in Boston, most of my friends and relatives still had no idea if I'd survived the catastrophe. I kept an American cell phone during the summers when I worked in Maine, but my teenage brother had the phone for the school year. That night, he'd forgotten it at his best friend's house and sixteen-year-old Tom had to play operator for hours until the phone ran out of battery after the 123rd call, telling people over and over that there was no news about Kez yet and please keep praying.

After the reporter called my parents, my younger brother posted the good news on Facebook and over the next few days, it trickled out to my friends. For some, word of my survival came another way. My summer boss, Dave, was awake in the middle of the night, searching the Internet for news of me and praying, when he heard my voice. He rushed to the living room where the TV was on and was amazed and relieved to see my name and a still photo of me on the screen. Thanks to the ABC reporter who had called Bill's phone, my voice was heard on the eleven o'clock news on ABC, CBS, and NBC, and it was repeated on newscasts throughout the night. I've received a number of emails from people who didn't sleep until they heard me on the news and knew that I was okay.

In Haiti, I was unaware of the prayers and the worried wishes that were aimed at me from far away. I settled into a rhythm: triage and emergency room care for an hour or two until the area under the tree was bare, a quick check-up on Bill and TiPatrick, a run to my house for supplies, then back to the tree as another group of refugees stumbled in. One man arrived, carrying his injured son. They'd come almost four miles on foot because this was the only place they knew about where the boy could get care.

My supplies started to run low, so I looked for my friend Abbey. Abbey worked at an orphanage behind the field and they had a small clinic. The American doctor who ran the clinic had flown to the U.S. that very morning, but thankfully, he'd left the keys with Abbey. I raided their clinic countless times that night and as the January air grew cooler, Abbey and I borrowed dozens of sheets and baby blankets for the crowd trying to sleep on the ground. The orphanage building was badly cracked in several spots and they'd moved all the children onto the field. Every time I walked into the building, I thought to myself, "I should probably be afraid right now." But I wasn't.

I used my last size three suture. All I had left was size fours, which, contrary to logic in numbering, are smaller than threes. Without a needle driver, I simply couldn't use them. My fingers couldn't grip them tight enough. I muttered a desperate prayer. "C'mon, God. You gotta do something. I can't stitch any more people up unless you get me some help here."

Five minutes later, a young woman approached me holding a Ziploc bag. "I'm a nursing student," she said. "And I have these. Do you need them?"

The bag held scissors, tweezers, clamps, and needle drivers.

At midnight, the men carried in a woman on a piece of plywood. Her head had been hit and she had open wounds on her face and forehead. Her eyes and her nostrils were full of fine white concrete dust. The woman was breathing, but she was unresponsive. A towel covered her lower legs and I bent down and pulled it off. Both her legs were completely crushed from the knee down, blood crusted and clotted, mixed with chunks of cement and dirt. I could see muscles, tendons, bones flayed open. I stood up.

"Cover her up. There's nothing I can do for her."

A few minutes later, she died. I told the men to move her body out of my triage area to an empty corner of the field. Our morgue was officially open.

In her wake came another woman, accompanied by her middle-aged husband. The husband was unharmed, but the woman's right leg was almost severed at the knee. It was twisted out of line and the bones were visibly shattered and sticking out of her calf. Blood pumped steadily from the leg, dripping down the wooden door she was lying on and turning to red mud where it met the dust below. She was conscious but very weak, and I was sure that she would pass away quickly. I ignored the husband's pleas for me to save her and I went back to the tree, to the people whose lives I could save.

They brought me a man several hours later. He was awake and talking, complaining of pain but showing no external injuries. His vital signs were stable and he appeared to be badly bruised but nothing more. I left him and went to other patients. Twenty minutes later, I checked him and he was dead.

His death scared me. If that man could seem stable and die so abruptly, Bill and TiPatrick could suffer the same fate. I hurried back to the camp and found TiPatrick shivering. I tried twice to get an IV into him but I couldn't find a vein. All I could do then was cover him with blankets and make a couple of the boys lie on either side of him to keep him warm. Bill was awake, and although stable, continued to moan in excruciating pain. I felt helpless and frustrated—there had to be something I could do for him! I marched back to my house for a final hunt, a successful one. I found a bottle of Vicodin with fewer than a dozen pills in it. I gave Bill two of them and he finally, mercifully, fell asleep.

In the last hours of the night, my neighbors rescued a little boy and carried him to his mother there on the field. I heard them frantically yelling my name and I hurried to them. The anxious crowd parted and I saw the limp, broken body laid across the woman's lap. The boy was looking up into her eyes, speaking to her, and she cradled him and whispered back to him. I looked at the sickly gray color of his face and I knew that I couldn't tell them the truth that I saw so clearly. Instead, I poured a little medicine into his mouth and told them to pray. Less than ten minutes later, that mother's anguished cries echoed across the clearing. Her son was dead.

The night seemed to go on forever. Each time I thought I could take a breather, a new group of victims would stumble in. There was always someone bleeding or someone screaming in pain or someone shivering or crying for water. I don't think I ever sat down. When the first pale streaks of dawn appeared over the destroyed city, I listened and realized that the singing had never stopped. Despite their fear and sorrow, a group of people near the center of the circle were singing songs of praise to God. I didn't sing. I looked in front of me at the children huddled together and behind me at the still bodies beside the stone wall. I looked up at a sky that seemed dark and foreboding. I looked down at my own hands. They were covered in blood.

Eulogy for Ben Splichal Larson

By Scott Ulring

Ben's uncle Scott was someone he greatly admired. Spontaneous and creative, Scott composed songs Ben treasured while growing up. Scott was asked to share a eulogy at Ben's funeral on January 22, 2010, on behalf of our family. Perhaps Scott understood Ben so well because of their similarities and playful nature, or maybe it's simply because of an uncle's love for a nephew. I think it's both. —RSL

HI, MY NAME IS Scott Ulring, Ben's uncle and godparent along with my brother James. I want to thank you all on behalf of the Ulring, Larson, and Splichal families for traveling to be with us. We are thinking of and praying for the people of Haiti. The horrible losses they have sustained. Our hearts go out to the dead and to their families. I want to say too that amidst our grief there is celebration. We are so thankful to have Jonathan and Renee back safely.

Ben was six months from finishing at Wartburg Seminary. He was just getting started. My view of Ben was less a rose already in bloom than he was a rosebud still gathered tightly, about to burst forth. His life was cut short on January 12, 2010. I'm sad, selfishly, because I won't get to bask in the sun of Ben's playful disposition. As Peter Samuelson said to me last night, Ben was an expert at joy. I'm sad too for the church, because what I was seeing and hearing from Ben, in my view, and from his professors at Wartburg, was important and fresh.

Ben was different. It was just in the last year or two that he really started to plug in seriously with his studies. Ben was actually a bit of a revolution-ary. In a good way. He loved people. He loved God. He wanted to mend the divisions within the ELCA; to reach across continents; to reach the people outside the box called "church" and bring them in. He had a fire in his belly for this work. Privately, I saw him as a kind of playful Trojan horse, a secret weapon, twenty-five years in the making.

My view, and I think perhaps Ben's too, is that the ELCA is like a lot of mainline denominations, caught betwixt and between—uncertain about its relevance today, still perseverating over old arguments. I think Ben was thinking forward; thinking deeply about what it really means to follow Jesus in this world, in a postmodern sense. And to that I say, Amen. It is a question that we need to address for our children's sake.

I think Ben was doing this work. I can hear it in most of his music and clearly in the first sermon I heard him give. It was among the best I've heard. This in a family that parses sermons like Italians slice onions. I think his first song on the recent CD "Made" hints at how he was just starting to pull these threads forward. Listen to his words as he sets out his own creation story:

"And so I was made, she breathed me life, and every breath I breathe now is a breath of grace."

Ben adds Renee, his Eve: "My love was made, her fingers wrapped perfectly and tight around mine."

And then together in motion: "And so we travel, with strength this path we feared when we were both alone."

The word "alone" is the right word to mark the last transition. The song arcs. Ben and Renee together invite us to come along, sweeping us in: "My Maker's arms are big enough for you / She breathed you too, she breathed you too . . ."

To my ear this is fresh. It's not just a ditty. It goes beyond "Jesus loves me this I know, for the Bible tells me so."

Ben knows God loves him, not only because the Bible says so, but because he feels God's grace in every breath, his heart is moved by the Spirit. And so he moves his understanding of faith *out of time*. He faces forward, not backward. He uses our traditions and the words of Scripture as his foundation.

My observation of Ben is that this understanding of grace freed him to clearly address the *what's next* . . .

I saw Ben, Renee, and Jonathan moving together in faith enjoined with and alongside the Spirit and with us too. Not just some of us: all of us, as many as are willing, traveling into the world, with good courage because we are not alone.

This song is not just an accommodation. You can hear the themes of complexity, uncertainty, ambiguity embedded. By accepting as givens (rather than resisting or denying these things), he validates the reality of this strange world we live in.

It's frustrating, because these are just hints. But this is what I hear in his music. I'm not Ben, I don't know where he was going. I would have liked to know. I do know this, when he got serious, he was becoming good fast. His systematics professor last night said Ben's paper was the best senior paper *he has ever read.* He told Ben earlier: "I didn't know you had it in you."[1]

We didn't either, but we suspected. Ben was an out-of-the-box thinker. But he was also a *very clear* thinker. That is a rare combination. What we didn't know was whether his playful spirit would plug into his calling like it probably needed to, but we were beginning to see that it was.

A quick example. In my experience when theological discussions are just beginning to get interesting, Lutherans instinctively pull out the "P" card. "Well, it's a Paradox." It's a tried and true Heresy stopper.

Lutherans are very fond of their Paradoxes. I found out last night that Ben wrote his senior paper on a BIG ONE: good and evil.

I also heard last night that Ben was fond of pointing out when people were Heretics. "Heretic!" he would say, but in a playful way.

One of the reasons that I imagine Lutherans play the "P" card is this. When people talk too much about their Heresies, the church risks the dreaded "S" word, Schism.

Here's a quick story. Our neighbor Steve Scott up at Juggler Lake is a thoughtful but conservative Christian from Atlanta. Ben, Jonathan, and Renee had dinner there one night and over drinks the conversation drifted to that age-old Schism, Free Will.

After Ben died, Steve called me and said he and his wife Sue have had some serious time to talk since the evening with Ben, Renee, and Jonathan. And he has since written a song that he plays in his group. Its name: "God chose us first."

Before the news about Ben, I thought I knew a little bit about grief. My parents, Joe and Aleta, are gone. I know those tears, those of a bereft, anxious kitten.

This past week I learned there are many more kinds. Tears that come on fast, pile up—angry tears, raw and jealous, relentless, lurking, anchor-weighted, sucker-punching, tears that go too far; tears that grab you by the throat; tears that can't reach far enough; tears that whisper of unnamed places, beyond the reach of words.

And I am made aware of how little I really know. I am aware that there are so many more lost, tens of thousands, hundreds of thousands dead . . . I can pray for them, but my tears are reserved mostly for Ben, for Renee, for Jonathan, for my sister April and my brother Judd, for Katie and Amy, for Marilyn and for the rest of us here.

When I go in my mind to Haiti, my mind can't fathom the scale. I imagine countless tears falling, drops into rivulets, rivulets into rivers, rivers

---

1. See Appendix C to read the paper.

into the sea. I see a pile of rubble on the TV. I understand the desire to dig until my fingers bleed. I am aware of tears upon tears. We are of like mind. I am used to being on the outside looking in. We are on the inside now, looking in . . .

In closing, here's what Marilyn Larson, Ben's grandmother, said when she learned about Ben: "How are we going to live without Ben?"

We don't know. We're going to have to start learning.

Recently Ben was going on about Original Sin. He was pestering Jonathan and Renee. "Jonny, I got it."

I for one would have liked to know what Ben was thinking. I can imagine that conversation up at Juggler Lake over coffee. Ben had a way of seeing things differently.

Renee said she's not mad at God, yet. I'm glad. They were called. We know that there are risks involved in following Jesus. Peacemakers are held up as "blessed" for a reason. I'm not privy to God's plan, but I just can't imagine Ben dying in Haiti was part of it.

We need your help. We need to learn how to live without Ben. A cynic might see it this way: "Look what happens when you follow Jesus." Or we could see it differently, like Ben would. Look around you, and see what happens when you follow Jesus.

APPENDIX C

Participation and Evil:
The Problem of Doing Evil When
Attempting to Fight Evil[1]

By Benjamin Splichal Larson

At Wartburg Theological Seminary in Dubuque, Iowa, professors warn their students to think long and hard before writing systematically on either the Trinity or the problem of evil. With these two subjects, the chances are high of slipping into heresy or at best talking in circles. Receiving an A on such an endeavor is rare.

In the first week of a senior theology course on creation, Ben set his heart set on exploring the topic of evil—its origin and our participation in it—for his final paper. I repeated the warning we received our first year in seminary, but he simply looked at me and grinned.

Central to Ben's theology is faith that God creates new life out of the most evil and devastating circumstances through the cross and resurrection of Jesus Christ. One month after submitting the paper below, Ben profoundly witnessed to the core of his faith as he died, singing, buried by rubble in the Haiti earthquake. Ben's last song is a witness to something that is greater than evil, death, and destruction:

"O Lamb of God, you bear the sin of all the world away; eternal peace with God you made, God's peace to us we pray."

Ben did not ignore the reality of evil in our broken world, but he proclaimed God's redeeming work in and through Jesus Christ for all of creation. May his paper intrigue, challenge, and strengthen you as we all look forward to God's reconciling work in the resurrection of the dead and the fullness of the New Creation.

Ben got an A. —RSL

1. Originally published in *Currents in Theology and Mission*, Vol. 39, No. 6 (December 2012), 449–56.

Introduction

ON AUGUST 17, 2008, the popular writer and religious leader Pastor Rick Warren asked Senator John McCain in a nationally televised interview, "Does evil exist, and if so, should we ignore it, negotiate with it, contain it, or defeat it?" McCain's answer was short, concise, and met with thunderous applause: *"Defeat it."* This answer came on the heels of five years of war in Iraq, where the United States had engaged in combat against a country it called part of the "Axis of Evil." Iraq, the Axis of Evil, lost far more noncombatant, dare I say innocent, citizens in that war than the United States has lost in its entire history.

Here we have a clear example of how humans, including Christians, often participate in evil when attempting to fight evil. This is why it is of utmost importance that we look deep into that dark and cold term, *evil.* This paper will not try to solve the problem of evil; it will not even try fully to understand evil. Instead, it asks: Are we able to participate in God's plan to bring about an end to evil, and if so, how? To tackle this question, we will look first at how humans participate with God. Then we will look at how humans participate with and understand evil. We will address the timeless questions: Where does evil come from? Did God create it? Finally, we will ask what we can do about evil, if anything.

What Is the Source of Human Participation in Evil?

To lay the groundwork, let us begin with an early Christian theologian who thought deeply about participation: Maximus the Confessor. Maximus "understands" God on two levels. There is God in God's essence, about which we can know absolutely nothing. Then there is God in God's activity out of God's essence, which is the revealed God. We cannot know anything about God apart from the activity of God.

When something is created, it cannot exist outside of the activity of its Creator. This means that creation is the initial and continued activity of God. There is no existence without God creating and sustaining that existence. Therefore, all communion with God is communion with the action of God. Participation with God and God's activity is done only through created reality.[2]

---

2. Tollefsen, Torstein Theodor, *The Christocentric Cosmology of St Maximus the Confessor*, ch. 5, "The Concept of Participation" (Oxford, UK: Oxford University Press, 2008), 190–224.

The source of human participation in evil is often called the "fall." What is the fall? It is usually summed up in this way: God gave humans free will. Since God honors that gift, God allows us to choose wrong. Therefore, God is not to blame for creating evil; God just allows it to exist. "God even knows, in a mysterious way, how to bring a good from the consequences of an evil, even a moral evil, caused by God's creatures; but for all that, evil never becomes good."[3] Yet, going back to the story of the fall, there is one character who throws this for a loop: Satan. It is impossible to discuss evil without discussing Satan.

The serpent in Genesis is never identified as Satan; however, throughout history, both Jews and Christians have read Satan into the serpent—"the tempter." If Augustine, Luther, and countless others attribute the fall to Satan as the tempter, we must ask: Why did God create Satan? Why did God create a tempter? If God wants us to choose right over wrong, why create someone or something to tempt us into transgression?

Theories about Evil's Place in Creation

Where does evil come from? Did God create evil? Christian tradition offers a number of answers to these questions.

In light of Scripture, Christians have commonly assumed that evil either originates in the tempting serpent or in humans' act of eating the forbidden fruit. However, although eating the fruit is a transgression, and it leads to suffering and death, Genesis 2–3 does not explicitly state at this time that "evil" has come into the world. Not even when Cain murders Abel does Genesis mention the presence of "evil." Instead, the first mention of evil comes in Genesis 6:5, right after the "sons of God" see the fairness of the daughters of humans and have children with them called the Nephilim. This is likely Genesis' interpretation of the origin of evil: it is related to the crossing of a boundary between the sons of God (angels) and daughters of humans.

This understanding creates a stark difference between transgressions and evil. Transgressions are punished; evil is destroyed. Evil here in Genesis 6 is not created by God. Instead, evil is a result of created beings breaking the boundaries of heaven and earth. If heavenly beings bring evil about by breaching the boundary of earth, since heaven and earth are created

---

3. Dutari, Julio Terâ, "The Origin and Overcoming of Evil: Original Sin and God's Suffering in Christianity," trans. Richard Schneck, S.J., in *The Origin and the Overcoming of Evil and Suffering in the World Religions*, Peter Koslowski, ed. (Dordrecht; Boston: Kluwer Academic Publishers, 2001), 49.

together with beings of their own, is it not also evil for humans to cross into the heavenly realm? Isn't this what happens when humans speak and act in place of God or pursue the desire to be like God—able to define the boundary between good and evil?

That is one option, and it is compelling. However, Genesis is perhaps best used as an interpretation of life rather than as a chronology of events. This approach adds value to the story of Adam and Eve. A common interpretation of evil is that it is what takes life from the living; it makes something that was alive into an object. In short, it is objectifying being: "[Evil transforms] living being into objects to be manipulated, and since a living being dies when it becomes an object, evil is a force against life."[4] This means that evil and death go together.

The real issue here is whether or not God created evil. This is fundamental. If God created evil, in one way or another, it is ultimately God's to deal with. This question of the source of evil kept some of our church fathers up at night: "It is more worthy to believe that God is free, even as the Author of evil, than that He is a slave. Power, whatever it be, is more suited to Him than infirmity."[5] Here we see that Tertullian finds more comfort in the idea of God being all-powerful and the Author of evil than God not being the source of evil. Tertullian chooses the idea he can live with—the idea that does not circumvent the power of God. Others, such as John of Damascus, are not willing to attribute evil to God, so they work their way around it:

> His permission, therefore, is usually spoken of in the Holy Scripture as His energy and work. Nay, even when He says that *God creates evil things,* and that *there is no evil in a city that the Lord hath not done,* he does not mean by these words that the Lord is the cause of evil, but the word "evil" is used in two ways, with two meanings. For sometimes it means what is evil by nature, and this is the opposite of virtue and the will of God: and sometimes it means that which is evil and oppressive to our sensation, that is to say, afflictions and calamities. Now these are seemingly evil because they are painful, but in reality are good. For to those who understand they became ambassadors of conversion and salvation. The Scripture says that of these God is the Author.[6]

4. Gustafson, Scott W., *Evil and the Followers of Jesus* (Bradwell Books, 1996), 31.

5. Tertullian, "Against Hemogenes," ch. xiv in *Latin Christianity: Its Founder Tertullian, The Ante-Nicene Fathers,* III, A. Cleveland Coxe (American Reprint of the Edinburgh Edition; Grand Rapids, MI: Wm. B. Eerdmans, 1951), 485. [Retrieved from http://www.ccel.org/ccel/schaff/anf03.v.v.xiv.html, December 2009.]

6. John of Damascus, *An Exact Exposition of the Orthodox Faith,* trans. S.D.F.

With these statements, John of Damascus separates evil into two ideas: that which is in opposition to God and that which seems evil at the time but is actually good. John of Damascus attributes only good to God; he emphasizes that what seems evil might not actually be so. The idea that evil is opposition to God is easy to agree with, but the argument that evil might not actually be evil is not so convincing to the post–World War II world.

Augustine makes room in creation for evil by saying that it is necessary. "There can be no evil where there is no good; and an evil man is an evil good."[7] This is an attempt, common in theology, to make evil and good dependent on each other. Augustine lays out the idea that good and evil cannot exist without each other. Knowing one means knowing the other. This, however, creates an issue with dualism. If good *requires* evil, then God must be both evil and good. If God is only good, then evil is an eternal power that God is dependent upon. That would mean God is not free.

Augustine has another idea that "What is called evil in the universe is but the absence of good."[8] This may seem to contradict his earlier statement, but it doesn't necessarily. Evil is not secretly good; instead, it is the lack of good. Evil exists only when good does not. This is a useful idea that will come back later.

Martin Luther is known for living with contradictory ideas, and he lives up to that reputation with his thinking on evil. Luther also speaks a great deal about evil in connection to Satan. Like most of medieval Europe, he considers Satan an evil being, an enemy of God:

> Thus God, *finding* the will of Satan evil, not *creating* it so, but
> leaving it while Satan sinningly commits the evil, carries it along
> by His working, and moves it which way He will; though that
> will ceases not to be evil by this motion of God.[9]

Salmond, Book IV, ch. xix, "That God is not the cause of evils," in *Nicene and Post-Nicene Fathers of the Christian Church*, Second Series, Vol. IX, ed. Philip Schaff and Henry Wace (Reprinted; Grand Rapids, MI: Wm. B. Eerdmans, 1983), 93. [Retrieved from http://www.ccel.org/ccel/schaff/npnf209.iii.iv.iv.xix.html, December 2009.]

7. Augustine, *The Enchiridion*, trans. J.F. Shaw, ch. 13, in Philip Schaff, ed., *Nicene and Post-Nicene Fathers of the Christian Church*, Vol. III (Reprinted; Edinburgh: T&T Clark; Grand Rapids, MI: Wm. B. Eerdmans, 1988), 241. [Retrieved from http://www.ccel.org/ccel/*schaff*/npnf103.iv.ii.xv.html, December 2009.]

8. Ibid., ch. 11, 240. [Retrieved from http://www.ccel.org/ccel/schaff/npnf103.iv.ii.xiii.html, December 2009.]

9. Luther, Martin, *De Servo Arbitrio* (*"On the Enslaved Will"* or *The Bondage of the Will*), trans. Henry Cole, 1823, section LXXXVI. [Retrieved from http://www.ccel.org/ccel/luther/bondage.xii.xi.html, December 2009.]

Luther asserts in *The Bondage of the Will* that evil was not created but *found* in the will of Satan. This means that God does not control wills, but uses even evil wills to do good. For Luther, God controls the entire cosmos, yet at the same time leaves the creature free. In this quote, Luther does not attribute evil to God, but he confesses that it is God who makes room for evil. However, Luther does not stop there.

Above we saw Luther's claim that God did not create Satan's will as evil. This seems to imply that Luther did not believe God created evil, but on the other hand, foundational to Luther's theology is the idea that "God works life and death, good and evil, everything in everything."[10] Luther's theology is consistent with Christian thinking throughout time: All that is, is God's creation. Nothing can exist apart from God. Luther agrees with Maximus the Confessor and most theologians on this point. I find Luther to be the most intriguing thinker on the problem of evil because he never lets himself be bound to systematizing, which both frees him and makes him impossible to represent in a paper like this.

So how can Luther do that? How can he say two seemingly contradictory things? Luther thinks about God on two levels. First is the revealed God, primarily revealed in Jesus Christ, and second is *Deus absconditus*, the hidden God. This reminds us of Maximus: the revealed God (Christ) is the activity of God, while God in God's essence would be the *Deus absconditus*. For Luther, God is also largely hidden in God's activity. If God works "everything in everything," what God is doing is largely ambiguous (see Ecclesiastes 8:16–9:1). It is only in God's Word spoken in God's Son that God's purpose is revealed. But even there, God's love is hidden under signs of God's wrath, God's power under the weakness of the cross, and God's life under death.

The God revealed in Jesus Christ is an enemy to evil. Jesus Christ reigns until all evil is defeated, and even death is defeated (1 Corinthians 15:20–28). Jesus Christ has power over evil and the power to work good through evil. However, when Luther speaks of the *Deus absconditus*, the "terrorizing hiddenness is so oppressive and unavoidable that the question is posed: Does God work not only indirectly, in evil, but does *God* also work evil?"[11] This is not to propose that the hidden God has a different will from the revealed God, and especially not to claim that the Son has a different will from the Father. That would be heresy. What Luther is saying is that our experience of God is twofold. We can only witness the hidden God with

---

10. Bayer, Oswald, *Martin Luther's Theology: A Contemporary Interpretation* (Grand Rapids, MI: William B. Eerdmans Publishing Company, 2003), 206.

11. Ibid., 204.

mystery and terror. It is through the revealed God that the terror is overwhelmed by love, for it is there that we learn that everything must ultimately
serve God's love. Therefore, God in the vast mystery of God is free to be the
author and worker of evil. Who is the creature to question the workings of
God in the hiddenness of God? Yet the God who is revealed to us through
Jesus Christ is revealed as love.

Conclusion: Chaos, Evil, Death vs. Creation, New Creation, Life

So, we have done the important and impossible task of thinking about evil
along with some of the great minds of the church's history. However, rather
than getting closer to understanding evil, we are actually only getting closer
to understanding the problem of evil. Therefore, in this conclusion I will not
pretend to answer the problem of evil. I will not be able to explain evil in
a way that gives humans the ability to control it. The goal here is merely to
understand evil in *a* way that is helpful to a creature of God.

Here is what I am convinced of: everything that exists is created and
sustained by God. Therefore, there are two options for contemplating evil
based on existence and nonexistence. If we believe that evil has being, then
we must believe that evil is created and sustained by God. If we believe that
Satan is an evil being, whether or not Satan is an enemy of God, Satan has
to be God's creation. So the first option is that evil does exist and God did
create it and does sustain it.

The second option is more complex and, I think, more powerful: that
is, that evil does *not* exist. Evil does not have being. The only way evil cannot be attributed to God is if evil lacks being. I will now argue this second
option biblically and logically.

When discussing evil, theologians usually go back to Genesis 2 and
look at the serpent, the forbidden fruit, and original sin; however, I would
like to take us back to Genesis 1.

> **Genesis 1:1–2** In the beginning when God created the heavens
> and the earth, the earth was a formless void and darkness cov-
> ered the face of the deep, while a wind from God swept over the
> face of the waters.

Creation is God's action over and against a formless void. Hence God
made existence. I am going along with Augustine and many others in assert-
ing that God created *ex nihilo* (out of nothing). By creating out of nothing,

God defeated nothingness with creation. Here's where I turn to Karl Barth. According to Daniel Migliore,

> Evil for Barth is the alien power of "nothingness" (*das Nichtige*) that arises mysteriously from what God does *not* will in the act of creation. As Barth explains, "nothingness" is not nothing. While neither willed by God nor an equal of God, it has its own formidable and threatening power. . . . God alone is able to conquer the power of nothingness."[12]

For Barth, evil is not a being but a power. It does not exist as being. In the language of Maximus the Confessor, evil has no existence of the essence. Evil is not a thing but an action, just as love is not being but action. This idea works. Love is not created by God but is the relationship God has with God's creation. Love does not exist as a being, but it has great power. Similarly, if evil is the "alien power of 'nothingness'. . . [that] God does *not* will in the act of creation," it can still have great power. Thus, the evil power of nothingness corresponds to the formless void in Genesis 1:2, over and against which God wills creation into being.

Genesis 1 is echoed in the Gospel of John.

> **John 1:1–4** In the beginning was the Word, and the Word was with God, and the Word was God. He was in the beginning with God. All things came into being through him, and without him not one thing came into being. What has come into being in him was life, and the life was the light of all people.

This adds a third and forth dualism to our discussion. There is creation against void, good (Genesis 1:4, 10, 12, 18, 21, 25, 31) against evil (nothingness), life (John 1:3) against death (implicit), light (John 1:4, Genesis 1:3) against darkness (Genesis 1:2).

If God defeated the formless void with creation out of nothing and defeated darkness with light, how does God defeat evil and death? Every Christian should know the answer to that question. The void was defeated by creation; evil and death are defeated by new creation. The Word through whom all things came into being, the Word through whom creation came *ex nihilo,* went into the nothingness of evil and death by way of the cross. The new creation comes through the action of *the one through whom creation came into being out of nothingness* going into the nothingness of death and

---

12. Migliore, Daniel L., *Faith Seeking Understanding: An Introduction to Christian Theology* (Grand Rapids, MI: William B. Eerdmans Publishing Company, 2004), 127. For Barth's discussion of this, see Karl Barth, *Church Dogmatics*, iii, *The Doctrine of Creation*, 3, trans. G.W. Bromiley and R.J. Ehrlich (Edinburgh: T&T Clark, 1960), § 50, "God and Nothingness," 289–368.

evil. Death and evil are defeated in Christ because it is impossible for death to hold Christ in its power (Acts 2:24).[13]

> **2 Corinthians 5:17–19** So if anyone is in Christ, there is a new creation: everything old has passed away; see, everything has become new! All this is from God, who reconciled us to himself through Christ, and has given us the ministry of reconciliation; that is, in Christ God was reconciling the world to himself.

Reconciliation, then, is not God's fallback plan for the sin of humanity, but rather God's plan from the beginning of creation. Creation from the very beginning is God's plan to destroy evil, death, and nothingness through the Word. This view makes the most sense to me. It has the most good news in it and seems not only to honor Scripture, but also actually helps much of it make sense in new ways.

So what does this good news mean for our original problem? What does the Christian have to say to Senator McCain and much of the United States? Based on his experience of history, Karl Barth believed that

> . . . [O]nly God is able to conquer the power of radical evil. When individual human beings, groups, or nations, sure of their innocence and convinced of the utter wickedness of their enemies, claim for themselves the right and the power to rid the world of evil, they often become themselves agents of evil.[14]

If humans participate in evil by identifying other beings as evil,[15] then it is of utmost importance that humans begin to understand that evil does not have being. Anything that *is* cannot be evil on account of the fact that it *is*. If it exists, then it is created and sustained by the activity of the Creator who creates and sustains over and against evil. It is not possible for any person or any part of creation to *be* evil.

All participation in evil is essentially participating in death rather than life. Evil makes a living being into an object. Evil makes God's creation into less than God's creation. We know this. In our society we participate in evil through the same process. We participate in evil through language in which a person ceases to be a being and becomes a label, such as "fag" or "slut." We participate in evil when we cease to see people as beings but view them

---

13. See Martin Luther, *Lectures on Galatians 1535: Chapters 1–4*, trans. Jaroslav Pelikan, *Luther's Works*, Vol. 26, ed. Jaroslav Pelikan and Walter A. Hansen (St. Louis: Concordia, 1963), 280–282.

14. Migliore, *Faith*, 128.

15. This would be entailed by the human desire to "be like God, knowing good and evil" as well as by our desire to pass judgment on others.

instead as consumers. We participate in evil when we think of third-world countries as sources of cheap labor and not nations of people. We participate in evil when we label other people or societies as evil, for example, in the political label, "Axis of Evil." This process of making being into object is not limited to humans, but could even be extended to all of creation. Nor is it limited to language. Evil is participated in by action, rooted in and supported by the language we use. All action that uses beings as objects is evil.

Martin Luther was clear about the link between the way we speak of others and the issue of evil. Satan "accuses us and makes our evil conscience worse in the presence of God . . . disparages what is good about us and vilifies our merits and the faith of our conscience." Satan is imitated by people who "exaggerate, enlarge, and expand the sins" of others and "minimize, find fault with, and disapprove of their good works."[16]

Humans can fight against the power of evil, not only outside ourselves, but also within ourselves. We are creation and new creation. "It is precisely confidence in the superiority of God's grace that empowers believers to fight against evil and suffering in the world against seemingly impossible odds."[17]

This confidence in God is faith. It is through faith, trust in God, that we are able to participate in God's action of creation, new creation, and reconciliation. It is through faith that we can give up trust in the objectification of being. It is through faith that we speak and live in new language shaped by God's love for the world in Jesus Christ. This is the language of the Holy Spirit, who, when our conscience accuses us, "protects us in the presence of God and comforts us by giving a good testimony to our conscience and to our trust in the mercy of God . . . excuses, extenuates, and completely covers our sins . . . magnifies our faith and good works."[18] It is through faith that we can fight evil as an already defeated power.

---

16. Martin Luther, "Lectures on Galatians 1519: Chapters 1–6," trans. Richard Jungkuntz, *Luther's Works*, Vol. 27, ed. Jaroslav Pelikan and Walter A. Hansen (St. Louis: Concordia, 1964), 388.

17. Migliore, *Faith*, 128.

18. Luther (Galatians, 1519), 388.

APPENDIX D

Photos

Benjamin Splichal Larson, Renee Splichal Larson, and Jonathan Larson at an
event in early 2008 in La Crosse, Wisconsin. They were there to support Ben's
mom, April Larson, who received an Iverson Freking award for ecumenical
action. *Photo courtesy of Renee Splichal Larson.*

Renee and Ben discuss a point of theology while visiting the lay school for the Eglise Lutherienne d'Haiti in January 2010. *Photo courtesy of Jonathan Splichal Larson.*

Ben holds Belinda, a three-year-old child with severe physical disabilities, at Wings of Hope in Fermathe, Haiti, in May 2009. *Photo courtesy of Renee Splichal Larson.*

Ben and Jon after receiving flowers from a group of Pentecostals who were visiting the St. Joseph's Home for Boys in Pétionville, Haiti, on January 10, 2010. *Photo courtesy of Jonathan Splichal Larson.*

Ben rubs medicated shampoo on the head of a child in the Port-au-Prince ravine on the morning of January 12, 2010. *Photo courtesy of Jonathan Splichal Larson.*

Keziah Furth, Ben, Jon, and Renee enjoy a meal at an upscale Chinese restaurant in Port-au-Prince hours before the earthquake. *Photo courtesy of Jonathan Splichal Larson.*

Two floors of St. Joseph's Home for Boys collapsed during the 7.0 magnitude earthquake of January 12, 2010. The roof of what was a seven-story building now sits on top of the rubble of the chapel level and the dance floor level, which were compacted from three stories to about six feet in the collapse. The remaining four stories, which included living spaces for the boys and the guests, were severely damaged and left uninhabitable. *Photo and description courtesy of Renee Dietrich.*

Another view of the collapsed top floors of St. Joseph's shows where Ben, Jon, and Renee were trapped. *Photo courtesy of Renee Dietrich.*

St. Joseph's at ground level the day after the earthquake. Kez's house (the "Shoebox") is visible in the foreground (lower right). Renee, Jon, and Al used a ladder to cross the alleyway from the collapsed roof of St. Joseph's (right of mural entrance) onto Kez's roof and then to the ground. *Photo courtesy of Renee Dietrich.*

Renee tried to work her way up this rubble-filled stairway to look for Ben the morning after the earthquake. *Photo courtesy of Renee Dietrich.*

The cross on the roof of St. Joseph's still stands after the earthquake destroyed the building. Jon clung to this cross during the aftershocks after escaping from under the collapsed top floors. *Photo courtesy of Renee Dietrich.*

A woman walks past a collapsed building in Port-au-Prince on January 18, 2015, six days after the earthquake that devastated the island nation. It was years before rubble from the earthquake was removed from most of the capital. *Photo and description courtesy of Renee Dietrich.*

Crowds stand outside the Caribbean Market on Delmas 95 in Pétionville, Haiti, following the January 12, 2010, earthquake. An estimated seventy-five to one hundred people were in the building, one of the largest supermarkets in the country, when the earthquake hit. Many were buried alive. Rescue efforts went on for days to find survivors and to recover those who died. Trapped victims were able to survive on food and drinks in the store and sent text messages out for days begging to be rescued. *Photo and description courtesy of Renee Dietrich.*

Simple homes on a hillside in Port-au-Prince are reduced to rubble following the earthquake. *Photo and description courtesy of Renee Dietrich.*

A makeshift tent city houses thousands of earthquake victims in Port-au-Prince following the January 12, 2010, disaster. Almost every open space in the capital was turned into temporary shelters for earthquake victims, for months to years after the earthquake. *Photo and description courtesy of Renee Dietrich.*

Hundreds of black crosses mark this mass grave in St. Christophe, just south of Titanyen, Haiti. Jon and Renee visited the site with Mytch and Louis Dorvilier in February 2011 and January 2012. *Photo courtesy of Jonathan Splichal Larson.*

Jon and Renee on their second trip back to Haiti in January 2012. *Photo courtesy of Jonathan Splichal Larson.*

Bibliography

Ackermann, Denise M. "Lamenting Tragedy from 'The Other Side.'" In *Sameness and Difference: Problems and Potentials in South African Civil Society*. Edited by James R. Cochrane and Bastienne Klein. Washington, D.C.: Council for Research in Values and Philosophy, 2000.

Annan, Kent. *After Shock: Searching for Honest Faith When Your World Is Shaken*. Downers Grove, IL: InterVarsity, 2011.

———. *Following Jesus Through the Eye of the Needle: Living Fully, Loving Dangerously*. Westmont, IL: InterVarsity, 2010.

Bell, Rob. *What We Talk About When We Talk About God*. New York: HarperCollins, 2013.

Berry, Wendell. *Jayber Crow: A Novel*. Washington, D.C.: Counterpoint, 2000.

Bonhoeffer, Dietrich. *I Want to Live These Days with You: A Year of Daily Devotions*. Louisville, KY: Westminster John Knox, 2007.

Buechner, Frederick. *The Hungering Dark*. San Francisco: Harper & Row, 1985.

Dietrich, Renee. *Dèyè Mòn: Behind the Mountains*. Dubuque, IA: Sustainable Land Development International, 2009.

Elliott, Michael, Jeffrey Kluger, and Richard Lacayo. *Haiti: Tragedy and Hope*. New York: Time Books, 2010.

Evangelical Lutheran Church in America. *Evangelical Lutheran Worship*. Minneapolis, MN: Augsburg Fortress, 2006.

Farmer, Paul. *The Uses of Haiti*. Monroe, ME: Common Courage, 2006.

———, Abbey M. Gardner, Cassia van der Hoof Holstein, and Joia Mukherjee. *Haiti After the Earthquake*. New York: PublicAffairs, 2011.

Girard, Philippe R. *Haiti: The Tumultuous History—From Pearl of the Caribbean to Broken Nation*. New York: Palgrave Macmillan, 2010.

Gloor, Carol. "Luke 24:36–42." *Christian Century* (November 1, 2011) 30.

Hall, Douglas John. *The Cross in Our Context: Jesus and the Suffering World*. Minneapolis, MN: Fortress, 2003.

James, C.L.R. *The Black Jacobins: Toussaint L'Ouverture and the San Domingo Revolution*. New York: Vintage Books, 1989.

Muggah, Robert, and Athena Kolbe. "Haiti: Why an Accurate Count of Civilian Deaths Matters," *Los Angeles Times* (July 12, 2011). http://articles.latimes.com/2011/jul/12/opinion/la-oe-muggah-haiti-count-20110712.

Norris, Kathleen. *Dakota: A Spiritual Geography*. New York: Ticknor & Fields, 1993.

O'Connor, Maura R. "Two Years Later, Haitian Earthquake Death Toll in Dispute," *Columbia Journalism Review* (January 12, 2012). http://www.cjr.org/behind_the_news/one_year_later_haitian_earthqu.php.

Passi, Peter. "Story of Duluth Pastors' Son Carries on Through Song After Tragic Death in Haiti." *Duluth News Tribune* (February 27, 2012). http://www.duluthnewstribune.com/content/story-duluth-pastors-son-carries-through-song-after-tragic-death-haiti.

Plantinga, Cornelius Jr. "Living By the Word: Reflections On the Lectionary," *The Christian Century* (October 2, 2013) 20.

Reeves, Nancy. *Found Through Loss: Healing Stories from Scripture and Everyday Sacredness*. Kelowna, B.C.: Northstone, 2003.

Rohr, Richard. *Things Hidden: Scripture As Spirituality*. Cincinnati, OH: St. Anthony Messenger, 2007.

Wiesel, Elie. *Night*. New York: Bantam, 1982.

Wolterstorff, Nicholas. *Lament for a Son*. Grand Rapids, MI: Eerdmans, 1987.

Wright, N. T. *Surprised by Hope: Rethinking Heaven, the Resurrection, and the Mission of the Church*. New York: HarperOne, 2008.

Index

Song Index

Ben's Songs

Other Songs

Scripture Index